MW00604793

Educating

Educating

A MEMOIR

LaRee Westover

BUTTERFLY
EXPRESSIONS

EDUCATING: A MEMOIR

Published in the United States by Butterfly Expressions LLC
500 N Main Hwy.
Clifton, ID 83228

info@LaReeWestover.net | LaReeWestover.net

Library of Congress Cataloging-in-Publication Data
Names: Westover, LaRee, author.
Title: Educating: A Memoir / LaRee Westover.
Identifiers: LCCN 2020914737 | ISBN 9781735486505 |
ISBN 9781735486512 (ebook)
Subjects: LCSH: Westover, LaRee—Family. | Home schooling—United States. |
Women—Idaho—Biography. | Christian biography. | Idaho Biography. |
Child rearing. | Homeopathic pharmacopoeias. | Herbs—Therapeutic use. |
Essences and essential oils—Therapeutic use. |

ISBN 978-1-7354865-0-5 (hardcover)
ISBN 978-1-7354865-1-2 (ebook)

Printed in the United States of America
10 9 8 7 6 5 4 3 2 1

Book design by Morgan Crockett | Firewire Creative
Printed by Book Printers of Utah, Inc.

NOTE: This memoir is not meant as a treatise or a teaching manual on alternative healing modalities of any kind. It is not to be used by the reader as a substitute for competent medical advice, and we take no responsibility for its use in any form. In this family, we seek medical advice when it is needed and encourage you to do so also.

DEDICATED TO ALL

WHO HAVE THE HEART

OF A TEACHER

Mountains behind the Westover house
in Clifton, Idaho, highlighting "The Princess"

Contents

Foreword

VAL WESTOVER

We are floating on the cloud tops at 12,000 feet. It is raining below us. Cloud cover extends as far as the eye can see below, and the morning sun illuminates the entire scene. There are no reference points; all is sameness—except straight ahead. We are approaching one startling solitary object. A massively huge behemoth is in our path. It is eighty-five miles away. The pilot does not need to point it out by saying something like, "It is the third one from the left." There is only one. No crowd, no competition, no companions. "The Great One," Denali, the highest peak in North America with a topographic isolation of 4,629 miles, is getting bigger as we approach. It is going up and up and up higher still. This mesmerizing sight makes our long journey worthwhile.

"The Great One" has been given many names, not all of them becoming. Some have sworn at her arrogance, her seeming invincible presence. She has defeated many. Even more have backed away. There may be taller mountains, but here in our view there is only one. In spite of cursing or praise, epitaphs or adulation, "The Great One" carries on. Alone.

Similarly, this memoir is about a unique, standing-alone, doing-it-myself, independent-of-accommodation-or-insult life. There will be critics of LaRee. They will be lost in the sameness. There will be those who admire, who are able to tolerate and appreciate the courage to be different, a pioneer, and a point of choice. The true story you are about to experience will be neither diluted nor enhanced by critique or applause. History is often rewritten, but the rewrite does not alter the truth or the past.

There are many themes in her narrative, but *being different is okay* stands out. Lookout points on the roads or trails we traverse are not chosen for their sameness. They are chosen and relished for the unique perspective they present. Herein is a lookout point of life itself. I remember unique vistas. I cherish the mountains rising above the plain. The unexpected becomes our focus. The punch line makes the story memorable only if you are surprised.

When I recollect my friends and my children, is it not their unique characteristics that first come to mind? When I describe their personalities to others, is it their sameness I focus on or their unique differences? If I am honest to myself, it is often their quirks, follies, and imperfections that make me smile and endear them to me. I love my fellow beings for their gifts and talents, but also for not being just like me.

If within yearnings and aspirations lie the seeds of greatness, it follows then that the glory of mankind is in diversity.

This is not the story of a road less traveled. It is the story of a woman walking where a path did not exist. She blazed her own trail and did not leave breadcrumbs for a retreat. Most of all, this story—if you come with an open heart—will educate.

Preface

I *have authored and published four books* that were written with the intent to disseminate information on particular subjects. This book, however, is different in both content and format, and as such, a different set of publishing protocols seems to apply.

There are significant differences between self-publishing a book and submitting a manuscript to a publisher. One important difference is that when an author signs with a publisher, the author may be relinquishing at least some control over the content of their book. Final editorial decisions often rest with the publisher, even if those decisions are contrary to the author's wishes. The motivations of author and publisher may not always be aligned.

Serendipitously, about the same time we were getting this explanation from our printer, our company lawyer approached us with much the same information. He explained that if truth were to be told, unembellished, we would need to maintain editorial control, and he recommended that we self-publish. The higher upfront costs of printing and binding, accompanied by the difficulties of marketing and distribution, often make self-publishing an unrealistic choice for many aspiring writers. But because one of my nonnegotiables was to retain absolute control of the content, I decided to accept the risks and challenges of self-publishing.

This book is *my* memoir—a memoir that for several years now, I have known I would one day write. But let's set the record straight right here. Part, but only part, of the impetus for writing my memoir at this time is the publishing of our daughter's book, *Educated.* I want to tell the story of my life as I really lived it and not in the dramatically fictionalized way others, based on my daughter's book, are telling it for me. I want my grandchildren to know who their grandmother is and was, and I want to be a force for good in their lives. Also, I feel a compelling desire to shine a light on homeschooling, herbal medicine, and the living of a conservative and Christian way of life.

I have drawn from my collection of loose notes, poignant personal memories, and years of journal entries. Sharing glimpses into some of the personal learning experiences of my life is intended to do more than just set the record straight; it is meant to educate. I hope to teach some of what I consider to be important principles. And I hope that those principles, coupled with the events and difficulties of my life, may inspire those who have chosen to live their lives differently from their neighbors.

I agree with what Gordon B. Hinckley, a former president of the church to which we belong, said when speaking to students at Brigham Young University: "You are good. But it is not enough just to be good. You must be good for something. You must contribute good to the world. The world must be a better place for your presence. And the good that is in you must be spread to others..." (Brigham Young University devotional, Marriott Center, 17 Sept. 1996).

As difficult as some of the events and circumstances in my life have been, I hope this modest memoir may bolster someone's resolve to achieve their own goals in spite of naysayers and roadblocks. I want the good in my life (as well as the things I have learned through the hard times) to contribute a measure of good to the world.

Prologue

BUTTERFLIES AND HOPE

If nothing ever changed, there could be no butterflies.
—*Wendy Maas*

M*y love of butterflies* began on a special day with my grandmother when I was six years old. Memories of that afternoon could have been sad and painful, but because my grandmother took the time to teach me about butterflies—and about hope—it became a treasured memory instead. This day has become so treasured that I have shared the story only a few times.

I grew up next door to my mother's parents in a house built on land my parents purchased from them. It was a joy to have my growing up years so intertwined with my grandparents' golden years.

My grandfather's health had been quite fragile for a long time, and he died when I was not quite seven years old. Just a few days after his funeral, I was "helping" Grandma get the last of the peach harvest into canning jars.

My grandparents' home had a large enclosed porch on the back. Underneath the porch steep wooden stairs led into the dark, damp root cellar. I didn't like going down there one bit. But I loved my grandmother. I had been told that her legs were "bad," and I had been asked to go into the root cellar for empty canning jars so Grandma wouldn't have to go. That was probably about as much help as a six-year-old could be, so I was determined to do it when I was asked.

I stepped down into that deep hole, gathered as many bottles as my little arms could carry, and started back up the stairs. As I reached the better lighting at the top of the stairs, I noticed something that looked ugly inside one of the bottles. To my young eyes it looked like a big, nasty worm. I didn't know what it was, how it got there, or how Grandma was going to get it out. So I asked her about it.

Her gentle hands took the bottles from me, and right in the middle of that busy day she sat down on the top step and pulled me down beside her. Her quiet, almost reverent tone held my attention. She explained to me how a caterpillar had climbed or perhaps fallen into that bottle, and it being "time"—I clearly remember her stressing that part about time—the caterpillar began to create a comfortable home for himself. She called it a cocoon.

Grandma explained that once the cocoon was finished, the little caterpillar would quite literally dissolve. I remember asking her what *dissolve* and *literally* meant—I was a very curious child. She also told me that in the Lord's own time it would emerge from the cocoon and would no longer be a caterpillar crawling in the dirt; it would be a butterfly. "Really?" I asked. This seemed like a fairy tale, and I wanted to watch this magic happen.

Grandma warned me that if the cocoon were opened too soon, if we even helped the butterfly escape just a little once we could see it, we would ruin everything. She put the bottle high on a small shelf and told me that I could check on it as often as I wanted, but I was not to touch it.

The lesson didn't end there. She knew that I had been grieving for my grandfather. I had been pestering everybody with questions about illness and death for days. Grandma told me that the unsightly cocoon was much like the coffin I had seen my grandfather in. This took me aback because I didn't know that she knew I had seen my grandfather in his coffin. I shouldn't have been surprised, though; my grandmother knew everything.

Grandpa's funeral had been held in the small living room in my grandparents' home—what Grandma called the *front room.* It had been decided that my cousin and I, just a month apart in age and best friends, were too young to attend. We thought this very unfair and decided to take matters into our own hands. First, we hid under the kitchen table. It was covered in a vinyl cloth that ended just inches above the floor (oh, the memories I have of playing under that tablecloth). Then we crawled quickly through the doorway and hid under the draped coffin that sat along the wall between the kitchen and living room.

Deep red roses were piled atop Grandpa's coffin and arranged in vases throughout the room. The air was heavy with their aroma. Ever since that day I have associated red roses with death. I don't care for them or their scent.

When my cousin and I thought no one was looking, we peeked up over the edge of the coffin. I have never forgotten the sight of my grandfather lying there, pale and still. Strangest of all, he wasn't whistling—Grandpa was always whistling.

Back on the steps of the root cellar, Grandma pulled me onto her lap. She explained that just like the caterpillar in the cocoon, my grandfather was in a private and snug place. I asked her if it was dark in there. She told me that yes, where his body was it was dark, but that didn't matter since my grandfather's spirit wasn't with his body. His spirit, the part of him that we loved, was now in heaven.

We discussed what a spirit is and more of what death means. Then my grandmother taught me about the resurrection. She told me my grandfather's weak and sick body would dissolve away, just like the caterpillar's body. But before I could say another word or even cry, she explained that, like the caterpillar, my grandfather would one day come forth. He would be like the butterfly emerging from the cocoon.

Grandma blinked away tears as she smiled. She said he would be like the young man she had loved and married, only better. He would still be the man she had walked and learned with for a lifetime. She said he would be wonderful, but I already thought that my grandfather was wonderful. He had made us corncob dolls and told us stories. He had made a bed for my little sister in a little red wagon and pulled her around and around until she fell asleep. He was always happy, and we knew that he loved each one of us.

Grandma and I sat together a little while longer, both of us crying just a little. I wanted to know how I could be sad if Grandpa was becoming like a butterfly. She explained to me that it was okay to be sad because sad meant that we loved him, sad meant that we missed him. But sad would be followed by a very great happiness when we saw him again.

I learned later that my grandfather had struggled with alcoholism during parts of his life. My grandparents had been through some hard times together, especially during the Great Depression. But they had loved each other and had triumphed together against great odds.

Grandpa had been sober for all of my young lifetime, but his health had been impacted—shattered, really—by his past actions and choices. As a teen I asked my grandmother about the stories I had heard about him. She then taught me about repentance and forgiveness—just as she had taught me about change and the resurrection when I was a child. She taught me about the Atonement of Jesus Christ, about love and hope. Although Grandma died just after I turned seventeen, her lessons have stayed with me all my life. And every time I see a butterfly—every time—I remember.

Educating

CHAPTER ONE

Introducing Us

When a day passes it is no longer there.
What remains of it?
Nothing more than a story.
—*Bashevis Singer*

M*y mother was a skilled seamstress.* Sometimes, however, she ran into difficulty when teaching others how to sew. She simply assumed that her students knew how to miter a corner or the proper way to pin a hem for stitching—things she knew so well that it didn't occur to her that the novices in her class didn't know them too. As I read back through this story of my life, I realized that in certain places I was also making similar assumptions.

There are certain aspects of my life that, while ordinary and easily understood by me, may seem unusual or confusing to you, the reader. I may assume that you are familiar with something that you are not. I may use a phrase that is specific to and well understood in the area and culture in which I live or in the religion I love. Because of this, I feel a need to introduce my family and explain some unique aspects of our lives. I will also define a few commonly used phrases.

Faith

First and foremost, Val and I are people of faith. We believe implicitly in the Lord Jesus Christ. Our faith, the church to which we belong (The Church of Jesus Christ of Latter-day Saints), service to others, and truth as we have come to know it are integral parts of who we are.

Prayer and the seeking of guidance and approval from a loving Heavenly Father is central to our lives and the choices we have made. We have tried to live our lives according to the counsel of heaven. We have tried to seek wisdom beyond our own and have done our best to live the things that we have learned.

As we were blessed with children, we recognized our responsibility to nurture and teach them all that we could. We taught them from an early age to seek their own answers and their own direction through study, pondering, and prayer.

We believe that priesthood power is the authority given from our Heavenly Father to His authorized apostles and prophets and is a central part of The Church of Jesus Christ of Latter-day Saints. Worthy men are ordained to the priesthood to serve and bless those around them.

Blessings by those who hold this priesthood authority have played an important role in my life and in the lives of my family members for generations. This is true of my husband's family as well. Such priesthood blessings are given at specific times in a person's life and for specific reasons; they are not an everyday sort of event. Some blessings are given to provide comfort during difficult times. Others are given by way of instruction or counsel. Still other blessings, very special ones, are given to facilitate healing in accordance with God's will.

These blessings—given when both the giver and the receiver are in the proper frame of mind—are considered personal messages from heaven to the recipient. They reflect heaven's view of our lives and our situation. Living worthy to give or receive such a blessing is a way-of-life goal for members of the church to which we belong and which we love.

Family

Family is of utmost importance to both Val and me. Our children's welfare is always our first concern. Having a family and rearing them well was our goal from the earliest days of our relationship.

My husband, Val, and I are parents to seven children. The oldest four are boys—Anthony (Tony), Travis, Tyler, and Lucas. Next is our daughter Valaree, followed by Richard and then Tara, who is our second daughter and youngest child.

Our children are very different from each other in both looks and personalities. For example, our first child, Tony, has very dark hair and brown eyes. Travis is very blond with blue eyes. Tyler's hair is a lighter brown than Tony's, and his eyes are neither brown nor blue. Lucas was born with blond hair and brown eyes. His hair darkened as he grew, much like mine did.

It was a joy to me to become acquainted with each of their amazing individual personalities. Our first four children were rowdy and rambunctious boys. When I became pregnant for the fifth time, I asked my mother what she thought I should do for variety this time. She replied, "Have a girl!" So I did. Valaree had very dark hair. For variety yet again, our second daughter, Tara, had very blond hair as a child. We had one more delightful son, Richard, born between Valaree and Tara.

Our children came into our lives at a relatively quick pace. The average span between them is twenty-one months, with nineteen months separating the closest two. Richard and Tara are a little more than three years apart in age.

As for my relationship with my husband, I consider our relationship is destined to continue forever. We hope to also share that eternal future with our children, their spouses, our grandchildren, and eventually our great-grandchildren.

We feel strongly that families are meant to support and love each other in this life and into the eternities beyond. Such a lofty goal has been easier to accept in theory than to achieve in reality sometimes. Nevertheless, as one of our prophet leaders once said, "the future is as bright as our faith." I look forward to each new day with—and for—this family of ours.

Alternative Heath Care

Our family has faced serious health issues for which mainstream medicine seemed to have no workable answers. We felt led to look elsewhere. I have spent considerable time studying and becoming proficient in the use of several alternative methods. Various alternative modalities have blessed our lives through a variety of injuries and health issues.

Among the issues our family has faced are head injuries, serious burns, illnesses, and a variety of more common health concerns. We know from experience that alternative methods and modalities work and work well.

Reaching for an herbal or homeopathic remedy is so normal to me that I often forget that this is not the usual response of most people. What I may consider helpful and normal may seem outlandish to others. Likewise, much of mainstream medicine, which often treats symptoms instead of addressing underlying causes of illness, seems odd to me.

Foot Zone Therapy

Foot zone therapy is based on the theory that there are signals on the feet which correspond to certain parts of the human body. The premise is that information can be gleaned by reading these signals as one works the feet in specific patterns with one's hands. The practice is ancient, and some health conditions can be eased by foot zone therapy sessions. I learned this amazing modality more than twenty-five years ago, and knowing it has blessed my life, the lives of those in our family, and the lives of many other people.

Midwifery

Most of our children were born at home with the assistance of an experienced and trusted midwife. When our children were old enough to allow me more flexibility, it was my privilege to become a practicing midwife myself for a time.

Home School

We intentionally chose to school our children at home for a great deal of their pre-college educations. At the time, it was certainly the road less traveled. Although our children were regularly involved in community activities, it was my great privilege to try to tailor their educations to their own specific interests, strengths, and weaknesses. I simply loved teaching our children and watching their minds expand and grasp new concepts. I still believe it was the right choice for our family.

I do not see how being homeschooled hampered our children in any way. Rather, it gave them unique perspectives and distinct capacities and attributes. Six of our seven children went on to college, and three earned PhD degrees. While the one who didn't attend college certainly could have, his interests lay elsewhere. All seven entered the academic world or their chosen professions as well prepared as any publicly schooled child from our community. They have, each in their own way, taken what we tried to give them and used it to become the good and productive people they are.

> You will never influence the world by being just like it.
> —*Author Unknown*

CHAPTER TWO

Beginnings

It is not the knowing what the right thing is to do;
nor is the journey the greatest challenge.
It is the faith and the courage to start;
the real struggle is in the beginning.
—*Val D Westover*

One of the luckiest things that can happen to you
in life is, I think, to have a happy childhood.
—*Agatha Christie*

I *was born in a beautiful valley* in the southeastern corner of Idaho. I am the second of my parent's five children and the oldest daughter. I have one older brother, one younger brother, and two younger sisters. The first four of us were born roughly three and a half years apart from each other. Our baby sister was born when I was fourteen years old, more than seven years after my youngest brother. Our home glowed with joy the evening that Mom and Dad informed us that this new baby (sister) was on her way.

My father worked for the postal service in our small town, but I think he secretly wanted to be a farmer. Although my parents' home was only four blocks off Main Street and within walking distance of local schools, my dad always had animals of some kind at home—chickens, pigeons, and a cow or two for milk.

As a very young child, I would sit on the cold lid of the milk can until my backside was frozen while dad milked the cows, just to be with him. Every night he would strain the milk, then line up full gallon bottles on our porch step for the neighbors. They left payment for the milk in a little box he kept on the porch.

I was born seven weeks prematurely and didn't acclimatize to this world very well or very willingly. My mom, being weak and anemic, was unable to nurse me, and no other liquid seemed to agree with me. I cried and cried with tummy aches except when I was lying face down on the large palm of my father's hand. He spent many a night walking the floor with me. I was born right at the time of the post office's Christmas rush, so all through December my father would work long hours, then come home to walk the floor with me at night. I finally settled in and felt content shortly after the new year. Only then could my exhausted father finally get some rest.

My childhood was a happy one. I remember long summer days, neighborhood parades and lemonade stands, and picking raspberries in a long-sleeve shirt because the plants made me break out in welts. My parents believed that busy children were happy children.

My parents lived by the adage *You can't raise your children properly in somebody else's yard.* They tried to provide every possible thing that would encourage their teenagers, as well as their younger children, to bring their friends to our house as often as possible. We had a big yard filled with all sorts of play equipment. As a teen, if a group of us ran out of something to do, we could always go to my home and Mother would throw us a party—with little or no notice. My friends and I had some great times at these impromptu events.

Another part of my parents' philosophy was especially fun: they believed in vacations, camping, swimming, hiking, roller and ice skating, and just about anything else you could do together as a family. We were expected to be able to do many things and do them well enough to enjoy it and share it with others.

My parents also believed that children and teens should be exposed to a wide variety of ideas and, when possible, cultural differences. They encouraged us to participate in school programs and activities. During my last two years of high school I belonged to a specialty sixteen-member choir that traveled for performances and competitions. We often stayed with the families of students living in neighboring school districts.

While I was still young and at home, our church leaders began recommending what they called "home evening." Each family would gather, usually on Monday nights, for a gospel lesson and fun activities. My siblings and I were encouraged to participate in preparing the lessons. My father took this program one step further.

Often my father would invite families whose church affiliations were not the same as our own to participate in these lessons. We would then go to their house for a lesson or activity on another evening. My father was never afraid to expose his children to philosophies and ideas outside those espoused by our church. He felt that truth, if it really were truth, would stand both the test of time and exposure to other beliefs.

I still remember watching my brother, seven years younger than me, flipping through his copy of the scriptures while a visitor was teaching from their copy of the Holy Bible. My little brother would stick his finger in his own Bible to mark references that he wanted to use in the family home evening presentation our family was responsible for the following Monday night.

These expanded home evenings with friends had one very strict rule: arguing with or interrupting the teacher—whether in our home or in theirs—was simply not allowed. My father was a gentle man, but he could be firm when the situation required. These evenings were enjoyable for all involved.

Mother often described herself as *persnickety*—fussy, meticulous, proper, refined, fastidious nice, tasteful. These wonderful words are excellent descriptions of my mother. She was an exacting housekeeper and workforce leader as we learned how to clean and do yard work. Mom would hide pennies in various places around the house on cleaning day.

We had better bring her all the pennies when we were done sweeping, mopping, vacuuming, and dusting. And substituting our own pennies did not work—she kept track of the dates on the coins she had used that day.

Neighbor friends knew better than to come to the house and ask if we could play before 1:00 on Saturday afternoons. After all, anyone who knocked on our door was likely to be put to work too.

Mom was an accomplished seamstress, cook, and housekeeper, paying far more attention to detail than I have ever done. She loved to sew but didn't particularly like to cook, even though she was good at it. I, on the other hand, have always loved to cook a great deal more than I like to sew. So Mother and I made a deal: If I could put in the first sleeve of a new dress or do the first quarter part of a hem to her exacting standards, she would then finish the dress while I cooked the next family meal. This arrangement suited both of us. Smart woman, that mother of mine! My desire to excel and do every project to the very best of my ability came from my mother.

My mother could look at a dress in a store window once, then go home and make a similar dress for me. Usually she did this by creating her own pattern from a pattern she already had in her drawer that only vaguely resembled the dress in the window. I loved wearing her creations.

The most incredible garment I ever saw my mother sew, however, was not for me. My piano teacher, a dear family friend, lost her husband quite suddenly. In her grief she was frantic about not having anything appropriate to wear to the funeral. She showed up at our door, arms full of horribly stiff taffeta, hoping my mother could make her a nice dress.

I remember seeing my mother kneeling next to her bed, pleading with heaven to help her complete this difficult, if not impossible, task. Usually Mom would have a woman try on a new dress, unpick a certain section, and resew it. But there was no time for that. This dress would have to fit properly the first time.

I could see no way that dress made from that fabric was ever going to hang on this woman's large frame and look like anything but a very big, very bright tent. But when Mom finished sewing it and the woman put it on, the dress looked stunning on her. I have tears in my eyes remembering my incredible mother, her talent, and her faith. I have watched my mother create many beautiful garments with her sewing machine, but I have never seen such a labor of love and grace.

Many of my most treasured memories center around canning seasons, when my grandmother, mother, aunts, and cousins gathered to peel apples, cut corn off the cob, and snap beans. As we worked, they told stories of their own lives and the lives of our ancestors. These priceless stories have nourished me far longer than any of the preserved food ever did.

My dad could never let anything go to waste. For example, it was not part of his Depression-era upbringing to leave apples to rot on the ground when they could be used to make perfectly lovely applesauce. We spent many fall evenings helping Dad peel a half-bushel of apples that had fallen to the ground. Our homework always got finished, but it sometimes had to wait until after the canning kettle was filled with bottles of fruit.

My dad never wasted an opportunity to teach us. Working on a project or simply spending time with him meant learning about the Roman legions, the Jews, other religions, and a host of other topics. You also learned a lot about Brigham Young University (BYU) sports, if you cared to listen.

My father is one of the most gentle men I have ever known. I only heard him use a cuss word once, and I don't believe I ever heard him raise his voice. He loved his wife, his family, his faith, sports broadcasts, and reading about nearly any topic. My love of knowledge—the quest I have had for facts all of my life—began at home with my father.

Every time I read the very first verse in the Book of Mormon, "Having been born of goodly parents, therefore I was taught somewhat in all the learning of my father," I think of my dad, and I smile.

My siblings and I were not homeschooled. We were, however,

schooled at home—in the evenings, on weekends, and all summer long. My parents tried to teach us almost every minute of every day by precept and by example. My childhood certainly convinced me that parents were more than capable of teaching their children nearly every subject under the sun.

Another lesson I learned from my father? *A person is never too old or too young to learn.* Because of the war and Dad joining the Navy at seventeen years of age, he finally received his honorary high school diploma. He was ninety years old.

CHAPTER THREE

I Can Do It Myself

I have two hands and everything!
—*Me, as soon as I could speak*

As you grow older, you will discover that you have two hands:
one for helping yourself, the other for helping others.
—*Audrey Hepburn*

I *was born with an inquisitive mind* and a need to do things myself, in my own way. I thank my parents for encouraging this in me as a child.

I have often been told I have an unusually well-developed stubborn streak. Many of the stories about my early childhood end with me having said, emphatically, "I can do it myself!" or "I have two hands and everything." Apparently, this happened every time my parents encouraged my older brother to help me do something they assumed was a little beyond my small fingers.

I saw no reason for my brother, who was three years older than me, to know anything that I didn't know. So I listened and I learned as he practiced his new reading skills with my parents. I also remember climbing onto my father's lap as he read to himself in the evenings. I would point to a word on the page and ask him what it said. Then I would ask him why it said that. Ever patient, he would answer: "That 't' says 'tuh'" or "that 'b' says 'buh.'" That was all I needed; I was off and running with reading.

Perhaps because I didn't want to upstage my brother, I kept my developing ability to read to myself. My parents were quite surprised when the teacher of a neighborhood kindergarten told them that I already knew how to read.

LaRee at age four wearing a coat and hat made by her mother

I have very little recollection of a time when I didn't have a book in my hands. As a child, I would often sneak a flashlight out of the junk drawer and read under my bed covers late into the night. Then I would tiptoe to return the book and flashlight to their places before morning.

While I eventually loved school as a child, I had a hard time at first. Already knowing how to read meant that I was just plain bored most of the time. I entertained myself by wandering the room, talking and talking and talking and talking.

My first-grade teacher, Mrs. Nelson, was a newlywed that year. Early in the year her husband came to school one day to take her out for lunch. She wearily told him that she could not go. In a dramatic stage whisper meant for me to hear, she said she had a student—me—staying in for talking during class. I was so embarrassed that she rarely caught me talking out of turn again.

Mrs. Nelson was an excellent teacher for a child like me. As a reward for my more diligent efforts to behave, she would walk with me through the park to the school for older children. We would check out books for me to read when I was bored in class. It was a bribe, of course, but it was a great incentive to be quiet.

Good grades seemed to come easily for me. I had good friends and got along well with my teachers. I usually worked ahead of the class, and, if I was quiet, I could pretty much work at my own pace on whatever interested me.

My parents did their best to provide their children with every opportunity that they could possibly afford, including piano lessons, voice lessons, and eventually for me organ lessons. I have always been grateful for their foresight and providing these special opportunities. Though I'm not as accomplished as I wish I were, music has always been a big part of my life. It is only natural that music was also a focus and a meaningful part of the lives of my own children.

As much as I loved school, summer times were even better—all that delicious time to read, swim, and ride bikes around the valley with friends. But these activities had to fit in between my chores and other jobs. As I grew older I worked hoeing corn and beet fields for farmers in our area. Several area farmers grew large fields of green beans, which were then picked and processed in the local cannery. As fall approached, troops of teens—myself and my friends included—moved into these large bean fields. This work provided the money we wanted for recreation as well as funds needed to purchase school clothes and supplies for the upcoming year.

Even during the school year, most teens in our valley regularly worked either on the family farm, for a neighboring farm, or for a business in town. I went to school with some teens who got up at 4:00 a.m. to work in a bakery before school. Many boys—and some of the girls—milked cows or took care of animals before school. Young people in rural areas tend not to have much time to sit around playing or getting into trouble—at least they didn't in those days.

Every summer our family took time to go on a vacation. It was usually to attend the three-day family reunion my father's family held every summer. Singing together—fun songs that my dad knew—and playing road games in the car are among my happiest childhood memories.

As mentioned, my parents taught by example as well as by precept. One such example was how to treat other people. My parents—and my Aunt Donna and Uncle Owen, who lived this principle in spades—showed me how to look out for the underdog or the mistreated and to make them feel welcome. Every fall as school began, Uncle Owen and Aunt Donna would ask us to look for children whose families appeared to be in need. We were to pay attention to details and report back to them—whether they needed gloves, coats, or winter boots, and the sizes. We were to ascertain what special items they wanted for Christmas and what their parents might need (if we could find out without getting caught). They never set a limit on the number of families we might suggest.

We followed this same holiday tradition every single year. Then a week or so before Christmas, my aunt and uncle would dress up in their Santa and Mrs. Santa suits, borrow a vehicle that wouldn't be recognized, and quietly start stashing Christmas gifts in the garages of these families. It was so much fun to be a part of. Going back to school after Christmas and seeing those children proudly wearing or talking about their gifts was far more gratifying than any presents we may have received.

My parents taught us to look for anyone who was being teased or left out at school or at church. This became a sort of creed among my own group of friends. We tried hard to include anyone who seemed alone or lonely. Sometimes this meant driving more than one car when we went to a movie or swimming in a neighboring town because we had gathered a larger group of friends.

At times as an adult, I have been approached by someone who gives me a hug and tells me how much she appreciated our friendship during her school years. I am not always able to remember their names, as many of the young people we befriended lived in our area for only a few months. But for the time they had been in our school or neighborhood they had been welcomed by my friends and by me. I am as proud of that part of my character as I am of nearly anything else I may have achieved. And again, this all began with my parents and my uncle and aunt.

My grandmother also did her best to instill principles of kindness and service into my young heart. She taught me the following short poem when I was very young, and it became one of my life's mantras. It is a rare week that I don't quote it to someone, somewhere.

> *I have wept in the night*
> *For the shortness of sight*
> *That to somebody's need made me blind;*
> *But I never have yet*
> *Felt a tinge of regret*
> *For being a little too kind.*

My mother suffered several miscarriages during my childhood and teen years. More than once my father called for an ambulance in the middle of the night. Mother's health was often tenuous in other ways as well. I remember her arm being bruised for what seemed like years from the shots the doctor gave her to, in her words, "bring up my iron." This anemia led to extreme fatigue and sometimes nervousness and shortness of temper.

I once asked my father why Mother would sputter in a loud voice for long periods of time. She used that word to describe it—sputtering—but it was much more than that. Such sputtering, when directed at me, usually came when I wanted to do something *my* way and Mother was equally determined that I would do it *her* way. My people-pleasing tendency was sometimes at war with my stubborn streak.

I asked my father why I was expected to be the adult and remain calm while Mother behaved like a child throwing a tantrum. In that calm way of his, but with sadness in his eyes, he replied, "Because you can, and, right now, feeling as she does [meaning the anemia], she cannot."

It took me years to understand what my father was trying to teach me: While we always expect ourselves and others to do their best and strive to be a little better than they were the day before, we cannot expect others to be what they cannot be at the time. People do not have to be perfect to be loved. Families support each other—even during the hard times when a family member seems difficult to love.

One day when I was about ten years old my mother was in the midst of one of her "sputters." We were running late and tensions were high. I dropped a large container of hairpins all over the floor, and Mother's sputtering increased exponentially. A few minutes later, I dropped the hand-painted glass butter dish my great-grandmother had brought over thousands of miles from Denmark to Salt Lake City and then eventually to Idaho. I had been taking it down from the shelf as I wanted to take it to school for show-and-tell.

The bottom plate shattered when it hit the floor, but the hand-painted domed top survived. I was heartbroken. I was also more than a little bit scared. My mother "set a great deal of store by" this family heirloom. If dropping the hairpins had provoked her so, what was going to be the result of breaking Great-Grandmother's prized butter dish?

Mother stopped mid-sputter. She knelt on the floor amidst the broken glass and took me onto her lap. Her voice was quiet as she explained that *things*—any *thing*, no matter how cherished—were only *things*. *People*, she said, were always more important.

She apologized for having been so upset with me all morning. Together we rummaged through the rest of the things in the china cupboard to find another glass plate to put under the intact dome of the butter dish. The one we found didn't exactly match, but to me it looked perfect. All thoughts of being late to school were forgotten. Mother lingered there with me and told me some stories about her grandmother, the original owner of the special dish.

After my mother's death I shared this story with my siblings and asked to take the butter dish home with me. It now sits in a place of honor in the glass-fronted cabinet in my home. I have never replaced the mismatched bottom, even though I have seen plates over the years that match the domed top better. This butter dish is a constant reminder to me of what I glimpsed about family relationships as a child, and what my father taught me later during my teen years: people matter more than things.

Striving to Please

One of my parent's most basic childrearing and life philosophies was *The middle of the road is the safest place to be.* This advice to stay in the middle of the road applied to both thinking and how we were expected to behave.

While I was never encouraged to "follow the crowd off a cliff if that is where they were going," to use my father's words, he often read these verses from the Book of Mormon to me: "It is not common that the voice of the people desireth anything contrary to that which is right." At the time I supposed this meant that it was always best to behave and dress as others did. Being unique and "thinking out of the box" was not encouraged much at all. (*What box?* I came to ask myself in later years.)

Mom's philosophy seemed to be that while being in the middle of the road was great, being out front and leading the pack was even better. She encouraged and expected excellence, being the best or at least highly skilled at whatever we set our hands to. Being "well-thought-of," to use Mom's term, was critically important. I didn't find this philosophy at all hard to follow during my grade school years. Like most children, I liked the praise and attention that doing well brought.

Life got somewhat more complicated when I entered junior high school. Suddenly, instead of just one teacher to impress, I faced a different teacher every hour of the school day. There were also Sunday School teachers, softball coaches, music teachers, and an ever-expanding group of friends to try to please.

How did I respond to these new challenges? I committed myself to pleasing each one of them! If a teacher tended to favor a student who sat in the front row and raised her hand often, I became that student. If a teacher preferred a quiet, studious type that rarely spoke, that was me. I was, almost without exception, every teacher's ideal student—the teacher's pet if they had one. I became a chameleon, not just blending in but remaking myself nearly every moment to be just right.

Looking back, I see that this philosophy of fitting in ran deep in our home. Mom would say to me, "Call Aunt Donna and see what she is wearing tonight." Being well dressed and always putting on makeup—both in public and at home—was simply expected.

My older brother, Lynn, was an enthusiastic supporter of my every endeavor. No girl could have asked for a better big brother. He encouraged me to do my best and would help me if he could. I remember sitting with him in the family car just before my first date. He was advising me on how close to—or how far away from—my date I should sit, what I should talk about, and other critical matters.

I interpreted his advice to mean that I should be exactly what my date for a certain night thought was perfect. Being perfect included knowing how to swim, dive, ice skate, bowl, play volleyball, and anything else a guy might want to do on a date. This, of course, was not what Lynn or my mother intended, but it was what I was learning.

I set a personal goal to be able to speak intelligently on nearly every topic. I was no longer learning for learning's sake; I was studying "to the test." I learned mostly to impress someone else—whether a teacher or one of my dates—rather than to quench my curiosity.

My self-confidence became dependent on what I thought other people were thinking of me. I began to lose who *I* wanted to be in the process of being what I thought everyone else expected me to be. And I began to judge myself by what I saw in other people's eyes: *Did they admire that dress I was wearing? Were my good grades impressing them?*

I don't fault my parents for the way they raised me. There is nothing wrong with expecting the best from your children, believing they are capable and amazing. Certainly, there was nothing wrong with my big brother's advice. I will be forever grateful to my parents for the legacy they left me and the many things they taught me. They were doing their best, and their best was very good indeed.

It was my own interpretation of perfection that led me from being an independent and confident young child to a teenager hanging her self-worth on the opinions of others.

CHAPTER FOUR

Losing Myself

Subtlety has more power to harm than does force.
—*Unknown*

Sometimes you have to lose yourself to discover
who you might yet be. Sometimes what feels like
breaking down is really just breaking free.
—*Cristen Rodgers*

I*t is the middle of the night.* Suddenly, I am wide awake. My heart is pounding; I am terrified! For a few moments I cannot recall why I am so afraid. But I am sure that if I move, even an inch, something horrible will happen to me. I feel as though I am lying on the floor of a dark and dirty van. I can't see the driver, but I know who I would see if I could. I can't breathe.

Slowly the reality of our bedroom comes into focus. I realize I am in my own bed in my own home. My husband is beside me. If Val is here, I must be okay. But I don't feel okay. I am still too frightened for words.

I sense Val is also awake. He speaks to me as he realizes I am rigid with terror. He takes my hand. It is all I can do not to flinch away. I am still caught between two worlds—both feel equally real to me.

Eventually, I calm down somewhat. My mind stops vacillating from one scene to another. We talk and I insist that he get up and check on our children. I insist that he check on his parents. I want him to go to town and check on my parents, also, but I don't ask. The more rational part of my mind is beginning to realize that the terror was only a dream.

Later, Val tells me that he woke up to a feeling of presence in the room—we were not alone. He describes what he sensed as warriors of light, which seems strange to me. I experienced threat; he experienced protection. Perhaps he experienced the protection that we have always known surrounds us.

Later that day, while using newspaper to build a fire in our wood-burning stove, I see a name in the paper of someone I have not thought about in many years: a former boyfriend of mine has been, and maybe still is, in the valley. My hands begin to shake. It has been nearly twenty years since I have seen this man. And I want it to be twenty times more than that before I see him again.

I find it hard to sleep over the next several nights. I startle at noises. I want my children where I can see them every minute. Val arranges a special priesthood blessing for me and for our home. Even with that, I am not completely at ease.

Who was this man who, after all these years, had appeared in my dreams, affecting me in such a way and to such an extent?

I share this story to highlight the impact of being abused or manipulated. There may be residual effects years later, even once healing appears to have occurred. There is no gender differentiation where abuse is concerned. Both men and women can be abusers; both men and women can become victims. Both victims and abusers will inevitably pay a heavy emotional price.

But it is possible to escape an abusive relationship. More importantly, it is possible to see such a relationship coming. I would like to offer some counsel based on lessons I learned the hard way. I want my granddaughters and grandsons to learn from my experience. And if anything I say reminds you of your own situation, please take immediate action.

Two Blankets—Two Very Different Men

Imagine two blankets. Both are vibrantly colored with shades of red and orange, beautiful hues of blue and green, and bright splashes of yellow. The pattern of one blanket is chaotic yet mesmerizing. I am drawn to it like a moth to a flame. It feels as though it will burn me if I touch it, but I touch it anyway. It burns me more than once before I can finally bring myself to set it down and walk away.

The second blanket also has a bold and compelling pattern of brilliant colors. I want to gather it up, wave it over my head, and march with it into the blazing sun. I want to be all that having such a blanket calls me to be—a woman with courage, faith, fortitude, confidence, and the ability to persevere.

This is the picture I hold in my head of two men who played pivotal roles in my life. The one contributed to the temporary yet dramatic loss of my self-confidence and is described in the following two chapters. The other is the man I married.

My Teenage Years

I loved being a teenager just as I had loved being a child. I especially loved turning fourteen. I was all grown up—in my own mind, at least. Mom made me an amazing blue wool dress, very simple but classy. I was allowed my first pair of high heels—rather low, to be sure—but I felt so *mature*. I wore this wonderful outfit when I was given my patriarchal blessing.

In our church there are men called as patriarchs, who serve by giving special blessings called patriarchal blessings. Unlike other types of priesthood blessings, church members receive this blessing only once. It is written down so it can serve as a guide and an inspiration throughout your life. My patriarchal blessing continues to give me great comfort and guidance.

Before long I discovered boys, and soon one in particular caught my attention—and I caught his. He was a gentle young man and much like my father in many ways. We met while ice skating over the Christmas break from school. I was barely fifteen years old at the time; he was two years older. He was absolutely the best sort of first boyfriend, respectful and kind. He thought I was wonderful, and he told me so, often. He never pushed against the standards I had set for myself or encouraged me to be anything but what I wanted to be. He welcomed and valued my opinions on every topic.

He respected my desire to follow the counsel of our church leaders and not formally date until I was sixteen. So in the meantime we participated in group events. He walked me to and from school. He was fun to be with and we had a good time together. We began officially dating when I finally turned sixteen.

He was preparing to serve a two-year proselyting mission for our church, and I supported his decision to go. But my older brother had left a girl behind when he went on his own mission, and I had watched his concern at losing her to someone else while he was gone. I had witnessed her confusion and pain as she dated other young men while waiting for my brother to return home. I had vowed that I would never wreak havoc on some guy's mission years by distracting him from his missionary work with thoughts of what I was up to at home.

It was a heart-rending dilemma because I didn't want this relationship to end. I wanted to share in his mission experience through letters we would exchange, but I didn't want to be the girl a missionary left behind. And besides, I was so young.

I ended the relationship with a heavy heart. I don't know whether it was my own decision entirely or if pressure from family and friends was the deciding factor. I began dating—quite a lot—but other guys seemed so immature after him. One young man showed up to our date drunk, twice.

Without really knowing how, I soon found myself in a new relationship. In our high school, if you went out with the same guy three times, you were "going steady" and were labeled "hands-off" by other young men. This new relationship would end up having a profound impact on me. This relationship is about the first vibrantly colored blanket I mentioned earlier.

Many years later I was given a book called *The Gift of Fear* by Gavin de Backer. This book is about predicting and avoiding danger, abuse, and violence by recognizing the subtle signs of dangerous people. It is about trusting your own "inner knowing" and wisdom. De Backer also speaks of dating, marriage, manipulation, and people who can't let go when the relationship ends. This new relationship would eventually prove to be a perfect illustration of de Backer's key points. I wish I had read it as a teen before I lived so much of it myself.

On our early dates, I sometimes felt vaguely uncomfortable. It seemed innocuous, the way he'd influence me to act in certain ways or to agree with what he had already decided. So often this was over the silliest of trifles—from what time he would pick me up for a date to when, or if, we would order popcorn at a movie. How could such small things matter? What am I getting upset about anyway? I would ask myself questions like these, and if I failed to criticize myself in this way, he would do it for me—with subtle put-downs. But he was charming and exciting and so fun to be with at other times.

Years of experience have taught me there are two kinds of uncomfortable feelings. There is the subtle feeling of knowing that something around you is not as it should be. This is what de Backer describes as the *gift of fear.* The other feeling is irrational or unfounded fear. Sometimes this fear is based on our feelings of inadequacy or fear of the unknown. This is not a gift—at least, not a good gift.

Fear can be used as a tool by the enemy of our souls. This kind of fear will keep us earthbound, unable to soar as we should. It is never wise to let unfounded fears influence our decisions.

It is our faith in ourselves, in the future, and in our Heavenly Father that should guide our daily decisions. Every child should be taught to trust their own assessments and feelings. A person's feelings and "inner knowing" should be respected by themselves and by others—always.

This young man was very attentive. I had experienced attentive behavior before, and I had liked it then. I felt having a boyfriend showering attention on me raised my status among my friends. I thought such attentiveness meant he was wonderful and caring. But in reality, this was neither wonderful nor caring. It was way over the top and sometimes even a little scary. There were constant phone calls, messages sent through friends, almost daily letters in the mail, and expensive and inappropriate presents. He expected me to be grateful for all of it.

He also expected me to reciprocate by lavishing similar attention and gifts on him. I was to praise him, both in his hearing and to other people, who would also lavish praise on him in response to my words. It was exhausting, expensive, and of course my efforts were never good enough. He regularly criticized me for not appreciating him enough. I came to believe that if only I could meet his expectations, everything would be all right.

All the while he was telling tales of other people's bad behavior: his being late for a date, or not showing up at all, was his cousin's or my best friend's fault. Other times he would blame my family for not giving me his message—a message they denied ever receiving. *Did I think he was a liar? Didn't I trust him? Why was I taking everybody else's side?*

I do not remember ever getting my way or having my opinion respected on any topic—and yet it all unfolded so subtly. For example, I would be asked what I wanted to do, where we should go, or what movie we should see. Then each of my choices would be discreetly ridiculed or simply ignored. Sometimes he would override my suggestions in favor of something he knew I disliked or felt uncomfortable with. Even though he was a member of the same church to which I belonged, he often criticized my personal standards. He would tease and humiliate me if I chose to attend church with my family rather than participate in something I would have been uncomfortable with on any day of the week.

Jealousy soon reared its ugly head. He accused me of being too friendly or flirting with any other young man I spoke to. So I began avoiding social situations and became wary of even being civil to other people when I was with him and, eventually, by myself. After all, I never knew when he might be watching. He would park outside my home and in front of the place where I worked. He wouldn't come in; he would just sit in his car hour after hour, watching and taking note of who came by. My job as a waitress—sometimes waiting on ball teams full of young men—became a constant source of trouble.

He would call at odd hours and inappropriate times just to see if I was home and thinking about him. If he called and I was not home, he would keep calling friends until he knew where I was and who I was with. If he could, he would show up there. And when he did, it always ended in a scene, with him demanding explanations and asking why I had not checked with him first. He would pitch a fit because I would not drop everything and leave with him. Was it jealousy? Was he trying to isolate me from family and friends and make me dependent on him?

When he accompanied me to an event I considered important, such as a family gathering or party, I would "owe" him. Without fail, the required repayment would be something that I had refused to do previously—my personal standards were almost constantly under attack. Sometimes the repayment might be doing a favor for one of his friends or family members. This type of manipulation is known as loan-sharking and creates a web of interdependence among the abuser, family, and friends that is difficult to break out of. This scenario happens among family members just as often as in romantic relationships.

He often told me that I had failed to meet him at a certain place when we had not made such a plan. I was accused of breaking a nonexistent and never-agreed-to promise to put him absolutely first, over everybody and everything else.

A more serious twist to these nonexistent promises was that I was never to disagree with his plans for my life. If I talked about going to college, I would be "reminded" that I had promised to keep my waitress job so that I could save up for "our future." I learned quickly to keep any future plans to myself.

This young man didn't pray about much of anything, but he claimed to be sure about us and our future together. He demanded commitment, claiming to know what was best for us both. His denial of my ability to make a decision for myself, or seek personal direction from heaven, became a source of contention.

Sometimes, he talked about running off to Vegas. At first, I thought he was joking. After all, we were so young and neither of us had any job skills. If we had been so foolish as to do such a thing, it was likely that neither of us would have ever obtained even high school diplomas. Looking back, however, I don't think he was serious. It was another way of keeping me off balance.

One particularly nasty technique he used is called the he said/she said game. This can drive wedges of misunderstanding between family members and friends that may never be completely resolved. Oh, the damage this game has caused in every season of my life—and not just by men in romantic relationships. Its other name is just plain gossip.

My boyfriend constantly created a multitude of upsetting stories to tell me. He would claim that my best friend had said such and such, or that a teacher or relative whom I respected had said that I should do a certain thing differently than I was doing it. This nasty game involved leveraging other people's purported opinions or comments to manipulate me into doing—or being—something I did not want to do or be. I began to suspect that nearly everyone was talking about me behind my back while pretending to be my friend and that nobody I liked or trusted really liked or valued me. Almost imperceptibly, I began to believe that the only support—the only true friend I had—was him.

I was angry all the time. I was angry at friends I had previously enjoyed spending time with. I even went so far as to look for things to be angry about as a way to please him. It was challenging to focus on my schoolwork, and I avoided spending time with other friends. All I could see was my anger. Keeping me in such a state of anger with family and friends was a way of isolating me. I was gradually getting cut off from people who could have helped me stand up for myself.

I began to rely more and more on this young man for my own opinion of myself, just as I had relied on my schoolteachers' opinions of me. I had learned his lessons well. This charming manipulator had me exactly where he wanted me.

When I did manage to push back and say no, it was simply not heard. As de Backer points out in his book, manipulative people are drawn to those who cannot say no or who do not know how to say it clearly and emphatically enough that it leaves no room for misunderstanding or manipulation. Every young person should be taught how to say no with authority. They should also be taught how to *hear and acknowledge* the word no.

Years before I read de Backer's book, Val told me, "No is a complete sentence!" I was delighted when I later saw that same phrase in this book. No really is a complete sentence. Anything more than that one word may be seen as an invitation for the other person to argue, challenge, or explain away.

Sometimes even mild disagreement on my part provoked yelling—temper tantrums, really. On the other hand, long silences were just as intimidating and just as difficult to cope with. Sometimes the silence extended for several hours while on a date. Other times it was a long, drawn-out, punishing kind of silence that went on for days—no notes, no letters, no presents, but plenty of stalking behaviors. Or the phone would ring but no words would be spoken when I answered it. He would follow me but refuse to talk to me if I tried to confront him.

It seemed like everything, always, was *my* fault. If I disagreed with him I heard, "Don't you trust me to take care of you?" or "You must think I'm stupid or something" or "You just don't think I'm good enough for you." He—and so many people I have known since—are very good at acting pathetic. The problem, I was told, was *me*—how I was hurting him, making him feel as though life was not worth living. And I bought it because I felt guilty—so guilty that I let him manipulate me even more.

If I wasn't sorry enough, if I didn't do what he wanted, the situation would escalate. Late one night he stopped the car in the middle of a busy highway, on a curve where oncoming traffic might not see him in time to stop. He got out of the car, shouting that he wanted to die because I had refused to go to a certain movie. I had told him I felt that movie was inappropriate, and besides, watching it would keep me out long past my curfew.

That I fell for such behavior, pleading and begging him to get back into the car, may look ridiculous here in print. But the reality at the time was far from ridiculous. I felt both trapped and panicked.

I am proud to say that I did not cave completely—no movie. I wish now that I had had the sense to drive off and leave him there. It was all a game to him, and he didn't intend to lose such a game by being killed or stranded.

He threatened to kill himself at other times. At the slightest show of resistance to anything he proposed, he would threaten to drive off the edge of the old quarry. (I had never been to the old quarry, but I had a good imagination.) Near the end of the relationship, when he could feel me pulling away, he even threatened to take me with him to the old quarry.

Why, you may ask, did I continue to put up with it? I have no idea, except that his appalling behavior was interspersed with good times. I only know that I began to tailor my words and actions to avoid triggering such reactions. Of course, it didn't work. But I was still convinced that if I changed my behavior, somehow things would be different. Things would get better.

One day my mother handed me a newspaper clipping as I walked out the door to school. Mother and I often shared with each other fun or inspiring stories and quotes. This one was different, however. It was Ann Landers's advice column. A young woman had written in about a man who was threatening suicide if she broke off their relationship. Ann's advice was something like, "If he handles disappointment of this kind by contemplating suicide, what will your life be like with him? Will he handle every disappointment or disagreement through the years by scaring you to death with threats of suicide? Will you ever have any stability and peace in your life?"

Then the clincher: "Can you rationally consider bringing children into such a situation as this would be?" She went on to say, "This young man needs professional help. You will be no more qualified to help him when you are married than you are now."

That article hit me hard. I knew exactly how that young woman felt: scared and powerless. I am not trying to be cruel or insensitive. I am not trying to tell you that threats of suicide or violence should never be taken seriously, but to use such threats as a manipulation tactic is the lowest of low behaviors. The very real possibility of suicide or self-harm is what makes such a threat so effective.

I would never presume to advise a person to leave a marriage or other relationship. But, as Ann Landers said, an individual in this situation is not qualified to provide help if professional help is what is needed. Ann Landers's words—delivered by my mother—convinced me that I was not responsible for his behavior, no matter what he said. Ann advised the young woman to send the troubled person to someone who could help him while finding her way to safety and sanity. Even though she wasn't talking directly to me, it felt like she was. This timely advice planted a seed in my heart, which, you will learn, eventually bore good fruit.

A Voice of Reason

This chapter has been just as difficult to write as I originally thought it might be. If you were disturbed by any of it because of your own situation, I encourage you to use reason, reflection, and rational thinking. Please do not act, perhaps unwisely, only on emotions, such as fear or even empathy. Please do not paint the people in your life with the brush of manipulation as I sometimes did to my own husband in the early days of our relationship.

Most of us—men and women alike—have some tendencies toward manipulation. We know what we know and we want what we want. It takes self-awareness and a measure of humility to feel confident that we are acting with the best interests of another in mind. Selfishness and self-righteousness have no place in any lasting relationship.

Few things are more frustrating than watching someone we love making choices that we are sure will bring them pain. There may be times when you can see what is in a friend or family member's best interest better than they can see it themselves. At such times, reasoning, even argument, may be appropriate. Even negotiation and enticements—I will do this if you agree to try this—may be called for.

But we must be careful. We must respect their right to choose. If we find ourselves telling lies, gossiping, playing the he said/she said game, or rewriting history to make a point, we have crossed the line into unrighteous dominion. We have become a manipulator extraordinaire.

People and situations can—and do—change for the better. There is great hope for any person willing to admit to themselves and to others that their actions may have been selfish, inappropriate, or just plain wrong. But a person who must constantly have his own way, or must always be right in every situation, is just as likely to change for the worse as change for the better. Being in control makes the manipulator feel safe. Power is addictive.

It helps if we can trust that God knows us all better than we know ourselves. I have learned that He will guide my actions—and reactions—if I can manage to listen quietly and to trust the direction He gives. There is no substitute for prayer in the great decisions of our lives.

Results

I hope my sharing of such emotional reactions nearly fifty years after the fact brings home to you the lasting impact that abusive and manipulative behaviors can have on one's psyche.

Because of the ongoing manipulation I experienced, I lost trust in myself. I lost trust in others. For years I tended to act irrationally and disproportionately in what seemed like similar situations. My behavior created tense situations and damaged some important relationships. Just as I grappled with the consequences of losing myself, I see the results of the things that I have described here in the lives of women nearly every day.

But over time I did change. I became more confident in my abilities and more certain that I was making good choices. I learned to speak and to act without gauging how others might react. I learned to trust my capacity to pray for and receive answers. I became opinionated. I even became impulsive at times! These were steps forward, or perhaps I should say they were steps back to who I was before I lost myself. Certainly, the lessons I learned through this difficult time helped me to become more of who I wanted to be.

The changes in me were not of benefit to just me. I learned that we need to encourage others and help them feel confident in their abilities. We need to trust ourselves more. We all need faith and loyalty more than we need criticism, blame, and manipulation.

CHAPTER FIVE

Breaking Away

Dear God, please help me break away from
the things that are breaking me.

—*Trent Shelton*

I'll spread my wings, and I'll learn how to fly
I'll do what it takes till I touch the sky
And I'll make a wish
Take a chance
Make a change
And breakaway

—*From the lyrics of "Breakaway" by Kelly Clarkson*

M*any people and events assisted me* in getting my head above water enough to see my relationship with my boyfriend more clearly. Several people provided just what I needed when I needed it. Although they were working separately and without each other's knowledge, they were united in purpose and spirit.

My big brother gently prodded. I valued his wisdom and was always willing to consider his opinions. He reasoned with me in actions rather than words by being an example of what a good young man is like and how such a man treats the women in his life. He began trying to set me up on dates with friends of his. They were also good young men who knew how to treat women with respect and kindness.

My religion and my relationship with my Savior have always been important to me. Even as a teenager, I did not like ridicule aimed at religion or religious people of any faith. I still get testy when I hear someone push people to act against their standards or poke fun at someone's beliefs, no matter how different from my own they may be. There was far too much of that in this relationship.

My boyfriend and I attended a church youth conference with a couple of friends. Toward the end of the day, all the youth were invited to stand and express their feelings and their convictions or testimonies. For those who chose to express themselves, it was a tender and emotional experience. Respectful silence and support are the only appropriate responses at such a time. Yet my boyfriend said something along the lines of "Next thing I know, you will be embarrassing us by running right up there and getting all sloppy and emotional too! Why don't all these idiots just join a convent?"

While his remark offended me, it also pushed my stubborn button. In a fit of temper and without much thought, I stood up, walked to the front of the room, and got in line—with absolutely no idea what I was going to say. As I waited for my turn, the most profound feelings filled my soul. I believe it was the power of testimony and what some term the witness of the Holy Ghost. I felt as though a loving Heavenly Father was reaching out just to me. It was a most singular and memorable experience.

This may not fit your belief system, but it fits mine. For me, it was a significant moment and a huge factor in the demise of this relationship. I wanted out! I wanted to live as I believed, without ridicule and without constant criticism. I wanted to be dating a man of faith, like my father and my brother and my first boyfriend. I just didn't know how to extricate myself from the situation.

Through the course of this relationship, my grandmother saw it all very clearly. She never hesitated to talk to me about the importance of choosing wisely, with the Lord's help, the man whom I would someday marry. She would say, among other things, "You marry whom you date. Be wise. Be careful. Be prayerful."

It is odd that I never resented my grandmother's many direct opinions. I knew she loved me and wanted the best for me. She was in the terminal stage of breast cancer and had a serious heart condition. We could both feel the press of time upon our relationship. I valued every word she uttered and everything she taught me. I loved living next door to her and wish she could have stayed with us longer.

Another event may have been the most compelling one of all for me. One Sunday morning at church, I ran into a young woman whom I greatly admired. She and her husband had rented my parents' basement apartment for a few years after they got married. I babysat for them many times after their first baby was born. In my early teens, she represented the type of ideal woman I aspired to be. She asked to speak to me. We stepped into a nearby empty classroom. The first thing she said was, "Your mother did not put me up to this." Then she added, "I do not know what is going on in your life or who you are going out with, but whatever is in your life that you need to move away from, *do it now. The light has gone out of your eyes.*"

Her words hit hard. I knew she was right, and I knew exactly what the problem was. This young mother's comments brought me up short and forced me to look intensely at my life. Where *was* I going? What *was* I thinking? I saw, plainly enough, that putting off getting out was not going to make it any easier. And I needed to get out.

I never saw that sweet young woman again. She will probably never know how profoundly her words affected my life.

A few days later, I spoke openly with my parents about my situation and the direction of my feelings. Since this increasingly unhealthy relationship had been going on for almost a year, it was past time to have such a talk.

There had been more than a little contention between my parents and me about this relationship. I had not taken their counsel as willingly as I did my grandmother's. My parents challenged me to pray about this young man and our relationship. Dad reminded me that, in order to get an answer to prayer, a person must be willing to live by the counsel received. He encouraged me to do as I had been taught: reason it out in my mind, then go to the Lord with a tentative decision.

My dad recommended only one possibility at first: walk away from this relationship entirely and, after a while, see how I felt. When he sensed my resistance, he suggested that I ask this young man to give me six months to clarify my feelings about our relationship.

My mother counseled me to pray that *I* would understand what to do, and not to pray that *they* would feel differently about the relationship. My mother's advice had a profound effect on me. Praying for understanding and direction became a way of life for me.

I dropped to my knees and prayed the moment they shut my bedroom door. Never had a sincere prayer been answered so quickly and so surely for me. I absolutely *knew* that I must walk away from this relationship entirely. And I also knew that I didn't have the strength to do it. So I chose the scenario my dad suggested and asked for a six-month reprieve.

I slept soundly that night, a first in some time. But I let my parents stew about it all night long. Shame on me! Perhaps they didn't stew. They were people of faith, and I had promised to pray about it with an open mind and sincerely wanting to know what the best thing was to do.

The next morning, I told my parents I was going to ask this young man to give me space to think. Then Mom asked me to promise that I would accept a date from the next guy who asked me. I agreed and, in return, she promised to call off my brother and his attempts to arrange dates for me.

Mom and Dad left to drive Dad to work, six blocks away. By the time Mom returned, the man whom I would eventually marry had called to ask me for a date for the following Friday night. Since the time between my promise to my mom and that phone call was suspiciously short, I asked Mom if she had been doing some backstage arranging—even though I knew she didn't know this young man or his family. She assured me that she had done no such thing.

I don't believe much in coincidences, but I do believe in miracles and in the intervention of a loving Heavenly Father in our lives. I also know, from years of personal experience, that prayers are answered. Did heaven understand that I would not be able to stand firm in my decision on my own? I think so. So He sent help: a knight in shining armor and a cowboy hat—a young man whom I barely knew and who was a complete stranger to my parents. Come to find out, this young man was also responding to a heaven-sent prompting, if you will, to call me at that early hour of the morning.

That same day I called my boyfriend. I asked him not to contact me for six months to allow me time to get my head straight about what I wanted for my future. My parents were relieved and happy for me. I felt a rather large sense of relief myself!

My relief didn't last long. Over the next few months, my now ex-boyfriend brought a lot of pressure to bear to change my decision. Even his family members got involved. I was pulled out of class at school for a visit from his father, and again for an uncle he had lived with, and then for a cousin, each in their turn. I received many phone calls, and all of them had essentially the same message: I was disappointing everyone. These people all thought they knew better than I did what was best for both of us.

I was informed that our relationship was the only worthwhile thing this young man had to cling to and was his only chance at a normal life. In light of his previous suicide threats, this was meant to scare me—and it did. Fortunately, since I had made up my mind to step away for a season, this sort of pressure only served to solidify my resolve. I had been pressured enough by this young man; I didn't need his family adding to it.

When his father visited me at school, he told me his son had been making payments on an engagement ring. "That's how serious he is!"—as if such "seriousness" should be enough to change my mind. He even offered to pay for the ring himself and put it on my finger. His unspoken message was *My son wants this, so you should want it too.*

Was being bribed with an engagement ring I didn't want supposed to make me stay in this relationship? Finally, I got angry and shouted loud enough that my teacher came into the hallway to check on me. Frustrated, his father left the building. I went back to my classroom more determined than ever.

Perhaps I should have been more patient with these messengers. Perhaps he had manipulated them into saying the things they did. Manipulators cultivate friendships with people who cannot say no; often they train their own family members, over time, to obey.

Angry was a good thing for me to be that day. I was finding my voice at last. I had found that I could boldly speak up for myself.

As you might expect—and as I should have expected—this young man completely ignored my request for six months of no contact. Every type of manipulation scheme he had previously used against me was used again, but this time with a sharper and more determined edge.

I also should have foreseen that my breaking it off completely would trigger a whole new level of stalking.

I was still working as a waitress. The restaurant had a dining room and a snack counter, and to move between these two areas waitresses had to pass by a set of large glass doors that led outside. My now-former boyfriend would sit parked in front of those doors my entire shift. Every time I walked by he would flash his lights and honk his horn. It was nerve-racking. My boss wasn't too happy about it either.

My parents had planned to go out of town, and my dad was worried about leaving me home alone. But I was determined and convinced my parents that I would be all right. Besides, I had relatives next door to keep an eye on things.

I was in the middle of refinishing my grandmother's kitchen table, which I had been given. I was working on it in the garage and needed to leave the garage door open for ventilation.

My former boyfriend parked his bright red sports car down the street where he could keep an eye on me as I worked. He stayed there for three days and three nights, leaving only occasionally for a few minutes at a time. I called the police. He would move on when he saw them coming but come right back after they left. I would call the police again and the scene would repeat itself. I didn't sleep well. I was nervous, on edge, every minute. It was more than a week until my parents finally returned home.

By the end of this frightening week, my resolve had hardened. I broke off the relationship completely. It was over. I wanted nothing more to do with this young man and with the fear that I had experienced.

A short time after this relationship ended, I attended a church meeting for young women. After the main speaker had finished teaching us, her husband spoke. I don't remember what her topic was, but his words stayed with me.

He told of pressuring his wife into marrying him when they were very young. He described having no job skills and little idea how to carry on as an adult. I wondered if he had been similar to the young man I had dated. Then he said that fortunately for him, she had taken a chance on him. I remember those words clearly—"taken a chance" with her future. Then he said with a smile, "Fortunately for her, I eventually grew up and turned out better than she had any reason to expect at the time."

He then asked the young women in the room, "What if I had not matured into a good husband and provider?" He added, significantly, "Please, don't any of you take the same chance with your future that my wife took with hers! It could have turned out so badly for her."

CHAPTER SIX

Finding Myself

If you are holding on to the past, let go!
What you are holding on to may be what is holding you down.
If you let go, you might surprise yourself by rising!
—*Val D Westover*

What if the change you have been avoiding
is the one that gives you wings?
—*Butterfly Express Christmas ornament*

O*n a brighter note,* I was enjoying going on dates with the new young man in my life. On one of our early dates we went to a dance, but, as I remember, we didn't dance much—not even when my brother asked me to dance with him. I was having such a good time talking and laughing with my date that I kept telling my brother "later" and "later" yet again.

Val recalls, however, that we danced almost constantly that night. He says he had us on the floor dancing so he wouldn't have to think of something to say. He claims that his hips were sore for days afterward!

When the dance ended, we drove to Logan, Utah, for dinner. We laughed and talked over dinner, having so much fun together that, without realizing it, we didn't start for home until way past my curfew.

My parents were quite strict about curfew. Because we had just started dating, they did not remember my date's name or what kind of car he drove. My aunt and uncle, my parents, and my brother were out looking for me when we got home. Was I ever in hot water—but I wouldn't change one minute of that night.

The next few months passed quickly. I was head over heels in no time. Our early courtship—the rest of our senior year of high school, the following summer, and our first year of college (me at Brigham Young University and Val at Utah State University)—were among the happiest days of my life.

Even though I felt joy and a renewed sense of self in this new relationship, it was also a nerve-racking time as pain and fear lingered from the former one; I spent too much time looking over my shoulder.

After a short while, Val quietly and efficiently took care of my former boyfriend's stalking. The result was a reprieve of more than a year, and gradually I relaxed. Eventually though, whenever Val was not with me, I would once again see my former boyfriend at the back of a church meeting or in other places. This new round of stalking lasted for only a short time, but I learned, once again, to be very wary and to travel in groups with other girls whenever possible.

My mother often remarked that Val had been an answer to her prayers. She rejoiced in the return of my confidence and naturally sunny disposition. She often said that she didn't worry about Val's obvious confidence in himself because "Val obviously thinks you are as amazing as he considers himself to be."

Early in our relationship, I see us sitting in his car in front of my parents' house. My mother is flipping the front porch lights on and off, reminding me that sitting in a car with a boy at the end of a date is not permitted. Val is trying to get me to form an opinion on something—perhaps a movie for next weekend's date. But I can't do it. For so long, nearly every opinion I voiced resulted in drama. Testing the wind for the right answer had become second nature to me. Pleasing people and transforming to match others' expectations had cost me dearly, but I hadn't learned how to stop doing it yet.

As a result, our relationship developed its own stresses. I was veering between a determination to avoid another relationship and experiencing absolute joy in Val's company. I wanted it to go on forever, yet at the same time I wanted nothing to box me in.

I learned later that women who have been deeply hurt by the manipulation of others often behave as I did. I painted this new relationship, and Val, with the colors of where I had come from. I met any kind of pushing—even pushing to think for myself—with silent resentment. It took time, but eventually—as Val loves to tell everyone—I prayed about our relationship, decided to trust, and *I* proposed to *him*.

We were sitting in his car before going into a wedding reception. Val was struggling with his tie, craning to see it in the rear-view mirror. I suggested that what he really needed was a wife to take care of things like that. I was only half joking as I didn't even know how to tie a tie. "Is this a proposal?" he asked. Without a moment's hesitation, I replied, "Of course!"

I had never seen anyone quite like Val. Not even my own amazing brother could compare. He was so full of life. Despite all his fun-loving enthusiasm, he had his priorities completely in line. I knew he was what I wanted in my future husband and in the father of my future children.

Val's goals matched my own. He wanted a wife and a family and to care for them properly. He had a strong testimony of the restored gospel of Jesus Christ, a deep love for his Savior, a knowledge of scripture, and a desire to live right by his fellow man and the Lord. And yet there was nothing stuffy or severe about him. And I was confident I was holding hands with the man I had held hands with in the preexistence.

Perhaps that phrase, *held hands with in the preexistence,* needs an explanation. One of the tenets of my religion is that we existed before our mortal birth. We lived as spirit children of a loving Heavenly Father and Heavenly Mother in a pre-earth state. Some members of my faith believe that we made certain covenants or promises while there. Val and I believe, firmly, that we knew each other there and made promises to one another. This belief has been a great strength to both of us during challenging times.

Some of my favorite memories of our courtship are things like messing up his mother's kitchen making no-bake cookies, using his own special no-recipe. They turned out marvelously, but then he splattered them all over the carpeted stairs as we ran down to share them and play another game of pool with our friends.

Imagine young people on dates playing run-sheepy-run in the grade-school yard! We did that more than once. We spent long, lazy days at Twin Lakes or at the local (thirty miles away is local here) swimming pool. We hiked the hills around our valley. We rode horses—quite an experience for this novice.

Yet it wasn't all fun and games. I got acquainted, to some extent, with farm life. I thought that since my dad had a cow or two, chickens, and pigeons, I knew something about "country life." I had fished, hiked, and even hunted. I had hoed beets and picked beans to earn money for school clothes. But I soon learned that I didn't have a clue about—or the proper clothes for—*real* farm life.

Nearly every time I went to Val's family farm, I destroyed another pair of the cotton pants my mother had made for me. So my future mother-in-law bought me a pair of sturdy Levi's to wear when I was on the farm, and they stayed at the farm. Only years later did I realize that neither of Val's sisters helped haul hay or brand cattle or do any of the work I did that summer. Sure, they owned Levi's, but they wore them for light yard work and gardening.

Why was I all over the farm, getting dirty and ruining my clothes? It was because I wanted to be wherever Val was. What was the point of being there if I was in the house visiting with the women while Val was outside? I didn't want to miss even one chance to be with him.

Val made our engagement official by proposing to me and putting an engagement ring on my finger just before he left to serve a mission.

CHAPTER SEVEN

The Best Two Years

By becoming the answer to someone's prayer,
we often find the answers to our own.
—*Dieter F. Uchtdorf*

Y*oung male members of our church* are encouraged to serve a two-year proselyting and service mission before they settle into marriage, college, or a career. This is all at their own expense, and their families may help. On their return, most of them describe this experience as the best two years of their lives. I can think of no better preparation for marriage and adulthood than such a mission experience. Today, thousands of young women in our church also serve missions—far more than did in my day.

It is unusual for a couple to get engaged before a young man's mission experience. In fact, it is advised against. Looking back, I see this step as the first of many other times when we would depart from the "middle of the road," walking together.

Many expressed concern about our engagement. Two of my brother's college roommates called to ask me out. I suspect it was because the girls they had left behind for their missions hadn't waited for them. They were probably thinking, *Why does this guy think his girl will wait when ours didn't?*

My parents, also, were not completely thrilled with me—in Mom's words—"putting myself on a shelf" for two years. And they weren't sure it was the wisest choice for Val, either. They needn't have worried about him in this regard. Val told me later that knowing what his future would be—and knowing who his future would be—made it easier for him to focus on his missionary service.

Because of my brother's experience, I had previously vowed never to promise that I would wait for a missionary. Nevertheless, after some time and much prayer, I decided to follow the counsel of heaven and trust that this relationship was right and that it would still be right when he returned.

Val's Experience with the Missionaries and Their Girls

When I was seventeen, I met a girl I liked. I prayed to know whether I should marry her. The answer was "yes." She was the first girl I ever dated. When she finally prayed and felt the same, she proposed. I accepted.

When LaRee and I became engaged, we were planning for forever. This was not to be a marriage of convenience. It was not based only on physical or even emotional attraction. The commitment was illuminated by prayer. I served a two-year mission, months after the covenant (our engagement) was made.

Engagements with departing missionaries were discouraged by some and ridiculed by most. I had a picture of my girl and my horse. When I got to the missionary training center, I was thrown in with several hundred young men. Most had girlfriends and pictures. The favorite activity was showing pictures of girls. This was accompanied by declarations of the certainty of the girl being there waiting when the young man got home. "She really loves me, and I know she will wait," could be heard everywhere.

The fear that their girls would not wait for them, but would marry someone else before they returned, was palpable. Those with the most fear were clamoring the loudest. It was as if their own convictions depended on convincing others. To calm their troubled souls, they needed to have others believe. It left a sickness in my stomach. My girl's picture stayed in the suitcase. We had something special; it was too sacred to spoil in that manner.

Instead I got out the picture of my horse. It was nice. It was in full color and in a gold frame. It was nicer than most of the pictures that my mates had of their girls. You can imagine the fun my companions had with that. They came from two floors down to see and make fun. Someone in authority came up to see what the uproar was about. "Please keep it down and act like missionaries." They all let off a lot of pent up emotions teasing me about my horse.

At first, I was intimidated. Then I was inspired. When a break came in the hoopla I quietly said, "I am sure she will wait." It was quiet. I had won after all. Suddenly, I was a hero. Amid claps on the back and cheers, I smiled. I remember thinking it would be nice to tell them the rest of the story, but I did not tell them my girl was wearing a diamond!

My horse waited. Unfortunately, LaRee's picture spent many weeks in my suitcase. And she waited too.

The Mission Years for Me

I expected the wait to be difficult, but I felt they ended up being the best two years—up to that point—in my life.

Those two years for me were good for me in many ways. I focused on my school studies and had the time and the desire to study the scriptures and the gospel of Jesus Christ. And I planned and prepared for my future roles as wife and mother.

I began to make my own decisions again. I even began to demand that my decisions be respected. Taking responsibility for and control of my life was an important step for me.

I was privileged to have a dear roommate at BYU who had temporarily given up on dating as she focused on her education. We had many memorable times together during those two years. My own wedding and hers occurred exactly one week apart.

I joined an on-campus group of girls who were waiting for their missionaries. They held monthly meetings, and sometimes special guests were invited to speak. I remember one in particular, who informed us that he was very opposed to missionaries leaving girls behind. But then he gave an amazing talk about the importance of learning to "wait well." He explained that, for much of our adult lives, we would be waiting for something—a new job, a new home, a child to be born. Then he counseled us on how to wait well, meaning with faith, patience, and service. His words have positively influenced my life for the last forty-five years.

Other experiences with this group were not so uplifting. The night of our spring formal dance, most of the girls dressed up in formal gowns, bought themselves corsages, and took their missionaries' pictures out to dinner. I refused to participate. Being curious, however, I observed from the restaurant foyer as the girls were seated around several large tables. Beside each young woman was an empty seat, with her missionary's picture on the table in front of the empty chair. Each girl in turn held up her picture to the group and spoke about her missionary. There were tears and protestations of eternal devotion—even though many of the girls were dating other young men while "waiting."

Again, as with Val and the young missionary men, the doubts these young women felt were palpable, as was their pain and fear. I could hardly get out of there fast enough.

What Val and I had, based on prayer and joy in an eternal commitment to each other, was entirely different from what I saw in that restaurant. I learned to wait well, and this has enabled me to wait upon the Lord and trust in his timing better than any other experience I could have had. Those two years were excellent preparation for my future life.

Pygmalion

While attending BYU the fall after Val left, I was assigned to read George Bernard Shaw's play *Pygmalion*. Based on the Greek myth of

Pygmalion and Galatea, which some describe as the most influential and inspiring of the ancient Greek myths, the play struck a discordant note in me. It offends me even more deeply now than it did then. I wondered how I had missed this myth's dark undercurrents during my Greek Myth Studies class in high school.

I read the CliffsNotes for Shaw's play to see if others reacted to this tale of manipulation as strongly as I had. Apparently, I was still looking, to some extent, for validation of my thoughts and feelings by checking with others. Realizing that by doing this I was discounting my own opinions made me almost as angry at myself as I was at the message put forth by this play. I became even more determined to think for myself and not be molded by other people's opinions.

One sentence from the CliffsNotes stood out so much I wrote it in my journal: "Eliza develops a soul of her own and a fierce independence from her creator." I wanted such fierce independence again. I knew I had possessed it as a child. I valued the progress I had been making in getting it back during the previous year.

I knew to the depths of my soul that the entire concept of anyone attempting to remake another into their own image of the perfect woman was wrong. This was the early 1970s and a time of unrest among women. Perhaps that influenced the intensity of my reaction. But I am confident that some of my initial aversion to this play stemmed from my toxic dating relationship in high school.

I realized, with a jolt, that being molded was exactly what I had allowed, and sometimes sought, then. I made a promise to myself right then to strive even harder to break the habit of looking to others for validation and approval. I understood, finally, what Val had been trying so hard to teach me when he insisted I give an opinion before I ascertained his wishes. I did not offer my college teachers the same spinelessly ideal student that I offered my high school teachers.

Even though I developed a deep and lasting aversion to people who manipulate the opinions and personalities of others, I still carried remnants of a deep-seated fear of conflict. I found that being my own person was a harder concept to live by than to aspire to. Sometimes, if I was not vigilant, going along to get along was still easier than standing up for myself.

A playbill for *My Fair Lady*, based on Shaw's play, reads, "A *misogynistic* and *snobbish* phonetics professor agrees to a wager that he can take a flower girl and make her *presentable* in high society." Was she better off being *presentable* to people who did not know and love her than being comfortable and happy among family and friends? This molding of another person into a prescribed form is, according to my observations and experiences over a lifetime, destructive to everyone involved.

Moving On

I had earned a large number of college credits during my high school years. I spent my first year at BYU completing general education classes. During my second year (which was the first year of Val's mission) I completed—except for one class—a two-year program in secretarial technology. I took first- and second-year shorthand during the same semester and aced both.

By the end of my sophomore year, I felt that I had gained what I needed from higher education. I was excited when I landed a job with a cutting-edge computer manufacturing firm. Many of the skills I had learned—shorthand, how to use mimeograph copying machines—were already obsolete in the computer world. I loved this job and the people with whom I worked. I learned much from them, and not just about computers. It was a productive way for me to finish out the final months of Val's mission time.

This new job was close enough to my parents' house to allow me to live there and drive to work. Mother and I used this season to prepare for my wedding. And I enjoyed spending more time with my younger brother and my youngest sister, who was seven years old.

CHAPTER EIGHT

At Long Last

We loved with a love that was more than love.
—*Edgar Allan Poe*

In you I found my best and truest friend,
the love of my life, and the
companion of my eternities.
—*LaRee Westover*

V*al, my fiancé, returned from his church mission* just before my twenty-second birthday. His parents and I met him at the airport. I don't believe I had ever been so nervous before in my entire life.

It had been two years since we had seen each other. Sure, we had exchanged countless letters and had even talked on the phone a couple of times. My mother took a picture of me on one of those occasions. She said she took the picture because I looked so happy. In the photo my whole face is literally glowing! I knew I still loved him, but I was nervous. I knew that we had both grown and changed in those two years.

Val is his parents' only son. While I was his fiancée and had missed him so much, I didn't want to be in the way of them welcoming their son home, either.

We waited and watched as various people streamed off the plane.

Suddenly, there he was—dressed in a missionary style suit with shiny new shoes and a brand-new *cowboy hat* on his head! As soon as I saw him, I knew that everything was going to be okay. He was older and more mature, obviously, but that cowboy hat spoke to me. He was still the same young man that I had grown to love so deeply—and he was home!

His mother dragged us all off shopping for my birthday. In a few short minutes, it was almost like we had never been apart. I still have the earrings we bought that day. They may be out of fashion now, but I love them.

It took some time for Val to muster the courage to get married. Getting engaged when the responsibilities of marriage were at least two years away proved easier for him than actually getting married. He loved me, but he had sense enough to know that marriage was a serious undertaking. Perhaps he saw—as he so often does—more clearly into the future than I could. I was blissfully happy and largely unaware that there could be bumps in the road ahead.

We had officially been engaged for nearly three years by the time we married. That had given me ample time to plan my wedding. I chose something to my taste for my wedding dress—plain white velvet, simply made.

My mother had been planning for her first daughter's wedding my entire life. She had a wealth of ideas. She had made many wedding dresses for others, all beautifully constructed, but intricate. After some tension and compromise, we agreed on a dress pattern that I liked and that almost satisfied her desire to create the most beautiful dress possible.

Mother even made a small version of my wedding dress to fit a blond-haired doll she had purchased. The miniature outfit matched every detail, complete with an intricate veil.

I have told few people about a memory I hold very close to my heart from the morning I was married. For you to understand it, a short walk down memory lane may be necessary.

My grandmother died right after my seventeenth birthday and a few short weeks before my first date with Val. She would have loved him very much.

While I was always close to my grandmother, this connection became even deeper during the final stages of the illness that led to her death. She would call our house when she was lonely or in a lot of pain. If I was home, I would walk next door and spend time with her. I often broke dates to respond to her calls, which had increased the stress in that already stressful relationship. Spending time with Grandmother was one of the few things I stood up for.

Grandma would tell me stories about her life. Perhaps she wanted to teach me as many of life's lessons as she could while she was still able. I wish I had had the good sense to record her stories.

Sometimes when she called me, she would want me to place my phone receiver on the piano bench and play her a song. The song was always the same, a hymn special to her because it had played a role in her mother's conversion to the church that she loved so dearly.

As a young woman in Norway, her mother (my great-grandmother) had met missionaries from The Church of Jesus Christ of Latter-day Saints. She became convinced that she had found important and eternal truths and badly wanted to join this restored religion. She was in her teens and still living at home. Her father was opposed to this new American religion his daughter wanted to join.

Eventually, she persuaded her father to accompany her to a meeting, and the hymn the small congregation sang touched her father deeply. He felt he was hearing truth, beautifully presented, and that a religion who taught such doctrine could only be a good thing. He not only gave her permission to join this church but also joined himself, along with his entire family. Their family later left everything behind in Norway and emigrated to the United States to join others who believed as they did. I will forever be grateful to my great-grandmother for her legacy of faith and the path that she chose.

The hymn that was sung in that meeting was titled "O My Father," and the lyrics tell a beautiful story about our Heavenly Parents, the love they have for us, our sojourn on Earth, and our longing to return home having accomplished all that He "sent [us] forth to do." This hymn also holds a special place in the hearts of many of my family members. I played it on the piano at my grandmother's funeral, and it was played by my sister-in-law at my own mother's funeral. I hope it will be played at my funeral when that time comes.

Grandmother almost always stood on her front porch and waved goodbye to us as we left for school each morning. The last year of her life, however, especially during that cold fall and early winter, she could stand only at her kitchen window. No matter how bad she felt or how much her legs hurt, she would wave a white handkerchief to increase the chances of us seeing her. Since she died before I met Val, he had never seen this loving send-off.

Early on the morning of our wedding, Val picked me up at my parents' home. I was feeling quite sad that Grandma would not be at the wedding with me. I was wishing she could have met the man I was marrying and could have seen who I had become in the years since her death. I wanted to ask for her advice and listen to her wise counsel as I embarked on this new chapter of my life.

As Val and I pulled away from the house, Val asked who was waving a white handkerchief from the kitchen window of my grandparents' home. I looked up and there she was, my beloved grandmother, sending me off for my special day in her own special way. She had been gone for more than four years. How I loved seeing her one more time and in this very personal way.

I also felt her presence throughout that special day. I have since come to understand that departed loved ones are often close to us during the most sacred—or most trying—times of our lives. I have often felt words of counsel and comfort coming from my grandmother. I look forward to seeing this beloved mentor in person again someday.

Val and I were married in the Logan Utah Temple. In our church, being married in the temple includes an ordinance called a sealing, meant to preserve a marriage and a family beyond death, for eternity.

It is a sacred and special privilege, lived for and earned by faithful members of The Church of Jesus Christ of Latter-day Saints. I had looked forward to being married there all of my life, and it met all of my expectations and hopes.

For years, Val and I have served one evening a week in the temple. This was also a lifelong goal and has been a great blessing to us. I had witnessed firsthand the greater peace, tolerance, and love that grew between my own parents through their service in this same temple. Although our marriage was already solid, I have seen much the same thing unfold in our lives.

Perhaps some information about temples and the work that is done therein may be appropriate. As temple workers, we assist patrons who are coming to make special covenants with God. These covenants, if faithfully kept, will bring blessings into their lives. We also assist patrons who act as proxy in the same sacred ordinances for deceased ancestors. One such ordinance is baptism, and another is the sealing of husbands and wives to each other for eternity. The blessings of these covenants are then available to be accepted or rejected by those ancestors who did not have this opportunity while they were alive.

In the New Testament, the apostle Paul was teaching the Corinthian saints about the resurrection when, in First Corinthians 15:29, he asks the question, "Else what shall they do which are baptized for the dead, if the dead rise not at all? Why are they then baptized for the dead?" Paul was referring to a practice in the early Christian church that the Corinthians were obviously familiar with. They were performing sacred ordinances, by proxy, in behalf of their dead, which is the pattern we follow today.

Our youngest daughter described us from our wedding photos as "intoxicated with happiness." In one of those photos, Val's expression looks just like mine did in the picture my mother snapped during my phone conversation with him while he was on his mission—supremely happy.

Even though our understanding of the breadth of covenants we were making was somewhat limited at that time, we knew that we were creating something much bigger than ourselves. Now, after nearly forty-six years of marriage, we understand better the depth of the commitment we made that day. Our faith in each other and in the two of us as a team has strengthened us to face challenges and even tragedies together.

Val's Account of Our Wedding

When I got home from my mission, we planned and prepared. When we were married, LaRee was a virgin, and so was I. We had waited. We went, as planned, to the temple of the most High God to be married. There, across the altar, we made covenants with God and with each other. Our marriage was designed from the very beginning to last forever.

The covenant we made was bigger than ourselves. It reached out into the millenniums ahead. It was charted to be more than just a marriage. It was promised to be more than just man and wife. Our marriage was sacred. It was blessed by the most High God. He sanctioned it. Although our understanding was limited, we knew we had created something bigger than ourselves.

An eternal marriage is more than just sharing. It is more than being mates. It is standing, leaning together when neither can stand alone. It is more than goals and yearnings. It is to believe together, when others doubt. It is faith in each other, in the combined, when others fear. It is to face tragedy together and survive.

It is also cherishing the results of faith—the miracles, the dreams, the impossible aspirations faced and obtained. It is miracles believed in and received. Yearnings achieved. Being in awe together of the majesty of the union. After a lifetime of being rewarded by faith, of feeling the approbation of God on the union and His intervention on behalf of the marriage, it has become something very sacred.

We were sealed by the power of Elijah for time and for all eternity. Could one of us change our mind? Of course. This was not a sentence.

It was an opportunity of epic proportions. We would have to work hard to keep it. We would have to love and forgive. We would have to be kind and considerate. We would have to become one in our desires and yearnings. We would have to reach the potential we had seen in each other. We would have to cling together above all else. This union would include children.

Together forever? An impossible star? Why rain on my parade? Would a commitment, a goal, or a plan have any impact on a marriage? It did not matter which road Alice in Wonderland took, because she was not going anywhere.

It will never work, some said. It cannot be done, from others. I have been accused of being a dreamer. If you are going to dream, why not dream big? Why not shoot for a star? Has our trying, our commitment, our unrelenting perseverance not had a positive effect? Do we need more divorce? Do we lack for more broken homes? You may not believe; you may not even be moving toward such a goal. But I do and am. I am getting closer to my star. My faith is turning into hope. Our marriage no longer can or will be interrupted by any earthly power or event.

The sweetness of our many years of marriage, of striving and reaching, has given me a hope that even death will not erase. It is a sweetness, an enduring peace, that shines through all the world's paltry and self-serving appeasements.

Take my money, my possessions, all that I have or hope to be, my life if you must. I will give it all for this one joy that springs eternal: I am hers; she is mine. Forever.

CHAPTER NINE

Wedded Bliss and Real Life

Being deeply loved by someone gives you strength,
while loving someone deeply gives you courage.
—*Lao Tzu*

Courage doesn't always roar. Sometimes, courage is the quiet
voice at the end of the day, saying, "I will try again tomorrow."
—*Mary Anne Radmacher*

V*al had worked hard to earn money* to support himself during his missionary service. He worked before and after school and during the summer months of his high school years. The year prior to leaving, he raised and sold baby calves and all but slept with the fragile critters the first weeks of their lives. He was tired nearly all the time. Sometimes I would ask to drive on our dates and would drive around aimlessly for a while just to give him an opportunity to sleep.

We expected that the money he had saved would be gone by the time he returned from his mission service. But his parents, bless them, had used their own funds to pay his mission expenses without our knowledge. That left the money Val had saved sitting in the bank, a nest egg with which to start our lives together. My own parents had done the same for my brothers.

What a blessing this sacrifice on their part was for us. With those savings, we were able to purchase a modest house in Logan, Utah, where Val had returned to school at Utah State University. There was even money left over, which we used to set up a part-time business to help support us. We were thus able to start our family *almost* as quickly as Val and I wanted to.

Once Val got past the fear of the responsibility he was taking on, he embraced marriage as he embraces all new aspects of life—with unbounded enthusiasm. He became very excited about the idea of adding to our family right away. Adding a child to our family the very first minute would not have been too soon in his estimation.

Having been raised on a farm with cattle and horses, he understood such things as conception and gestation. He knew that it would take time; after all, nine months was almost half the time he had been away from me on his mission.

We had been married for only a few weeks when Val came home and showed me an application to be foster parents. He had even tried to get the agency to give him an application for adopting. We were both delighted when, not long after, I became pregnant with our first child.

At first, Val said that he wanted our expecting a baby to be a secret for a little while. But his excitement got away from him as soon as my parents walked in our door. He couldn't wait another minute to share with them the good news.

That first summer, with me pregnant and still working full-time, Val and I experienced our first canning season together. An acquaintance had an orchard of pie cherries he offered to us gratis. Val took our new little Chevy Luv pickup and a large box to fill with these free cherries. He not only came back without the box, but the entire pickup was full of cherries. Enthusiasm and an attitude of *If a little is good, a lot is a lot better* are hallmarks of his personality. But how many cherries could we get into bottles and process before they started to spoil? We found out the hard way—and it was a lot of fun.

Val rounded up his sweet Aunt ReNee to help us, and they set to work pitting the cherries. I prepared the pie filling sauce and tended the cookers for the next two nights. They continued to work on the cherries during the day while I was at work. By the second night, they were both falling asleep over heaping bowls of pitted cherries. But we got it all done and lived to tell about it.

A few weeks later my parents brought bunches of Concord grapes to be made into juice. And when that canning party was nearly finished, Val sent my parents home, me to bed, and cleaned up the kitchen—every dish, cupboard, every square inch of the sticky floor—before going to bed himself. He was singing the entire time. Even though he was still attending classes at the university and was also working full-time himself, my health and our baby were his first concerns.

Married life was happy, but it came with normal challenges and setbacks. The winter before we were married, Val had broken his leg while we were walking back to his car after a campus event one very cold night. We had tucked our clasped hands into the warm pocket of his coat, and then I slipped on the icy steps. In trying to keep me from falling, Val slipped. He hit the ground, and I came down on him—right on his leg that lay at an angle against the edges of two of the concrete steps.

When people asked how he broke his leg, he would answer, "My fiancée fell on me!"

Even though Val got his cast off in time for our wedding, his leg had not healed properly. Walking was painful if he wasn't extremely careful. The following summer, he rebroke it along the same fracture line while playing tennis. This time, we consulted the best specialist we could find—the team doctor for the Utah State football team.

The doctor told us it was too bad Val was not a member of the football team so that he could treat his broken bone properly. What he would have done involved removing the cast every day so that the leg could be soaked and massaged. He explained that muscles atrophy while in a cast, and bones do not fare very well either.

We certainly couldn't afford such comprehensive treatment, as it wouldn't be covered by insurance. So we did what we thought was the next best thing: Val committed to staying off the leg for as long as necessary, and, after a few days, we cut the cast off ourselves. Val had brought an herbal book home from his mission called *Back to Eden*. We had both read it but had not tried using herbs yet; we decided to try them now. Every day, we soaked his leg in a mixture of herbs—comfrey, predominantly—and massaged the leg muscles. His leg healed perfectly and in a shorter time than we dared hope. We had witnessed our first herbal miracle. Our learning journey within the herbal world had begun.

Our home in Logan was not large, but it was brand new and included an unfinished basement. Val sister's fiancé and his roommates were given notice to move out as soon as possible, as their apartment was needed for the owner's daughter and her children. Six college men needed a place to live, and quickly. So my generous husband invited them all to live with us in our unfinished basement. I should have expected this, as his mother had warned me long ago that Val's first words as a baby might just as well have been, "Guess who followed me home for dinner, Mommy?"

The young men moved in and quickly threw up walls for bedrooms. But construction on a kitchen and bathroom in the basement proceeded too slowly for my liking. In the meantime, they shared ours on the main floor.

I was newly married and newly pregnant; having six extra men underfoot, sharing my bathroom and my kitchen, was a novel experience for me. Oh, the stories I could tell you! Having found my voice, I made sure the construction downstairs progressed, and they also learned to leave the tub clean and the kitchen tidy.

They really were great guys, and we all settled in nicely.

I began reading all I could find about pregnancy and new babies. I was going to be ready for this adventure. I thought I had a good idea of how arduous labor would be, and when I expressed concerns about it, one dear woman said, "Labor is not so bad. I've had bowel movements that were worse." I was so naïve and uninformed that I tended to believe her.

The birth of our first child was a nasty experience for both of us. I remember lying in bed a few days after the birth while Val was on the phone, commiserating with a friend whose wife had just had their first child the week before. Val was going on and on about what a miserable experience they—the fathers—had gone through. I was more than a little peeved. Then I listened. I have since learned that it can be just as difficult to stand by and watch someone you love suffer as it is to suffer yourself.

As a result of a clerical error, I was released from the hospital only a few hours after Tony was born. I didn't know any better or I would have stayed there longer. By the next evening, our tiny baby was having serious trouble breathing. He was growing lethargic and was difficult to wake.

We rushed him back to the hospital, where doctors found that Tony had a connecting passageway between his trachea and his esophagus. Fluid entered his lungs every time he nursed, and it was likely that he would develop pneumonia. Because the doctors knew that I was allergic to most antibiotics, they were reluctant to give Tony any antibiotics until tests determined which kind would be safest for him. Apparently, to them, the fear of an antibiotic reaction was more frightening than the possibility of advancing pneumonia.

A few days later we took Tony home, with instructions to "let his lungs dry out." Then we were to take him to McKay-Dee Hospital in Ogden, Utah, an hour to the south, for surgery. Sadly, nobody explained how I was supposed to dry out his lungs and still feed him when part of the milk he swallowed was going into his lungs. Not sure where else to turn, I went to the local health food store, where the two caring and informed men who owned the store gave me sound herbal advice. I felt somewhat reassured.

Val unwillingly left to set up for a summer logging job in Wyoming. I remember lying on our living room floor during those few nights, my hand on my week-old son's chest to feel it rising and falling as he breathed. I lay on the hard floor because I knew that I wouldn't sleep soundly that way; I wouldn't have to fear not waking if my baby needed me. I kept the phone next to me just in case I needed to call the pediatrician, but I wondered all the while what he could do if I did call.

I was grateful that we had those fine young men in the basement. It made me feel safer to know that they were only a shout away should trouble arise.

We took Tony to church on Sunday, two days before the scheduled surgery. It is customary in our church to give an infant a blessing, often within a month or two of birth. The baby's name is officially given for church records, and a blessing is pronounced that includes promises for the future. In giving the blessing, Val assured Tony that all would be well. I breathed a sigh of relief—perhaps that meant the surgery would be successful.

The next morning, I insisted that further pictures of his chest be taken prior to the surgery. Everyone was shocked by what these pictures showed: the connection between the trachea and the esophagus had fully closed and fluid was no longer leaking into our tiny son's lungs. Call it coincidence if you will; we call it a miracle. Many people had been praying for our baby son.

My maternity expenses were covered by my work insurance. But because we had taken our baby home—albeit briefly—on the same day he was born, his subsequent hospital stay and tests were not considered maternity expenses by the insurance company. Even though we managed to settle our bill with cash as we left the hospital with our baby son, doing so left our financial reserves seriously depleted. Real life was once again seeping into our wedded bliss.

The young men living in our basement became instant big brothers. We could leave our sleeping son with them for an evening to attend a movie or the temple. Even though the baby never woke up in the evenings when we were with him, we would almost always return home from a date and find six guys sprawled on the living room carpet, playing and laughing with one happy baby. Maybe they were hungry for families of their own.

Tony was born in February, and the following summer Val took a small logging crew into the Wyoming mountains. We packed a small camper so Tony and I could go along. I expected to return home with Tony when the colder nights of fall approached. We discovered that Tony thrived in the fresh mountain air, and he had no problem with his lungs even when the nights turned so cold I had to break the ice in our storage containers to use the water.

Val didn't consider much of anything as strictly "women's work." As an infant and toddler, Tony would wake up early nearly every morning. When we heard Tony making morning noises, I would jump out of bed and start breakfast while Val got Tony out of his crib. He would dress Tony for the day, bring him into the kitchen, and either feed him or take over breakfast preparations. This was our routine between the summer spent in Wyoming and Val taking a job in Logan when we returned home.

Val left early in the mornings for his new job, grabbing something to eat on his way out the door, leaving me to sleep until Tony woke up. It took about three days for me to realize that Tony's diaper smelled particularly nasty first thing in the morning. I asked Val if he knew about this. What a silly question, since I had not been changing any morning diapers all these weeks. Did I think that the child had suddenly changed his bowel habits?

I realized that my young husband had been changing his diaper every morning and not uttering one word of complaint. I then asked him what he had been doing with the smelly diapers, as we were using hand-made cloth diapers we had been given. He looked at me like I had sprouted a second head and said, "I've been washing them out and putting them in the diaper pail. Isn't that what you want me to do with them?" I protested and told him he hadn't needed to do that. He answered, "Do they smell any better to you than they do to me?"

When I got pregnant the second time, I vowed I was not going back to the hospital to deliver my child. I told Val—and I was only half kidding—that I would go to the small space between the house and the back fence (where no one would be able to see me) and do it myself. He could come if he wished.

We looked at options, including traveling to a birthing center in California. We had no way of knowing if a birthing center would provide a better experience than we had had at the hospital. But at least it would be different. Val couldn't leave work long enough for such a trip, so we kept looking.

About six weeks before my due date, somebody told us, "I don't know why you need this information, but I feel impressed to tell you . . ." He then gave us contact information for the first midwife we had ever heard of. You may call this an answer to prayer, coincidence, serendipity, or anything else you want to, but it felt like divine intervention to me. We immediately scheduled an appointment.

I loved this dear woman from the very first moment we talked. She was an herbalist and had certain protocols she wanted expectant mothers she worked with to follow. I followed every herbal preparatory suggestion she made. I only had six weeks left to prepare for a birth at home. We "went herbal" in a big way, and in a big hurry.

Because this good woman was still in training under the guidance of a doctor, they both attended my labor and birth. Prior to the birth the doctor puttered around the kitchen and kept us all fed. He stayed close by, giving advice and keeping an eye on things, but he was not in my face (or any other part of my anatomy). I believe he had immediately recognized my connection with the midwife and my trust in her skill and calm in her presence. I was very grateful for his perception and for his kindness.

This birth was a wonderful experience. Peaceful, inspiring, and much less painful than what I had gone through the first time. Being up and about instead of lying flat on my back during labor made a world of difference. The midwife was with me throughout the labor, monitoring and assessing both baby and me. I was given sips of juice during labor so, unlike during Tony's birth, I was neither dehydrated nor suffering from fluctuating blood sugar levels.

Val was right there with me also, holding pressure points to relieve my pain. He encouraged me every step of the way. We held our son the moment he was born—even before Val cut the umbilical cord. The emotional and spiritual high of such a birth must be experienced to be understood. Right then, I knew what I wanted for any future births.

This experience was so different from lying on my back, unattended except for occasional visits from a nurse, hooked up to a monitor that nobody realized until later was showing my baby in *extreme* stress. My first child was lucky to have survived being born. It had taken several months for my back to fully recover from labor endured while lying flat on my back and from the epidural I had been given.

I later learned that the hospital had experienced both a serious emergency and understaffing that night. Perhaps that knowledge should have brought me some comfort and more confidence in hospitals as a birth setting, but it didn't.

Now I had discovered what birth was meant to be like and how wonderfully rewarding and empowering it could be. I knew that someday I wanted to be a part of providing this amazing birth experience to other women.

When our second son was born, Val was being treated for diabetes, a family inheritance from which his father and grandfather had also suffered. At about that same time, we realized that things were not as they should be with his digestive tract, as he was experiencing severe and almost constant pain. Between the diabetes and the digestive issues, my energetic and hard-working husband was now in acute distress.

He described the pain as knives twisting in his gut, and it was becoming more difficult for him to attend classes at the university. During intense episodes, the slightest movement or pressure on his abdomen made the pain even more intense. Val continued working, despite the pain, whenever he could. We were still doing okay financially, but the almost constant pain sapped some of the joy out of our lives. And for me, at least, fear was beginning to replace faith in our future.

We sought the advice of several doctors. We were informed that the only solution was to remove some of his stomach, some of his small intestine, and a substantial portion of his large intestine.

Val was not yet twenty-six years old, and I remember his response well. He stood up to leave, and at the door he turned back and said to the doctor, with bleakness in his brown eyes that I love, "You may have at that sort of thing, right after you put me in a pine box!"

Val walked away that day from all medications and all discussions of surgery. It was not a simple or easy thing. I didn't know what to make of his decision at the time. I also knew that there would be no changing his mind, even if I had wanted to. It was his body, his choice. I could only help him find other options as quickly as possible, as our future, our family, and our dreams were at risk.

I was proud of his choice to keep searching for answers, even through his pain. If removing an organ doesn't fix a problem you are, for the most part, out of options after that. I didn't want Val to live his life with the consequences of the recommended surgeries.

People had differing opinions regarding what we should do. Some expressed their opinions loudly and repeatedly, and such constant haranguing was neither helpful nor appreciated. Their intentions may have been good, but it was not their call to make.

To make matters worse, Val also suffered a nasty accident around this same time. He was repairing an engine in his father's shop. The engine was hanging on a chain, about seven feet in the air, to make it easier to access. The chain broke, and a sharp edge of that massive engine landed on Val's foot, crushing his big toe. Two joints, the one in the toe and the one connecting the toe to the foot, were crushed. At the hospital, we were informed that there was no way to save either of the joints because the bones were shattered.

The doctor pulled out as many splinters of bone and small pieces of the joints as he could. After sewing it back together, he put a cast on Val's foot. He explained that the joints would calcify, becoming solid bone as they healed. Since Val would not be able to bend the joints in his toe and foot, he would have to swing his leg out to the side as he walked, for the rest of his life.

After a week, we decided to remove the cast ourselves, just as we had done with Val's previous broken leg. We soaked his foot in herbs daily. Today, we are not completely sure which foot was injured, as his foot fully healed, even the joints. There was no scarring, and it never troubles him at all. Neither his gait nor his balance is affected in any way.

I acknowledge that claiming to heal an injury this severe with herbs may be stretching credibility somewhat in your mind. We were more than a little astonished ourselves, even though we had witnessed such incredible healing previously with his rebroken leg. We have seen similar instances of healing in the years since. There really are herbs that will encourage the healing of muscles, ligaments, tendons, skin, and joints.

Val returned to supporting our growing family by working part-time in his own business while continuing to attend classes at Utah State University. While he loves to learn, he had never enjoyed school—actually, he had barely tolerated it, both as a child and as a teenager, and he was not much happier at the university. He loves to learn, but classroom situations only delay his learning and hamper his style. We began to seriously consider having him leave school altogether. He enjoys and is very good at being his own boss. A business of his own would have the added advantage of allowing him to work on his good days and slowing down on the days he was in the most pain.

We visited with the bishop (ecclesiastical leader) of our congregation, who owned a successful hardware store. His advice was to be prayerful and take some time to consider all aspects of our situation. If we decided to leave college and build a business of our own, he counseled me to support and assist Val in every way that I could.

There were many things I liked about living in the city of Logan. We had great neighbors; we could make a quick run to the store if we forgot something. I loved being just a few blocks from the temple. But we began to feel the pull of farm life and felt we needed more space for our children to grow up in. Our cute little house had a small yard and was on a main road that led to and from the college campus.

We began to consider making a move to Clifton, Idaho, where Val was raised. One of the young men who was renting our basement apartment was working part-time as a real estate agent and knew of our interest in moving to Clifton. One day, he told us he had a buyer for our current home if we wanted to sell it. We jumped at the opportunity.

We then purchased a thirty-five-foot travel trailer and backed it up to the front door of our house. We backed up an old semi-trailer to the back door of the house and began sorting through our possessions. Items for storage went out the back door. Things we needed while our new home was being built in Clifton went out the front door.

Living full-time in our trailer was rather fun. Sometimes we parked it in Clifton, on the farm. Often, we parked it in an open field next to my parents' house. My mother was undergoing chemotherapy at the time. Being next door meant I could be there for her and drive her to treatments. I could help my eleven-year-old sister get off to school each morning. Mom's fight with breast cancer was a difficult time for my little sister; she was the only one of my siblings still living at home.

Mom's cancer diagnosis was frightening, as she was given very little chance of survival, even with extensive surgery and chemotherapy. She and Dad had waited to tell the family about her cancer and upcoming surgery until after my youngest brother left for his church mission to Canada. I was pregnant with our third child.

My father had given my mother a priesthood blessing soon after she was diagnosed. In this blessing, Dad was impressed to bless her that she would recover and live to raise their youngest child to adulthood. Mom's faith in this blessing, along with her determination to live, became legendary. Not only was she determined to live, she was determined to live well.

The doctor told her that they would be removing lymph nodes down one arm in their attempt to contain the cancer. It was likely she would have only a small amount of strength and gripping power in that hand for the rest of her life. Mom bought several spongy balls of various sizes and brought them with her to the hospital. Her first words to my father as she emerged from the anesthesia was to ask him to hand her the largest of those balls. She started right then to work on rebuilding her grip.

Mother had been told some statistics that showed that people who manage to eat—even gain a little weight—while undergoing chemotherapy had the best chances for survival. Mom took this counsel to heart. If she was able to keep any particular food down, Dad would go out and buy it in bulk. When she could no longer keep that down, they would find something else. She had tended to be too slender, but for the first time in her life my mother reached what most women would consider a normal weight. In fact, she gained extra weight. Being a very determined woman, she quickly took the weight off once follow-up tests showed no residual signs of cancer.

Mother lived more than forty years after her cancer diagnosis and treatments. She not only lived to raise her youngest daughter to adulthood, but she lived long enough to see her daughter's children grow to adulthood.

CHAPTER TEN

Joy and Pain

We didn't give up and close the book when bad things happened in our lives. We simply turned the page and did our best to begin a new chapter.

—*LaRee Westover*

We have become accustomed to living our life with joy amidst pain and challenges.

—*Dana Reeve*

O*ur first years in Clifton, Idaho*, were both wonderful and difficult. Southeast Idaho felt like home to both of us, and it felt good to be home. But Val's health deteriorated even further, and our finances were often precarious as a result.

The births of each of the rest of our children were obvious high points in our lives—fountains of joy and spiritual renewal. Nevertheless, they came in the midst of worries over finances and discouragement about Val's health.

Despite our wonderful experience when our second son was born at home with the help of a midwife, I insisted on delivering our third baby in the hospital. My reasons seemed valid at the time. Construction on our new home would not be completed by my due date, as we had been promised. The brand-new travel trailer we were living in would have been more than adequate for giving birth, but I still made it part of my excuse to deliver in a hospital.

Looking back, I regret that decision. Once again, I set aside what I knew to be the right choice and caved under pressure from others. My parents, Val's parents, and just about everyone else was opposed to what they considered an outlandish and even dangerous intention to have our child anywhere other than a hospital. My husband honored my decision without argument.

Things went differently at the hospital for this second birth. Val and I were older and wiser, and we had studied a great deal. We had some practical knowledge as a result of our two very different previous birth experiences. We made a birth plan and saw that it was followed.

This birth may not have attained the spiritual high compared to our previous home birth, but it was nothing like my previous hospital experience, either. Had my first birth experience at a hospital gone as well as this one did, it is doubtful that I would have ever had reason to deliver any of my other babies at home.

All was not well with our new son, Tyler, however. When Tyler was about a week old, after I had just finished feeding him, I handed him to my mother. He seemed to be sleeping peacefully, lying on his tummy across her palm. Tyler—and his tummy—seemed to like lying in that position for a few minutes after eating. Suddenly, my mother realized he was not breathing. There was no motion of his little chest against her hand. She placed him across her shoulder and massaged his back and yelled at me to get the car keys and my shoes.

The hospital was just five blocks away from my parents' home, where we were that afternoon. By the time we reached the first street corner, Tyler had begun breathing again. When we arrived at the hospital, the doctors checked him out thoroughly. They speculated about possible causes but found nothing concrete to account for his lapse in breathing. We were so shaken by that experience that we had Tyler sleep with us until he was somewhat older. Lying on his father's chest to sleep was his preferred position the next several weeks. Val continued this pattern when our other children were born.

After Tyler, our other four children were born at home under the tender and very competent care of the same midwife who had delivered our second son.

The birth of Lucas, our fourth son, was wonderfully uneventful. It reminded us what a tremendous bonding and spiritual experience home birth can be.

Before our next child, Valaree, arrived, I had almost resigned myself to having all sons. I was okay with that, as our boys were beautiful and incredible children, and we loved them with all our hearts. We would have been delighted to have had another boy. Farms are fantastic places for boys to grow up.

As Valaree made her appearance, Val said with reverence and awe in his voice, "Honey, honey, it's a little girl!" I guess many men secretly want a daughter. I replied, "That's sweet of you, hon, that little thrill you just gave me with the girl thing. Now, hand me my son, as I want to get better acquainted with him." I was surprised when the midwife assured me that we had a new baby daughter.

Valaree's name is a combination of Val's name and my own, LaRee. I had planned to give this name to a daughter long before Val and I were married. We had kept that name in mind through the births of our four sons.

Our fifth son and sixth child, Richard, came next. This pregnancy was harder for me than the previous ones, since I struggled with anemia and experienced nausea in the afternoons if I became fatigued. Imagine, me feeling tired while raising four rambunctious boys and their equally energetic sister?

Worse yet, I went nearly seven full weeks beyond what I thought was my projected due date. My midwife kept insisting that my estimated dates were wrong. She would smile as she advised me to "leave that dear little babe in there baking" for a while longer. She was right because when he arrived he was perfect, a healthy and normal full-term baby.

I miscarried a baby between the births of Richard and our daughter Tara. This was a heart-breaking experience for the whole family. My pregnancy with Tara seemed harder than any of my previous ones. Nevertheless, the alternative therapies we had learned by this time made a positive difference to me and my baby during the pregnancy and her birth.

Reading through personal journals I kept during this time, and even accounting for the fact that I often used journaling to unload stress, I found far too many instances when I gave into discouragement or resentment. Often, these nasty emotions were the direct result of conversations I had with others about our sometimes-difficult circumstances. Too often, my journals show I was still struggling to distance myself from the opinions of others, especially family members.

During these years, I often wondered how one heart could hold both so much joy and yet so much pain. And compared to what my husband was going through, I think I had it easy.

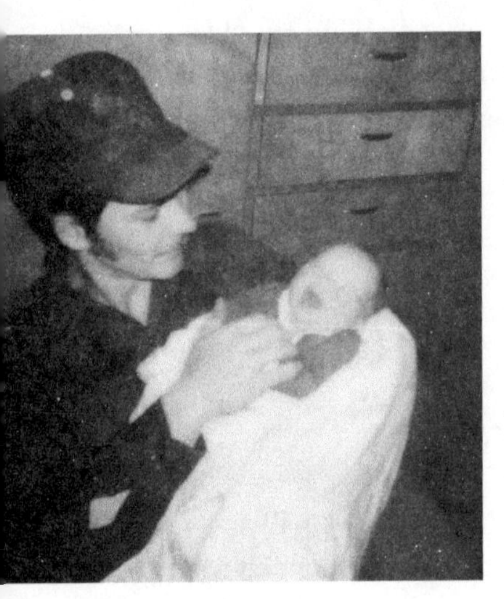

Val taking care of his three-day-old son, Tyler

For years after our move to Clifton, Val's days were mostly filled with pain since his digestive difficulties had not improved. I remember watching him slowly walk up the driveway one summer day, holding himself carefully, something I had never seen him do before his illnesses. The characteristic bounce in his step was gone. He looked older than his years, incredibly tired, and so very thin and hollow-cheeked. This sight of him moving so slowly nearly broke my heart.

Only occasionally would I see the enthusiastic, get-it-done-now and get-it-done-right man I had married. Our home life, the lives of our children, and our financial situation were seriously impacted by Val's health concerns. Survival—keeping the bills paid, a working vehicle in the driveway, and the electricity on—felt like all there was to life on some days. But our love for each other, and the emotional and spiritual highs that the births of our children provided, sustained us. And the joys of raising and educating our seven curious and energetic children kept us focused and moving forward together.

We learned that dairy products made Val's pain much worse. We tried to understand why, but there was not as much information on the subject then as there is today. We lived in a community with many dairy farmers, and diagnoses of lactose intolerance would not ever be in vogue. All the doctors we consulted never mentioned such a possibility.

We had been told that goat's milk was proving effective for some newborn babies with allergies or sensitivities to cow's milk. We began raising goats with the hope that goat's milk would be easier on his digestion. We also kept searching for other answers.

We tried every alternative therapy we could find that might relieve his pain and promote healing. If we had known then what we know now, it would have been a much shorter walk back to health for him. We learned as we went along, just as everyone is forced to do.

Although he was hurting more terribly than I can imagine and must have felt discouraged and despairing at times, Val did his best every day. The work ethic ingrained in him by his parents and his own personal moral code allowed for nothing less.

To make our modest funds stretch, we had to be frugal and waste nothing. We home-preserved everything we could to save money and extend the grocery budget, just as our parents had taught us. We ate a lot of venison during those years. My father liked to hunt, and venison was something I grew up eating—and cooking—so this was not difficult for me to manage.

We raised our own beef and chickens. The children would build huge chicken runs in the fields near our house using bales of hay as walls. The chickens ate the weeds inside the runs, which saved on feed bills and made for larger, healthier chickens. And once the chickens had eaten all the weeds in one area, the children would move the bales and build a new run. The chickens—fifty or more some years—had to be put in higher fenced runs at night so the coyotes wouldn't get them.

A few of our laying hens decided that getting out and roosting on the back of a small bench on the patio was a good idea. But I wondered who needs chicken droppings on a patio where children often play? So I thought I would train our dog to chase the chickens off the patio, and he became quite proficient—in his own way. The dog would sleep under the bench while the chickens roosted on the back of it. But when I would open the back door of the house, the dog would jump up and chase the chickens around and around, all the while barking very convincingly. As soon as I closed the door, however, dog and chickens would return to their previous posts, just as though I had yelled, "At ease!"

When our children misbehaved, I would tell them that my dog training skills must closely resemble my mothering skills since they all seemed to know how to behave just fine—as long as Mother was watching.

Our children helped with household chores from a very young age. I have a photo showing my two oldest sons secretly scrubbing the ring from the bathtub to surprise me. To reach the far side of the tub, their little feet could not even touch the floor. Their wide grins as they saw me there with a camera recording their efforts illustrate how proud they were of themselves.

In my experience, the woman of the house can do things much faster by herself than she can by teaching a child—or several children at the same time—how to do them. But efficiency is not the point in child-rearing. By patiently educating children, they can be a great deal of help, and working together blesses the lives of both children and parents in countless ways.

Most of our children seem to be natural entrepreneurs. Our children raised chickens, pigs, and calves. Tony once remodeled a shed to raise rabbits, and worms to sell to fishermen. He designed it to have two layers so the rabbits above would drop their pellets to nourish the worms below. Valaree later reroofed and remodeled that same shed during a competition with one of her older brothers—he did one half, and she did the other. She won.

Out of necessity, our family worked together and worked hard. But we also played together whenever we could. Each winter, usually in February, we would load everyone into our van and drive from Idaho to Arizona, where Val's parents had a winter place. It was so nice to escape from the Idaho winter weather, even for a few days. Driving a Jeep in the desert or going on four-wheelers was often the highlight of the trip for the children.

On each trip to Arizona, we also attended one of the area swap meets for an auction. This auction was held inside a huge red and white striped tent. Val and I would save every penny we could beforehand to make this trip—and this auction—fun and memorable. If something came up for auction that made a certain child's eyes light up, Val would bid on it and buy it for them if he could. We developed quite a reputation in that place over the years.

We also crossed the border into Mexico during these trips to Arizona, where we would wander from stall to stall in the open-air markets. I was never good at bargaining, but Grandma was a pro at what she called "dickering."

On one visit to Arizona, we drove on to California. Our children were full of teasing and high jinks—especially toward their parents—and this trip was no different. For one of the shows at SeaWorld, one of our sons persuaded us that the best view was on the very front row. When the star of the show, an orca whale, made a tail-flipping pass around the pool, water sprayed on all the guests—especially those sitting in the front rows.

Our son who had suggested we all sit on the first row had a flash of what he thought was brilliance. When he realized the spray would be coming, he ran forward instead of running away. He crouched behind the clear plexiglass wall that surrounded the pool, thinking that the salty water he knew the orca would soon splash out would miss him while getting the rest of us wet. We could see him grinning as he anticipated his masterful practical joke. But much to his surprise, this clever orca slowed as it rounded the tank near us and flipped its tail just enough to roll a wave of water over the edge, completely drenching our son without splashing any of us. The saltwater in his Levi jeans chafed his legs for the rest of the day.

I wondered, *Are these large creatures really that intelligent? Can they have such a wicked sense of humor?* If the gleam in the orca's eye as he swam by was anything to go by, I would have to answer yes.

After the first year of swimming lessons for our older two boys, we used the money—and thrifty spending habits—to purchase month-long family passes to the local swimming pool. I consider myself an excellent swimmer, and Val had taught swimming as a counselor for the Boy Scouts program. Having enough food to feed seven hungry children during a day at a water resort was a challenge. I got creative with these meals, and the children rarely complained. We had a lot of fun on those outings, and all our children learned to swim well.

One summer when we were rafting down a nearby river, the water started running too fast for the children's safety so we steered the raft to shore. Four-year-old Tara, who was wearing a life vest, jumped into the river from the upper end of the raft that was tied to the shore. I grabbed her arm, but the current caught her and she went under the raft. I lacked the strength to pull her back against the current. Val was standing in the water at the downriver side of the raft and told me to let go of her arm, and he would catch her. So, having no other workable choice, I let go and Val scooped her out of the water two seconds later. She was safe but hysterical, relieved but scared and angry.

The following summer, we purchased a family swimming pass two months in a row. But five-year-old Tara refused, at first, to get in the pool. Even safely in a swim ring and with water wings on, she would only get her little feet wet. Little by little, however, her siblings coaxed her down the steps and into the water. By the end of those two months, she was swimming all over the place. She would just take off—swimming underwater like a little fish. When she ran out of air, she would hold onto whatever unsuspecting swimmer's body happened to be close by and pull herself up. It was challenging to keep an eye on her and be close enough to rescue her if she needed it. Tara simply hated her life vest and water wings and had no fear.

Val's health gradually improved, even though it was often two steps forward, one step back. But eventually, he was able to get a successful construction business off the ground. Soon, he was once again doing "what could not be done," and doing it well.

Unfortunately, Val's health issues were not the only problems we experienced during those years, as I had my share of medical issues as well. I suffered repeated bouts of gallstones and kidney stones. And I had been plagued with multiple allergies since childhood. My reaction to antibiotics and other medications became even more extreme as time passed, and I experienced some heart-related difficulties as a result. Migraines laid me up from time to time. My health issues created added stress for our already beleaguered family.

We kept educating ourselves regarding alternative medicines and modalities that might improve our quality of life. One of my sons once remarked, "Don't let Mother read that new book. If she reads it, one of us will have to provide her with an opportunity to practice it—and it isn't going to be me this time." It often was, however, that child who provided me with opportunities to make use of the things I was learning,

We learned a great deal while dealing with childhood illnesses and the injuries that active children can incur. Even though injuries on work projects were very rare, our children, my husband, and I tend to play hard. If twenty teens were to ride jet-skis at the lake or go roller skating, it would likely be one of mine that would get run over or fall and break something. We were easily recognized by emergency room personnel at the hospital. These professionals became the closest thing we had to a family doctor.

I sometimes felt during these times that our family had more than our fair share of challenges. But the passage of time, and a closer acquaintance with the struggles of other families, has convinced me otherwise. Life, while full of joys, can also include much of pain.

From My Own Journal, dated June of 2001

It takes a lot of faith to put your life into the hands of another person the way that we do when we commit to spend the rest of our lives

and our eternities with another person. In marriage, we become a single unit. What happens to one, happens to the other, in very real ways. Attitudes, good or bad health, wise or unwise business decisions—everything about our spouse impacts our lives for the rest of our own life. [Sometimes, the hardest things we share are relatives, according to Val.] *How do we, with our limited range of sight into the future, dare risk it?*

In my case, I had the absolute assurance, given me after much prayer, that this man was the man I was meant to spend the rest of my existence, forever, with. I knew this shortly after we met, although I was only seventeen years old. I knew this throughout the two years of his missionary service. It was reiterated to me in a very special way in the temple on my wedding day. I have known it every day of my life since!

This knowledge, gained by faith, is very special to me. It has sustained me through the darkest and most discouraging moments of my life. Because of this knowledge, I have learned patience ... somewhat. Eventually, I learned to wait upon the Lord's timing for answers to prayer. This knowledge has given me courage when giving up looked to be the least painful option.

I have known, in sunshine and in shadow, that no amount of effort was too much effort to sustain the relationship that I have with the wonderful man I married. Knowing we can be together forever brings indescribable joy to my heart. Knowing that our children can be ours forever, also, is an indescribably sweet blessing.

This mortal life is full of so many struggles, for all of us. Things often do not turn out as we planned. There is sickness, financial struggles, children who face difficult challenges, and a whole lot more. It can, sometimes, be tempting to drift along, not working at our relationship with our spouse as we should. Perhaps we are even tempted to give up altogether on our spouse or one of our children.

The faith—the knowledge, really—that I have of the eternal nature of my family relationships limits my options to those that will strengthen and sustain these holy bonds. There is only one workable option available to me in every single difficult situation or when I am discouraged with my own or someone else's behavior. That option is to seek the wisdom of my Heavenly Father and act upon His counsel.

I have learned through hard experience that every time something becomes difficult or challenging in my relationship with my husband or my children, some change is going to be required of me. This is true every time. Even when I think that most of the problem lies with them. Almost always, when I ask in faith, I am counseled by Heaven to concentrate on changing me. This is not counsel to conform or to "go along to get along." It is simply that the only behavior I can really change is my own. I am instructed to stop whining and get back to living and loving, doing the best that I can, and remember that my family members are probably doing the best that they can do at the moment also.

I have also learned that the sooner I bend my will to that of my Heavenly Father and just get on with it, the less difficult and painful the journey will be. I have learned that if I listen and obey, there can be great joy in even the most painful parts of life's journey.

Once, when my husband's health issues seemed to be especially trying, I said to him, "Hon, I wish you would just learn whatever it is *you* need to learn from the trial of *your* poor health so that we can move on already. I am so ready to move on!" He looked at me patiently, yet somewhat sadly, and replied with characteristic wisdom and dry humor, "Sweetheart, what makes you think this lesson is just for *me*?"

Of course, Val was right. So many times over the years, I have learned lessons from his pain and sacrifice that has benefitted me and our family. But I do not tend to learn as readily when I am the one hurting. Pain seems to toughen me, but not necessarily in a good way. I seem to learn heaven's lessons best when I am nursing or helping someone else through the struggles of their own lives.

We may no longer have the stars in our eyes that we had on our wedding day. We may no longer believe that life will always be a bed of roses as long as we make all the right choices. We may no longer believe that it is possible to raise perfect children by being perfect ourselves. Were we once that naïve and confident? Life may have knocked some of the stuffing out of us, but Val and I are still very much in love, contented and happy in each other's company.

Gathering at the Westover house
in the valley during the 1990s

Westover house with internet antenna in the 1990s,
and "Princess" mountain in the background

CHAPTER ELEVEN

Educating Our Own

The more that you read,
the more things you will know.
The more that you learn,
the more places you'll go.
—*Dr. Seuss*

Education's purpose is to replace
an empty mind with an open one.
—*Malcolm Forbes*

A*s a freshman at Brigham Young University (BYU),* my declared major was early childhood education. This choice was, in part, the result of a phrase in a special priesthood blessing I had been given that indicated that I should "continue my education" in order to be a "teacher in the arts and sciences." Interesting phrasing, considering my lifetime of learning and teaching. "Arts and sciences" certainly describes the teaching in our homeschool as well as my line of work these last few years.

Later, at BYU, I met a professor whose wife was educating their children at home. The notion intrigued me. I reflected on my own school years: the wasted time, the way I worked ahead in classes, the topics I studied at home in the evenings, the long conversations I had with my father about things he knew much about but had not learned in school. I wondered if I could have learned almost everything I learned at school faster and more efficiently at home. I had loved school, but even back then, I felt there was a better way.

I thought of the things my mother could have taught me if we had been able to work together more often than just evenings, weekends, and summer breaks. Most of all, I thought of the influences I may have avoided if I had not allowed the opinions of teachers and friends to become more important than the teachings of my parents.

The idea of homeschooling children that I might be blessed with later in my life was in the back of my mind from that day forward.

Almost from the day we met, I was aware that Val had hated every minute of his public-school experience. So it was not much of a surprise when we talked about our future to learn that teaching his children at home was something he also envisioned for his own family.

As I pondered the notion, the idea scared me more than a little when we began to seriously consider it. Homeschooling is a huge responsibility, especially for the mother. The phrase "Mothers make us most" is perhaps particularly applicable to homeschooled children.

Because homeschooling daunted even my I-can-do-it-myself attitude, we did not begin homeschool when our oldest child reached school age. Instead, we sent him to regular kindergarten and his brother followed the next year. And two years after that, our third son also boarded the school bus each weekday morning.

The kindergarten was about ten miles away, and Tyler, our third child, did not do well with the bus ride. I noticed he was groggy and nauseated when he got off the bus at the end of the day. His teacher confirmed that he felt the same when he arrived at school.

I finally said to myself, *How hard can it be to teach the skills taught in kindergarten to one very smart little boy?* And with that, homeschool began for Tyler. We carefully considered all angles while deciding whether to homeschool the older two boys as well. A few factors stood out to us.

First, I wanted to teach our children myself, as I had dreamed. I wanted to be there when new ideas caught hold. I wanted to witness the development of their minds.

Second, Travis (in the second grade at the time) was not coping well with the teasing and bullying he saw during lunch hours and recess periods. His teacher told me that she couldn't decide whether to punish Travis or give him a medal for the fights he kept getting into while trying to protect other children.

For example, a young Native American student was almost constantly being harassed by some sixth-grade boys, and Travis simply could not bear to stand by and watch this happen. He would wade right into the middle of it, no matter how many were on the other side. Though he usually emerged victorious, witnessing this type of bullying was taking an emotional and physical toll on our young son. We felt that such a situation could not continue.

Although these were compelling reasons, I might have continued to put off teaching our children at home for who knows how long except for one final factor.

We had not yet found answers to Val's digestive and diabetic health issues, and the previous winter had scared me badly. He was in so much pain so much of the time, and his energy levels were often at a very low ebb. He easily caught any sort of "bug" that came through our area. I didn't have the courage to let the thought of losing him and raising our children alone completely take form in my mind. But deep in my heart lurked a horrible fear: I wondered whether by the time the ensuing winter passed, I would be working away from home to support my family because my husband would no longer be with us. He just wasn't getting any better.

Val's best time, such as it was, usually occurred in the middle of the day. And my boys were missing that time with their father because they were away at school. I wanted them to create some memories with their father in case the window to do so was closing.

This is a look into my thought processes of deciding whether to homeschool not just one, but all three boys. Val and I both felt settled about our decision, and with that, the Westover homeschool began.

I can still picture those first days of homeschool, my husband lying on the floor with his boys huddled next to him, reading an encyclopedia. They started on the first page of volume A. He would read them a title and then ask, "Who wants to know about such-and-such?" and off they would go. This only lasted a few days while I gathered what I thought was a more proper curriculum. I didn't recognize the value of such readings at the time, and now wish we had made it a regular part of our school days.

We had done our legal homework before bringing our children home. Some homeschool parents not far from our area had been jailed under very strange pretexts. Authorities were insisting that each homeschool in their county be licensed—even though such licensing was not required by Idaho state law. Homeschool families were then prosecuted for not adhering to the particulars of those licensing requirements. No homeschool that I was aware of had the resources to meet such regulatory requirements because most involved the structure of the building—ramps, boys' and girls' bathrooms, etc.—which were meant for public school facilities. We learned that the *law* is often different from the *regulations* of state agencies.

Our own local officials also insisted that we license our homeschool. After considering these recent cases, however, we chose not to put ourselves under these regulations by applying for a license that, under the laws of the state of Idaho, we were not required to have. We chose instead to follow the law as it was actually written.

When we were ready, we made an appointment to meet with the local school board. The meeting was stressful, but it went the only way that it legally could go. We simply presented the law as it was written in the state of Idaho. We were careful not to criticize or belittle the efforts of local teachers—neighbors and friends who, for the most part, were doing their very best. We recognized that they chose to be teachers because they wanted the best for the children in our community.

Our case was written up in the local newspaper after this meeting with the school board. In small towns like ours, even routine school board meetings tend to be big news. Neither the meeting nor the article was particularly contentious, but the slant of the article nearly scared my mother to death. She was convinced that we were on our way to jail. A great many people in the community, being rather uninformed, were certain we were breaking the law by schooling our children at home. At the very least, they considered what we were doing to be irresponsible.

Personally, I laughed—ruefully—when I read the article. The article simply didn't represent the facts or report the meeting accurately. If the word "not" had been placed in most sentences in which it wasn't found and deleted from most sentences in which it had been placed, the article would have been more accurate.

Shortly after we began homeschooling, the local school board received a letter from the Idaho State attorney general giving his opinion about our homeschool. We gently educated this man concerning the difference between his opinion and the laws of the state which he represented. The local school superintendent dropped by our house, unexpectedly, from time to time that first year. I would send my school-aged children into the basement to play for a few minutes until he had left. Eventually, I met him at the door. He quit coming after I teased him, somewhat unmercifully, wondering out loud what the neighbors must be thinking about his frequent visits when my husband was not home.

There were many who thought we were wrong to homeschool our children. Both sets of our parents disapproved—more so at first than when our children began to succeed in what they considered to be the "real" world. I never understood what was so "unreal" about family life or being taught by your parents.

Our parents may not have approved, but they certainly got right in and helped us in any way they could. If any of our children completed all of their schoolwork before the end of a week, they had a standing invitation to ride into town with Val's mother when she went to work and spend the day with my parents. Something fun, such as playing chess with Grandpa, was always lined up for those special days. Both Val's parents and mine were helpful in countless ways.

At first, I may have had some trepidation about the sheer enormity of the responsibility involved in teaching children at home, but once I got going, all doubts disappeared. We were living our dream by educating our children as we felt prompted to. My taking a paying job and contributing to the family income might have taken some of the pressure off my husband and allowed us to buy a few more "things." But homeschooling our children came to be more important with every passing day and with every small experience we shared with them.

Part of our curriculum that first year consisted of finishing the books the boys had been using at school when we brought them home. The school district, though not happy with our decision, was generous and helpful once we stopped wrangling over legalities. As a result, this first year was much like the running of a public school—but under a much smaller roof.

The following summer I attended my first Utah Homeschool Association Conference, which was eye-opening. I met families who had been schooling at home for years. I met bright, confident young people who spoke with adults on a wide variety of subjects—both intellectual and practical. Those exchanges portrayed an interest and level of respect that was different from what I had previously seen between other teens and adults. This aspect fascinated me.

As I attended classes and talked with more experienced homeschooling parents, new ideas began to take hold in my head. I learned that many families believed creating a mini public school, in your home, was not the most effective way to teach children. That sort of environment, they said, became tedious for children and difficult for Mom to maintain without the children becoming stubborn and rebellious. While I prefer to call it *persistent*, *stubborn* should be my middle name and is my children's natural inheritance.

I was taught that children learn more quickly and more enthusiastically when given greater autonomy. Of course, basics must be taught and taught well, but the majority of learning should happen when a certain subject catches a child's interest. Such learning then becomes almost a constant, continual, family-wide way of life.

"How many hours a day should a child spend learning?" I asked. The answer came back, not surprisingly, "Well, how many hours is that child awake?" Even play—no, especially play—can be a fruitful learning experience. I continued to be intrigued and excited.

Despite my excitement, for the next two years or so, I struggled with implementing these principles. I would focus more on learning together and less on individual interests and needs, as my public school and university training seeped back in. And the children and I inevitably got bogged down in the rigid structure.

When we began homeschooling, we had three school-age children, including one in kindergarten. It quickly became apparent that each had his own learning style and that tailoring our methods to their learning styles would help our children immensely.

So we studied various philosophies and styles of learning. The effectiveness of many of those concepts was validated by educators as the years passed. Val and I learned how to teach well by teaching our children. We also discovered that if you want to obtain a good education for yourself, homeschool your children.

I also discovered that one of the most effective ways to learn is to teach a principle to someone else. And the family is a wonderfully conducive learning environment, because there is often someone older for younger children to emulate and someone younger to serve and to teach. We found that our older children gained confidence and solidified their own understanding of a concept when they helped teach their younger siblings.

The Life of a Homeschool Mother

Homeschool mothers are busy people. This is especially true with a lifestyle such as ours. It wasn't as though I could get up each morning and have nothing to focus on but teaching for the rest of the day.

Our youngest daughter, Tara, once told me that she was flabbergasted after noticing that I spent nearly every day, all day, serving others, with little thought for myself. I observed in our children a similar desire to serve each other, for the most part. I am delighted to see it in them still today. And I am delighted when I see it in our grandchildren.

School days included spelling, math, science, history, social studies, making trips to the library, and many other educational endeavors. My days also included trying to keep the house clean and putting meals on the table. I worked to help my husband with his health challenges, to enable him to make a living for his family and enjoy schooling his family at home with me. And not least, I dealt with the nonsense and injuries of five boys and their equally active and competitive sisters.

In our house, being homeschooled was considered a privilege for both the children and for Mom. The children knew they had to do their share for homeschooling to work. At the end of the school day, before going out to play or work on their own projects, they helped put the house back in order—perhaps not quite my mother's version of "order" most days, but it sufficed.

Getting the children to do their schoolwork was more tedious and time-consuming on some days than others. I wondered why our children could not see that just getting it done would give us both more time to do something more enjoyable and give their mother more time for necessary household tasks. An hour or two, or even a few minutes some days, between school and preparing the evening meal was always a welcome respite.

On most days, however, our children were happy to get their schoolwork done. On good days they would get so engrossed in some aspect of learning that they wouldn't want to be pulled away for much of anything.

Unfortunately, children may not always be as anxious to learn as parents may be to teach. Grammar was the least favorite subject of most of our children. I remember Tara sitting in front of the computer one day in a snit. I am standing behind her, pretending to look for a book on the nearby bookshelf. She is pitching a fit, telling me that she needs a "teacher." I am equally determined that she is going to reread the instructions and learn to think. I have explained the concept to her, and she has read the instructions. I also know that if I lean over her, she may cajole and manipulate me into giving her the answers instead of applying her own brain to the task. This is not going to happen, even if I must spend the rest of the morning waiting for her to give in and think for herself. I fought similar battles with each of our children more than once.

I learned that proper behavior can be taught, but that behavior, especially as children grow into adulthood, is a choice. One of my sons expressed this very well when I informed him one day that he had been taught better than a certain behavior he was displaying. He said, "Mom, well-taught is not the same as well-learned."

Acquiring new skills—and remembering old ones—was a part of everyday life. We acquired one of the first personal computers in our small town. Only a contractor working from a home office had one before we did. And he used it specifically for his business—his children weren't allowed to use it, even for their schoolwork. I had to learn to operate the computer before I could teach our children to operate it.

While children learn best when excited about a subject, educational materials have to be available to them to pique their interest. We had a full set of the *World Book Encyclopedias*, *Zoobooks*, *National Geographic*, and other educational magazine subscriptions. On our often-limited budget, having these materials consistently available was sometimes a challenge.

We have always had more than one floor-to-ceiling bookshelf in our home. I may have put more books away in labeled storage boxes than many people own during a lifetime. There is never enough time to read and study all we may want to—for either Val or myself. I think this is also true for most of our children.

We made weekly visits to the library in Preston, Idaho. The librarians there had a special shelf under the check-out desk specifically for our family. We checked out and returned so many books at a time that we often returned books by mistake that were not theirs. The librarians kept those books stacked on this shelf until we returned in a week or so.

We also obtained a card for the Utah State University library in Logan, Utah. We spent many a long afternoon there, taking advantage of their larger and more complete research and magazine areas. We felt it was a blessing to live reasonably close to a college town and that wonderful library.

In the early days, our homeschool was held year-round. Since fewer children directly under Mother's thumb tend to get a lot more work done in less time than a roomful of children, we often had time to spare. We soon developed a floating free day for visits to libraries, museums, planetariums, or historic sites. Sometimes, in the early spring and late fall, those days were spent in the yard, getting the garden in, or preserving produce in canning jars and freezer bags. As the boys got older, that plan changed because of summer work schedules.

Sometimes we shifted schoolwork to the evenings. I could never see what difference it made whether school subjects were covered in the morning, the afternoon, or the evening. On the days that some of the older children were out with their father, I could devote my time more completely to the younger ones—in much the same way that the older ones had been given my attention when they were younger.

I made it a point to be available in the evenings to help with schoolwork as much as possible. In this way, my evenings were not much different from those of mothers of publicly educated children who spend time in the evening helping their children with homework assignments. Striking a balance between spending time with their father or on other activities and making up for these interruptions was a priority.

One of the greatest strengths of schooling your own children is the amount of time that children and parents get to spend together. In many homeschool families, this extra family time is mostly spent with Mom and other siblings. Because of the nature of Val's work, our children were able to spend a great deal of time with their father. Since time with their father had been one of my primary motivations for homeschooling, this brought me great satisfaction.

Often the boys were sidelined from school for a morning, a day, or even a week at a time to help their father. Due to the nature of our family businesses, this happened often during the summer. They were not allowed to let their schoolwork completely slide, however. While I was responsible for most of the "book learning" of our homeschool, our children were also blessed with practical, hands-on experience working with their father.

I have said *boys,* but Valaree also spent time working with and learning from her father. Valaree has always believed that she could do anything that her brothers could—and has often proven it. From a very young age, Valaree rarely asked for help with such things as changing the oil in her car or changing a tire. She frequently took on gardening and yard work projects. Driving heavy equipment or working high up on a construction project never gave her pause. These days she can often be found plastering, painting, or even taking on small remodeling projects.

Our youngest daughter, Tara, was usually busy with her pursuit of anything music related—voice lessons, theatrical productions, and performances of one kind or another. Tara did work for her dad for a couple of weeks during one college summer break when she needed extra money. While Tara certainly had no fear of getting dirty, she could usually find other things to do instead.

Working with their father was a great educational opportunity for our children. One of my sons who went on to earn his PhD recently told me about some training he had been involved in at work. For the rest of the team, there were many new skills and procedures to be considered, learned, and mastered in a very short time. Our son realized that most of these skills and ways of approaching a problem were second nature to him. He had acquired them while working with his father.

> Do we love ourselves and our fellowmen enough to defend their right to believe differently than we believe?
>
> —*LaRee Westover*

CHAPTER TWELVE

True Education

The capacity to learn is a gift;
the ability to learn is a skill;
the willingness to learn is a choice.
—*Brian Herbert*

There are few things more pathetic than those
who have lost their curiosity and sense
of adventure, and who no longer care to learn.
—*Gordon B. Hinckley*

W*e worked to provide our children* with a good education. But we also wanted them to develop skills, attributes, and attitudes not always taught in public school settings. But how on earth and under heaven do you teach children to think rather than just to memorize a series of dates and facts? How do you teach them to apply what they are learning? How does a parent help their children develop attitudes such as gratitude and attributes such as confidence and persistence?

Our desire to teach our children such basic life skills and help them develop character traits that would serve them well for a lifetime shaped our everyday life and impacted the focus of our homeschool. Some of the most important principles we tried our best to teach in the minds and instill in the hearts of our seven children are listed below.

1. A Desire for and an Ability to Discern Truth

One of the reasons I fell in love with Val all those years ago was his desire for righteousness. His love for the Lord was the most important thing in the world to him. It meant doing things in the Lord's way rather than his own, like serving a mission rather than staying home and marrying me. And this righteousness he so desires includes the love our family has for one another.

Val teaching Primary class at church

One way to show your family that you love them is the desire to teach them the things that you know to be true. For Val and for myself, *truth* is not confined to matters that pertain to the nature of God, our relationship to Him, and His commandments and covenants with us. Truth refers to *all* things that are true, whether it be a scientific principle, history, mathematics, or the best way to construct a steel building.

Truth stands the test of time and will be as true tomorrow as it is today. Truth brings peace and happiness when applied to one's life and allows us to live with joy even in the face of extreme trials and challenges.

Val discerns truth from sophistry better than any other man I know. He doesn't abandon his ideals and opinions easily, as he worked too hard to arrive at them through study, pondering, and prayer. He only relinquishes them when he acquires greater knowledge, greater light. This happens through further effort on his part or when someone who really knows takes the time to enlighten him.

Members of our church believe that agency—the right to choose one's own path—is God-given and essential. Unless I am free to choose my course of action in life, I can neither be held responsible for my actions and choices nor take advantage of opportunities for growth and development.

As any parent knows, it is often difficult to tell where your role begins and ends. We may develop a just-do-it-my-way attitude because of our age, experience, and sense of responsibility for our children. But that attitude runs counter to helping our children become autonomous, responsible adults.

I don't pretend to have all the answers to this dilemma, and neither does Val. But we do have strong feelings about this topic. Agency, or the right to choose, is a key principle of heaven. And we tried very hard to make it a key principle of our home as well.

2. An Attitude of Gratitude

We wanted our children to understand that gratitude and appreciation make what you have enough and what others do for you enough—a joyous interchange. This attitude is a guarantee of a happy life.

3. A Desire for Knowledge

The desire for knowledge burns hotly within me; it always has. The topic itself is not nearly as important as satisfying my curiosity. I am often amazed—appalled would be a better word—when I see people encounter something new or unfamiliar and feel little desire to know more about it. This attitude was as completely foreign to that young man who caught my eye, my heart, and my mind at age seventeen as it is now. Val has always loved to learn and continues to read and study.

Not too long ago, an employee of ours brought his 3D printer to work. Next thing I knew, Val had studied nearly every aspect of this technology and was devising ways to utilize it. The employee, a young tech genius, was amazed at how quickly Val could grasp facts, tie them together, and become knowledgeable about something he had never seen before.

Leaving Val on his own for a few moments at a homeschool convention usually meant having to help him haul boxes of books to the car. They were not very expensive since he purchased them used at the stalls of other homeschool families, so I didn't mind. Finding more bookshelf space in our house was often a challenge, however.

We expected that our homeschool would foster this sort of hunger for knowledge in our children. We believed that one of the most important things we could teach our children was *how* to learn. I wanted to instill in our children a desire to learn at least as fierce as that of their father and mother.

For the most part, our children have met our high expectations in this regard. I am often astounded by the insights or exciting information they share with us and with each other. It is satisfying to watch them hold their own in discussions with their father. Watching one of our adult children become interested in a certain new subject, often bringing their own children into the learning experience, continues to be one of my greatest joys.

> Education is not the learning of facts,
> but the training of the mind to think.
> —*Albert Einstein*

4. Problem-Solving Skills

We wanted teaching our children to include problem-solving skills—how to solve life's daily problems on their own.

5. Logical Thinking

Getting to the end of a road begins with the very first step. We wanted our children to acquire some foresight and be able to think logically about the task ahead, whether great or small. Whatever walk of life they chose, we wanted to show them how to plan, organize, and carry out a project—or even just a thought—to completion.

By our definition, an educated person is one who can think and analyze and not be "driven by every wind of doctrine" or by the siren song of the popular philosophies of the time. Because they read, study, and *think*, they are not overly influenced by other people's opinions. Sound judgment is rooted in being able to foresee the end from the beginning.

6. *Critical Thinking*

We wanted them to learn to think critically when presented with information, whether in written form or when listening to a speech or a news broadcast. This is an essential skill, but I sometimes lament that it is becoming a lost art. Applying truth and core values to the analysis of information—*pondering* is the word Val uses for this important skill—keeps a person from being misled or manipulated.

> The function of education is to teach one to think intensively and to think critically. Intelligence plus character; that is the goal of true education.
>
> —*Martin Luther King Jr.*

Many years ago in high school, I had a demanding English teacher who invited the most advanced students to demonstrate our knowledge and analytical skills by critiquing books from suggested reading lists. These critiques could earn us college credits.

We spent an entire day in a testing center where we were given the titles of three books considered to be great literature; it was assumed we would have already read them. We were to write essays about the books. No reference materials were provided or allowed—not even copies of the books themselves. If we had not already read all three of them, and if we did not analyze them critically enough, we would fail to earn college credit.

The purpose of this exercise was not to demonstrate that we had read a lot of books. It was to show that we had been taught to *question* and to *analyze*. We had been taught to look for the author's purpose in writing the story, why they wrote it from that perspective, and what they were trying to have the reader think or feel. I did quite well on these tests and began my time at BYU having already earned college credits.

It was therefore important—and natural—for us to expect that our children also learn to read critically—regardless of what they were reading. When children really think about what they read, it encourages them to be open to considering many opinions, then ponder and pray and decide for themselves what is true and what is not. I have followed this with nearly every book I have read, including books of scripture, for a lifetime.

7. Reasoning Skills

We hoped to be able to teach our children to avoid bias and prejudice in their thinking. Teaching our children to look at a situation or a problem from as many angles as possible before making a final decision was our goal. We hoped they would be unafraid of trial and error and to be willing to learn from their mistakes as well as from their successes.

We wanted them to be able to evaluate situations, cultures, people, and varying philosophies open-mindedly, but also without being taken in by hype and hyperbole. Following the crowd, being in the *middle of the middle,* was not taught or practiced in our homeschool.

8. A Capacity for Creativity

We wanted them to be able to think creatively and let their imaginations have sway. Our children tended to be very imaginative in their play. They were also finding unique ways to learn—and sometimes unique ways to get out of doing schoolwork.

If nothing else, a homeschool should teach that it is okay to be your own person, go your own way, think your own thoughts, have your own opinions, and live your life the way you think is best. It should also teach you to respect other people's choices.

Sometimes, whether in a household or in our homeschool setting, a person might have to work rather hard to be heard, because in a family of nine, others may also be trying to express their opinions at the same time. But each person is expected to have opinions.

One of our primary parental goals was to instill creativity in our children. I like to think we did that. I have rarely seen any of them hesitate to take on a new task just because they didn't know how to do it. Something hard or new is usually considered—as it should be—merely a challenge.

9. Productivity and a Work Ethic

Part of our success, I believe, came about because we wanted so badly for our children to grow up to be productive and hard-working adults who thought for themselves and contributed in positive ways to the family and to the communities in which they lived.

I have often been heard to say that "I taught my children to work, and work well, and then Val (or the neighbors who later hired them) stole them away from me." I say this mostly facetiously, but there is more than a little truth to it. Even as young people, our children had reputations for being excellent workers, and today our children are known for their work ethic.

10. A Can-Do Attitude

Many of the skills described above are a part of what we call a can-do attitude. It does little good to know things if you don't know that you know them and have confidence in your ability to put your knowledge to use. Val is a great example of someone with this life skill. His primary profession for many years was the construction of metal buildings, which often included demolishing the existing buildings on the property before new construction could start.

One job they did was more than a little unique. What follows is Val's own account, which illustrates his attitude in challenging situations. It also gives you a glimpse into the sorts of things Val and his crew—often his own sons—did as a matter of course.

The Last Chance Canal—A Can-Do Attitude Being Lived

The bridge over the Last Chance Canal in Grace, Idaho, had collapsed into the river nearly fifty feet below, and the river itself was nearly as deep. This water-carrying bridge was among the longest in the state at over two hundred forty feet in length. The bridge carried more weight than any overpass in Salt Lake City, or so I was told by the engineers.

A firm in South Carolina was fabricating the new bridge. The collapsed structure needed to be removed before the new bridge could be installed. Until then, they could not release irrigation water back into the canal. Thousands of acres of Idaho potatoes were soon going to need water. They were special. They were seed potatoes. Failing to reconstruct this bridge in time for the growing season could threaten the potato crop and affect the price of potatoes across the nation. It could be catastrophic.

I was invited to take a look at it. I was told that a large firm with several D-9 cats (caterpillar tractors) had said that it could not be done. I only had a D-7 cat, which is about one-third the size of a D-9. After praying and getting some ideas, I thought I would venture. So I submitted a bid and was asked to come for an interview. The job was ours—if we could do it.

It seemed like half the town of Grace, Idaho, was watching us when we moved the old bridge the first foot. And over the coming days we did the impossible and successfully removed the entire collapsed bridge. My crew was preparing to leave when I was approached and asked if I would consider assembling and installing the new bridge. Time was of the essence, and sections of the new bridge were beginning to arrive. The farmers had been watching us, and they had confidence in my old equipment. Or was their confidence in me and my crew?

We fully assembled the bridge on the west bank, then mounted it on massive rollers. The idea was to cantilever the bridge out over the river and into place. We rigged a nose (a long lifting beam) on the east end of the bridge. I then pushed the bridge out into space with my JCB extend-a-boom forklift. We counter-weighted the west end of the bridge with my step-deck trailer, loaded with all the highway concrete dividers we could find.

Soon after the far end of the bridge reached about the halfway point over the river, we hooked the largest crane in southeast Idaho up to the east end of the extended bridge. The operator began to lift up the bridge to keep it from tipping into the river below. The closer we pushed the bridge to the crane, the more weight the crane could lift. But, of course, the farther the bridge went from us, the heavier it became for that crane.

Finally, we removed the lifting beam, as the bridge was hovering above its final resting place. The top of the new bridge was now more than one hundred feet above the river. Large cranes supported it on both ends. The cranes were both red-lined (past the safety margins). Somehow, the bridge weighed more than the engineers had calculated.

The crane operators slowly lowered both ends about eight feet, and we saw that the mounting bolts did not match the holes on the bridge. The bolts were set in concrete by a contractor with the latest and greatest GPS equipment. The bridge was hoisted back up slightly, but there was no going back across the river. We had left the point of no return more than eighty feet ago.

The engineers on site were beside themselves. They argued; they blamed. Then the wind began to blow. When the wind blows here, it does not take hostages.

I considered the options, grabbed a cutting torch, and was soon making modifications to the bridge. Then they shouted for me to stop. They asked each other what they should do. One asked the other, "Can he do that?" They could not believe that I was really doing what they could clearly see me doing. My attorney was filming the drama.

We had quite a large crowd of onlookers. If the wind started to gust, it would be a disaster of epic proportions. Everyone's fate was hanging in the wind. The crane operators were getting ready to jump and run when I finished the modifications and motioned for them to again try to lower the bridge into place. Everything fit. The engineers were talking to their lawyers as we mounted the transition plates.

In the end, a few hours of additional welding made the engineers satisfied. There were not as many people there on the day the irrigation water was released, on time. Disaster was diverted to another day.

The president of the Last Chance Canal Company at the time is now an Idaho State legislator. My attorney and I had a meeting recently with Representative Gibbs. He remembered me—imagine that. And after almost twenty years, he recalled the reason I was given the job: "It was your can-do attitude," he said. Sometimes, we do need to tilt at windmills.

One of my faults has been chasing rainbows, the impossible that was only a prayer away. I had a business card once that read: "Any problem handled immediately. Impossibilities take a little longer. Miracles by appointment only."

Maybe I am a braggart, but I try to give most of the credit to my God. My job is to believe.

CHAPTER THIRTEEN

Our Students

Curiosity is one of the permanent and certain characteristics of a vigorous intellect.
—*Samuel Johnson*

Believe you can and you're halfway there.
—*Theodore Roosevelt*

O*ur children—like all children everywhere*—are unique and individual. I knew I needed to adjust my way of teaching to fit their way of learning if we were to experience lasting success. When Travis had joined Tony on the school bus each morning, I discovered that their younger brother, Tyler, was a quieter child, one who would happily spend an entire morning coloring. Who knew? Up until then, Tyler had always been in motion, trying to keep up with his older brothers.

Tony usually did his schoolwork quickly and quietly so he could move on to something else. Like his father, Tony usually had multiple small projects going. Some were just for fun, and others were ventures to make a little spending money. Besides raising rabbits, worms, chickens, and calves, he got a part-time job in a sign-making business with the understanding his wages would be used for the supplies and training he needed to go into business for himself.

When we first began homeschooling, people expressed concern about our children's socialization. Since the negative aspects of public-school recess was one of the reasons we decided to homeschool, such concerns about socialization seemed strange to us. I thought my mother's oft-repeated advice that "you can't raise your children properly in someone else's yard" applied to the schoolyard just as well as the neighbor's yard.

Tony was, and is, inherently very social. He liked to make plans with friends, either going out with them or inviting them home, whenever he could. Since our older boys are fairly close in age, these groups often included a younger sibling or two. As the oldest child, Tony's patterns became a model for our other children. Thereafter, our home was often filled with our children's friends after school hours, on weekends, and during the summer.

When we first began homeschooling, there was a homeschool group operating about forty-five miles away in Pocatello. Eventually, a group was started a little closer to us. For the most part, however, our children preferred to make friends with people in the community, whether they were being homeschooled or not.

Participating in music and a local theater group was a big part of our younger children's school years. I now wish I had involved our older children in this more when they were younger. Participation in this theater group was fun, time-consuming, and sometimes expensive. Tara, Richard, and Travis made theater a big part of their lives during their teen years. Valaree also occasionally participated. Now, Valaree's children, along with many of our other grandchildren, enjoy these activities a great deal.

Travis had an incredibly wide range of interests. He completed his schoolwork chart dutifully, but, except for mandatory subjects that kept his mother happy, he worked on his own and in his own way. He wanted to try it all—from cooking to tanning leather. If Travis read about someone, somewhere, in some century, doing something, he wanted to experience—and master—it for himself.

Tyler tended to be studious and focused. Even as a child, he was a list maker and an organizer. He had a plan for his education from the very beginning. He worked steadily toward that goal with little need for encouragement or much oversight by his parents. If there was a part of his education where he felt he was falling short, he would find a tutor or a computer program to help him.

Our delightful and kind-hearted fourth son, Luke, showed signs of some rather severe learning difficulties quite early on. He couldn't seem to grasp and retain numbers and letters. Reading had come so easily to his older siblings that I was baffled. Our research led to more learning, especially about brain quadrants and crossing the mid-line of the brain. The whole family became involved in helping Luke succeed.

Luke loved animals and being outdoors. Sitting at a desk for any length of time was agony for him. His shoulders would slump and his brow would knit in concentration. But his eyes would light up and his whole body would fly into motion whenever I would say, "Enough for now, Luke. Find your dad or grandpa and see if they need your help."

The thought of going outdoors when his schoolwork was finished was usually motivation enough for Luke to get his work done despite his dislike for it. He was never happier than when he was out on a horse or a tractor with his grandfather. Luke would happily spend hours with his grandpa, even if it meant getting drilled with the alphabet the entire time. I bless that grandfather's patience. While it wasn't something he was necessarily known for, he was endlessly patient with Luke.

It became obvious early on that Luke was a very tactile, hands-on learner. I cut letters and numbers out of materials with different textures—sandpaper, fur, corduroy, whatever I could find. His older brothers *crawled* the shapes of the letters with Luke in our sandbox.

Luke's siblings played endless games of Uno with him, which gave me an idea. I began covering the pages of books and worksheets with transparent plastic in bright colors. Putting colors and numbers together seemed to connect the creative aspects of his brain with the more linear parts. Then, at a homeschool convention, we learned basic Brain Gym techniques. This modality became a great blessing in our family, but especially for Luke.

We also bought Luke a ride-on mail truck, patterned after the big one my father drove as a postal employee. The older children then made dozens of houses out of poster board and put numbers and letters on them. And they made mail for Luke to deliver. They spent part of each day helping Luke "deliver the mail" until the shapes of the numbers and letters finally became clear in his mind. After that, they relabeled the houses with simple three-letter words and kept on helping their brother learn by delivering mail. My older children were amazing to watch, and I see much of the same practices in the next generation as our older grandchildren see to the needs of younger siblings.

A family—and a homeschool—can be an especially beneficial learning environment. Within the family unit, children have someone to imitate in their parents and older siblings, and they have someone to serve if they have younger siblings or nieces and nephews.

One fall, I got bronchial pneumonia. This sort of thing often happened as the weather changed. After I recovered, a bad cough lingered for weeks. Whenever I coughed, I felt so lightheaded I would have to sit down. A neighbor made me an appointment for a foot zone therapy session—something I had never experienced before. I went because I didn't want to offend my neighbor, because I was curious, and because I was getting desperate. Within less than an hour, the therapist had identified an old knee injury of mine. She made a difference in both the pain level and the mobility of the knee without any prior knowledge of the problem. She was also able to make my chest and lungs feel better—I quit coughing for the first time in weeks.

She really grasped my attention, however, when she said, "Smile, please." I smiled. "Odd," she said. "You are not missing those teeth." "What teeth?" I asked. "Your eye teeth, on both sides. Perhaps the ones next to them, but I don't think so." A genetic trait from both my mother's and my father's family lines causes our baby teeth to come in fine, but the eye teeth in the permanent set do not come in to replace them. Several of my cousins and a sibling or two have the same issue. I was astonished—and more intrigued. How had she known? I wanted to learn more about what she was doing and how she was doing it.

I made an appointment to bring Luke in for a treatment. As she worked the area of his foot that corresponds to the brain, she asked me what I knew about brain quadrants and the limbic bond that connects the left and right hemispheres of the brain. Realizing that you don't learn much when you act as if you know it all, I replied, "A little." She shared with me some of what I had already learned from months of personal study, then suggested a host of new resources to learn even more. This woman's skill and knowledge made a real difference in our young son's life. Immediately after this, I decided to learn foot zoning, which has been a blessing in all our lives ever since. Both Luke's wife and Travis's wife have also learned to foot zone.

Luke's challenges changed the chemistry of our homeschool. Memorizing poetry was something we had focused on and enjoyed. But memorizing did not come easily to Luke. The older boys still memorized verses, but more quietly, with less of a production made of it and less praise given for it. Luke persisted and we praised his efforts, and today, he memorizes as well as anyone.

Val often pointed out that learning should be a lifelong pursuit and that we all learn differently. Luke had plenty of time to learn in his own way and at his own pace. Val would also remind me that the single most important aspect of being able to learn well is attitude and that once a child becomes convinced that he cannot learn, hope is lost to them. Until faith in themselves is restored, they will not be able to learn as they should.

I don't believe that Luke, schooled at home as he was, ever lost hope. While he knew that he learned differently from his brothers, he also knew that he had his own unique skills and that he could do some things as well as—or even better than—his brothers. He did tell me once, however, that he was not sure he would ever be all that his oldest brother, Tony, thought him capable of becoming.

Who has this young man become? Watching Luke research information on farm equipment or other subjects and then educate his father is a thrilling thing for this homeschool mother to witness. I see Luke and his wife accomplishing miracles with their own boys, some of whom struggle with learning challenges that are similar to those their father experienced as a child. I see their children loving and helping each other learn, just as Luke's siblings did for him.

When Tony was fifteen years old, he came to me and said that both Valaree, nearly five and a half, and Richard, not yet four, were ready to learn to read. He said they both knew their letters well, both the shapes and the sounds. Apparently, they had been paying attention as their older siblings and I worked with Luke. Tony thought it would take only a little bit of effort to teach them how those letters and their sounds combined to make words. I explained that I had no time at the moment to help with this, because my focus needed to be on Luke. "If you think it needs doing today," I told Tony, "then do it." It took Tony only a few weeks to get both Valaree and Richard reading.

Several of my highly intelligent children would probably have been labeled ADHD, had we asked anyone's opinion. Unless the subject really engaged their attention, it was almost impossible to keep them sitting still in a chair. This certainly applied to Valaree. She was a busy and fast-paced child and picked up on new concepts very quickly. She could get more accomplished in a day or an hour than most people could in a week. Valaree could sit still for long periods of time only if the topic intrigued her and only if it was of her own choosing.

If she really wanted to know something, getting information into her head was the easy part. Getting her to sit still long enough to take a test and prove that she knew it was much more difficult. I was frequently astonished by the knowledge and skill Valaree displayed in normal everyday life since her testing results made me wonder if she was retaining much of anything from her books and lessons.

Our youngest son, Richard, was the very definition of ADHD as a child. He learned best by obsession—one subject at a time. He was not yet old enough for us to expect him to sit still in a formal classroom setting by the time he had learned to read at four years old. I gave him more leeway than the others as far as structured education was concerned. He loved to read so much that keeping him equipped with new reading material became a challenge. Family trips to local libraries became even more frequent.

He was still a young boy by the time he had read nearly every book having anything to do with animals in the Preston, Idaho, library's youth section. He filled notebooks with his detailed drawings. First, he just drew the animals; then he drew their habitats, then their bone and muscle structures. Then he moved on to another subject, until he felt he had learned everything he could about it.

He loved making models, either of the universe or some other area of study. He often bored his younger sister to tears, talking at her (yes, *at* her—as she was not always listening) about subjects he was learning. He was almost constantly learning, but he could no more sit still and be forced to learn than he could sprout wings and fly.

Richard was not aware of the terms ADD or ADHD until after he reached adulthood. He had no idea that the concept of a learning disability might apply to him. He came across this possibility after he returned from serving a church mission and was enrolled in college. He was alarmed when his roommates pointed out the "problem" to him. It wasn't so much trouble with school; it was that he was constantly in motion, either going from one concept or task to another in rapid-fire succession or obsessing on one project until it was completed, just as he had done as a child. I saw it as a nonissue. His style of learning had served him well, and I was confident that it would continue to do so. Richard received bachelor's and master's degrees in Inorganic Chemistry from Idaho State University, and was Master's Student of the Year in All Disciplines. Four years later, he earned a PhD from the University of Oregon in Materials Chemistry. He works for Intel.

Richard also has an amazing talent for music. He likes to add extra runs and chords to nearly everything he plays, and it sounds amazing. He has always picked up new musical instruments, fiddled with them a few minutes, and taught himself how to play them well. From a young age he played the piano almost constantly and could play by ear almost any song he listened to first. If he was awake, he was making music—or noise of some kind. After he was married and he and his wife had a baby on the way, I delivered our Clavinova digital piano and headphones to his house. I hoped that this might help his wife and new baby find a few minutes of quiet every once in a while.

Stories about Richard, by His Father

One day, Richard and a friend were discussing a certain spider that his friend had learned about in school. Richard told his friend that the information he was sharing about the spider was wrong. Eventually, his friend's teacher showed us her manual in order to prove Richard wrong. We then went to the Utah State University library and checked out a large book on spiders, written by a leading authority. By that, our son was vindicated.

When Richard was not much taller than my waist, we went to the Hogle Zoo in Salt Lake City, Utah. As we started the tour, somebody asked a question that our guide did not know the answer to, but Richard did. And he added information on mating habits and other trivia without any prior preparation. Soon our group grew as others joined in. The tour guide graciously acquiesced and even asked Richard questions herself. We had a most enlightened tour.

Richard could learn. What was even more important, he knew he was smart enough to learn anything that he wanted to, but he just needed the proper motivation. He matured differently than others; maybe he just needed some time to be a boy. He was interested in and knew different things than most children his age.

Richard may not recollect some events as I do, and he might even resent some of his time spent at home. But I believe we gave him the best we could, and we hope he got what he really needed, including a can-do attitude. We are so pleased that Richard eventually went on to earn a PhD in chemistry.

Both Richard and our daughter Tara have astonishingly beautiful and full-ranged voices. They often sang together at special events all over our valley. Tara, in our home and in our homeschool, was both a delight and a challenge. Like all our children, she is very intelligent. She was intensely focused on music and on performing nearly anytime and anywhere.

Tara could rarely see a practical use for basic school subjects—at least as they related to the pursuit of her personal interests. Fortunately, she has a quick mind and retains information easily. She also very much liked to be first and best. Her competitive nature demanded that she master, to the best of her ability, the information and basic school subjects her older siblings had. It was an ongoing challenge to help her balance book learning with her several musical pursuits.

Tara, like Tyler, always had a plan for her life. I have a copy of a list of goals she wrote, listing subjects she needed to complete and what she needed to read in order to "graduate" (her word, not mine). At the bottom of the page is written, "Finish before you turn 16. Go!" And below that are the words "Done List."

Tara, probably more than our other six children, might have benefited from a more structured, focused, and intensely monitored educational environment. Because her learning style and Richard's were so very different, it was a challenge to structure our homeschool in such a way that met both of their unique learning needs.

Looking back with the advantage of decades of hindsight, I can see things that could have been improved upon in our homeschool, of course. If I could go back in time, I would specifically focus on each of the attributes and principles mentioned in the previous chapter and make our children aware that these attributes were being focused on. I would try to tailor each child's education even more completely to their particular learning style. I would also start doing that at an earlier age than I did. Yet, considering what a new concept such tailored learning was in public school settings and even at homeschool conventions, I think I was actually pretty good at it. I would try to be a little less tense about all aspects of our children's educations. I would try to enjoy these critical early learning years and help our children enjoy them, even more than I did at the time.

TOP: Mountains behind the Westover house in Clifton, Idaho, showing Buck's Peak, and "The Princess" left of center, "seeing it for the first time"

LEFT: Young LaRee and her mother LaRue Hunt vacationing in Yellowstone

RIGHT: Portrait of LaRee that Val took with him on his mission

TOP: LaRee and Val prior to his departure for a church mission

BOTTOM: Joyful LaRee speaking with her fiance' Val on his mission

CENTER: LaRee and Val cutting the wedding cake LaRee made

LEFT: Val working at a welding shop

BOTTOM: LaRee and Val with sons Tony, Travis, and Tyler

TOP: Val with LaRee who was expecting Tara

BOTTOM: Val with his son, Tony, at a Boy Scout Court of Honor

MIDDLE: Westover family (left to right): Lucas, Richard, Tony, Tara, LaRee, Val, Travis, Valaree, Tyler

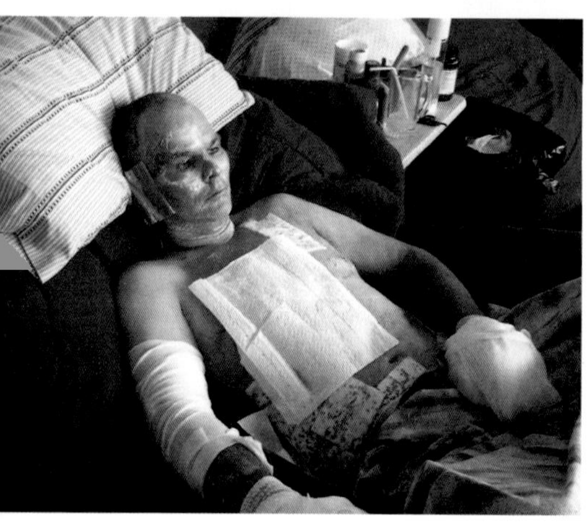

TOP: Westover children (left to right): Richard, Lucas, Tony, Travis, Tara, Tyler, Valaree

LEFT: Val on the mend about six weeks after being seriously burned

RIGHT: Valaree, Tara, and Richard in Halloween costumes

TOP: LaRee and Tara at Niagara Falls

MIDDLE: Val and Tara at Niagara Falls. Tara labeled this picture and others from that trip, "Friends"

BOTTOM: Tara as a teenager sporting braces

TOP: LaRee teaching class at Butterfly Express headquarters

BOTTOM: Butterfly Express employee team

CHAPTER FOURTEEN

Beyond Homeschool

You're off to great places!
Today is your day!
Your mountain is waiting!
So...get on your way!
—*Dr. Seuss*

Be a Student as long as you still have something to learn,
and this will mean all your life.
—*Henry L. Doherty*

V*al and I were living our dream.* We had wanted to school our children at home, and we were doing it even in the face of significant challenges. Nevertheless, at the beginning of each new school year in late summer, our children were encouraged to pray about where to attend school and make up their own minds. We honored their decisions, even though we felt strongly that homeschooling was the better way. When our children did attend public school, they not only did well, they excelled.

Tony decided to return to public school his eighth-grade year. I am not sure if it was an answer to prayer or the call of friends and fun that drove his decision. The following school year he chose to stay at home because, according to him, public school took too much time away from his "projects." After staying home again for his freshman year in high school, he decided to return for his sophomore, junior, and senior years.

Tony would come home from high school questioning something he had been taught, get books out, and dig into it himself. He did this with everything from the summaries of famous poetry he had been assigned to read in class to historical facts. I loved seeing him figure things out for himself.

I think Travis went to public school because his older brother was going and because he wanted to prove himself in wrestling. He did well in academic subjects and very well in wrestling, placing in the state wrestling competition that first—and only—year of his high school attendance. This would have been considered his freshman year, although he only signed up for those subjects he was most interested in.

As I recall, I encouraged Tyler to give public school a try his eighth-grade year. I knew how intelligent he was; I also knew what he knew. But I wasn't sure that *he recognized* that he knew enough to begin thinking about and working toward a college education. I thought the experience of seeing how he compared to his peers in the public school would help him move forward.

One young woman told me that she had planned to be valedictorian at her high school graduation—until Tyler returned to school. She recognized that keeping up with him academically would be challenging.

Tyler completed just one year of public education and resumed his education at home. He was approached by high school administrators and was asked to participate in a statewide academic competition. The vast amount of knowledge he had acquired through his personal dedication to learning was recognized by many teachers and students in the school district, even though he was not attending public school at that time.

The best student in each subject tested—from the entire state of Idaho—was to be given an expensive engineering calculator as a reward.

Even though Tyler took first place in more than one category, they allowed him to receive only one calculator.

After he finished his two-year service as a missionary, Tyler attended Brigham Young Univeristy where he received a bachelor's degree in Mechanical Engineering—without ever obtaining a high school diploma. Five years later, he earned a PhD in Mechanical Engineering from Purdue University, and did post-doctoral research at Sandia National Laboratories. He is a senior scientist for Idaho National Laboratory.

Luke showed no interest in going to public school, to put it mildly. Valaree didn't care to attend either, except for a released-time religious instruction program sponsored by our church and held during the day near the school campus. Richard and Tara were interested only in the music programs offered by our local high school and in school plays and performances.

Tara became convinced that the larger high school on the other side of the valley had a better music program than our local high school. She would have been willing to attend classes there if it had been required to participate in their music program. I spent a considerable amount of time trying to enroll her there for her junior year. My lack of success was not from lack of effort.

As parents, our goal from the start was to sufficiently prepare all our children for a lifetime of learning; we wanted them to be able to go in whatever direction they chose. We always knew that our children *could* go on to college from our homeschool. Just because graduating from college had not been the path for Val and me did not mean it would not be the correct choice for our children.

Depending on what a certain child wanted for their future, we could see the advantages of a college education. We could also see some aspects of college life that might have a negative influence on susceptible young people. Val and I had been there ourselves, after all. We also knew that because of Val's health issues and how it had affected our financial standing, those who attended college would need to obtain scholarships. We structured our homeschool with these goals in mind.

Preparing our children for entry into college, if that was their desire, was a great concern of ours from very early on. Tony was in the third grade when we began homeschooling, and we learned that college entry was possible and that scholarship opportunities were just as available to homeschooled children as to those that attended public school.

The easiest way for homeschooled children to get into a college was to score very high on the ACT or SAT tests. An impressive score on these tests can also help them qualify for a scholarship. It is also beneficial to have already earned some college credits before applying to a university. Participating in extracurricular activities and service opportunities and having good references from leaders in your community is also important.

One year while we were attending a homeschool convention, we heard a report from a Texas family whose oldest child was the youngest person ever to be accepted to Brigham Young University. From time to time after that, we would hear an update about this child or about a younger sibling who had entered BYU at an even younger age.

Our educating philosophy includes the premise that a young person needs to study everything they can and they need to be taught to ponder. They need to form opinions about things after looking for evidence and information on all sides of a topic. They need to learn how to explain, or even defend, their point of view. And they need to learn to write well. Only after they have gained a measure of proficiency in these things are they ready to learn the skills that will enable them to do well on standardized tests.

Test-taking is a skill that can be learned. Learning facts just to take a test, as I had been taught to do in my own public-school education, is not much of an education, really. I have never considered getting an education and preparing for standardized tests to be even remotely the same thing. But given how important scoring well on certain tests is for getting into college, improving test-taking skills became a priority.

I tried to teach our children test-taking skills by having them take and retake end-of-unit tests and end-of-book tests until they got them right. They took these tests even though I knew how they were doing in each subject from working with each child every day. I tried to remember and guard against what I had learned from my own experience, that facts learned only for a test can be immediately and completely dismissed from one's mind.

During our first year at college, though at different universities, Val and I each took classes that used the same textbooks. I aced the classes, as did Val. Many years later, I asked Val a practical question about something, and he answered it in great detail. I asked him how he knew so much about such things. He replied that he had first read about it in a class in college. We had both taken that class and read that textbook.

Not only did I see the difference in his way of learning compared to mine—and in his memory—I also noted the phrase *first read about it.* He took an idea that was new to him and studied it thoroughly. He still does that today. And he seems to remember whatever he has studied forever.

What a great illustration of the difference between learning to take a test and putting something useful in your mind to draw from for a lifetime. I hope I accomplish that type of learning better now than I did when I was younger. These days I tend to be almost as obsessive as my husband is about learning as much as possible about subjects that interest me.

Motivating Richard to study for the ACT test was challenging. I assigned Tara to help him, and as I had hoped, working together got them both underway. Both went on to attend universities, and both earned master's and PhD degrees. Tara obtained her advanced degrees at Cambridge University in England. Tyler, as I have mentioned, also earned a PhD degree.

I remember taking an ACT preparation test right along with Richard and Tara one day. Although they each did quite well that day, I outscored them both. I should hope so—after all, I had been a homeschool mother for many years by then.

I believe we met many of the educational goals we set for ourselves and our children. Our neighbors, even the high school principal, acknowledged—frequently and vocally—that the Westovers ran a homeschool that worked. The graduates of this homeschool learned how to learn and how to work hard to follow their dreams.

We like to think our homeschool produced intelligent, inquisitive, and successful children. It also helped one child surmount serious learning disabilities—disabilities that professional educators said could not be overcome. The personalized approach of a well-run homeschool played a part in the wonderful, intelligent, and successful man this child became.

We could see that our children were under almost constant scrutiny. Failure to impress the neighbors and the authorities with our efforts did not seem to be an option. We felt a burning desire to see our homeschool succeed. The can-do attitude we fostered in them was a large part of the eventual success our children enjoyed. We sought to instill a strong work ethic that helped them in their early years and beyond.

During that time, I was often heard saying—and I still say it now—"I taught our children to read and to want to know things. Then, with a minimum of guidance from us, they charted the course of their own educations." I believe that this is the way education should be.

The Next Generation

Time rolled on, and our children grew up and went out into the world. They began to marry and have children of their own. As of this writing, the six of our children who have children have provided us with thirty-six wonderful living grandchildren. And there is one more on the way. Our family has also suffered the tragedy of some special little ones that did not survive the perilous journey into this world.

Like every parent, we were hopeful that as our children matured, they would be appreciative of the things they learned at home. We hoped they would at least appreciate that we tried to do what we thought was best for them individually. We hoped they would know that we gave it our very best efforts, even during the most stressful and challenging times of our lives.

If I had my life to live over again and knowing what I know now, I would absolutely homeschool our children all over again. I think it might be easier, however, since there are more resources now than were available when we were teaching our children. I think there would also be less stress because I would know that things would work out with Val's health. I would try to enjoy the journey even more than I did the first time around.

Most of our children have chosen to school their own children at home more than they have sent them to public schools.

Tony and his wife, Michele, homeschooled their youngest for part of one year. Their five children are intelligent and marvelous and each one excels in learning. The oldest two have obtained college scholarships, and there is no reason to assume their twin girls, coming up next, will not do the same. I hope they know how proud we are of them and how much we love them.

Travis and Megan homeschooled their children for a time. They live close to us and are doing a splendid job giving their children quality educations. Their oldest, Thomas, would tell you that he loves to read even more than we do.

I could write pages and pages about the phenomenal ways in which Tyler and his wife, Stefanie, are teaching their eight children. They are both master educators, and their children are very well taught. What they are doing with their children is nothing short of amazing. They have adopted three children—a blessing for us—making eight total for their family.

Our son Luke and his wife, Samberly, also homeschool. Each of their boys has struggled with mastering reading skills, and there have been speech difficulties as well. The way they have sought answers, found and worked with speech therapists, and done whatever was necessary for the sake of their children is very impressive. Their twin boys, the oldest of their children, are outstanding young men. Like their father before them, it is becoming difficult to tell that they ever struggled with learning at all.

Luke now lives next door to us, and watching his children grow up has been such a blessing in our lives. Still being a small part of their education has been our great privilege. Even when they are with their friends, they never see us without stopping to give us a hug—or two or three.

Our son Richard and his wife, Kami, are doing a mix of homeschooling and taking advantage of public and private educational resources. Kami's advanced degree in education adds to her capabilities to teach her own children. They do not live as close to us as our other children, but there is no doubt that their children are well-taught and thriving.

What is our daughter Valaree's homeschool like? I consider myself something of an expert on this topic because some of her children's education takes place here, under my roof, while Valaree supervises aspects of the businesses we own. Let me share a few stories from the time I spent with her children about a year or two ago. I recorded this in my journal at the time.

Valaree came to me with twelve-year-old Kendra in tow, asking if I had time to explain a math term to Kendra and show her how to complete the problem. "I could, BUT . . ." I replied.

"I know, Mom!" Valaree responded. Then she turned to Kendra and instructed her to go back through her math book until she found the term and the instructions and could solve the problem herself.

I watched with heightened interest as young Kendra started thumbing through pages. I suggested that she find an unused computer—this isn't hard to do because we have a bunch of them—to look up the information. I watched her google the math term on three or four websites, including YouTube, work on some of the problems demonstrated, and then go back to her mother to tell her what she had discovered. Now, to my mind, that is getting an education. That is learning how to learn.

Would Kendra have understood the concept as well if her mother or I had given her the answer when she first asked? I don't think so. Kendra received the very best kind of instruction she could get.

> The best teachers are those who show you where to look, but don't tell you what to see.
> —*Alexandra K. Trenfor*

When our son Luke was young, I responded to a question he asked me by telling him to go look it up. He then said, "Mother, why is it that when an adult calls you on the phone with an herbal question, you tell them the answer, but when I ask you a question, you tell me to go figure it out?"

This observation did not change my response to my children, but it certainly changed my response to neighbors and students in my classes who would later ask me questions. It was a personal reminder that educating is not about providing answers. It is about encouraging opportunities to learn and mastering the skills necessary for living an abundant life.

One day Valaree's sixteen-year-old son, Matthew, came to our house looking for another history book to read. He had read his favorite one twice, from cover to cover, a *huge* volume and one of the best I know on American history. Our local library used to let us keep one of their copies checked out for months on end. Matthew scanned our many bookshelves, asked his grandparents for advice, and left with two new books to read—one of them very large and detailed. He also sat down with his mother at the computer and ordered two more books he saw at our house, ones he wanted to own rather than just borrow.

This burning desire to know is the high road to education—the kind that continues for a lifetime. I was delighted to witness that this fire had been ignited in my grandson.

The same day that Matthew went on his book hunt, I had agreed to take his fourteen-year-old sister, Tavanna, shopping. As we drove, we got to talking about Matthew's love of reading. Tavanna began expounding on the topic of education. She told me that Matthew was just about the smartest person she knew, but that her Uncle Richard (our son) was the smartest. She went on and on about the things that Richard knows. She said that he "knows something about everything, and most things about many things." She was particularly effusive about Richard's ability to twist balloons into animal shapes and play lots of different musical instruments.

With no coaching on my part, Tavanna added that the kind of education she received depended on herself. She explained that she very much liked to read but "not like Matthew does." She told me about her plan to read a certain number of books and the topics she was interested in learning more about. She then showed me a book in her bag that she hoped she would have time to finish reading while we were visiting some friends of mine later that day. While we were shopping, she bought yet another book she was very excited about reading as soon as possible. She also wanted to share this new book with a friend she thought would really like it—just as soon as she had finished reading it herself.

The most impressive thing to me of the entire afternoon occurred after we arrived at my friend's home. Her husband had been suffering from ill health for some time, and she was weary from caring for him. Tavanna went to the downstairs family room as soon as we arrived and pulled out the book she wanted to finish reading. She noticed that the family room, which doubled as the grandchildren's playroom, was, in Tavanna's words, a "disaster." So she put her books back in her bag and spent the time organizing and straightening up this room.

When her service was discovered, it brought tears to my friend's eyes. I think I was as proud of Tavanna in that moment as I may ever be, even if she earns her own PhD someday. Knowledge, compassion, and a desire to serve—what a combination, and in one so young.

Who would Tavanna be with a public-school education? Who would our children have become if we had made different educational choices? There is no way to know. It is impossible to take two roads at the same time, or even to foresee all the consequences of two different decisions. Many will remember the words in a well-known poem by Robert Frost, "The Road Not Taken," which reads, "Two roads diverged in a yellow wood, and I—I took the one less traveled by, and that has made all the difference."

There is nothing our children could not have achieved with the preparation we gave them as homeschool parents. We lacked money much of the time. We had struggles and setbacks of many kinds. Yet despite all of this, our children got the best start in life that we knew how to give. And they have capitalized on this start admirably, each in their own way.

Returning to the question of sociability. It has been my experience that on the whole, homeschooled children (and I have known many of them) are quite well adjusted. They know how to respectfully converse with adults in their lives and even seem to enjoy adult company. They also tend to respect and relate well with their peers.

Feeling that homeschooling was best for our children does not give me the right to an opinion about your choices for your children. I am not even entitled to make that important call for my grandchildren. Parents must seek guidance in deciding how to educate their children.

Nevertheless, there are those who seem to have fixed ideas about how being homeschooled is a detriment to a child. Val and I were criticized frequently, and our children were sometimes belittled for not being part of mainstream public school.

Not long ago, Val was sitting in a waiting area inside the Logan Utah Temple. A person whom Val didn't know was sitting next to him, talking to someone else about a certain neighbor of his. This man said of his neighbor's children, "They are worthless. They are homeschooled"—as if being homeschooled explained everything there was to know about these children. Also present in the waiting room and who was part of this conversation was the man who had been the public school superintendent during our children's school years. He made a valiant attempt to change the subject. Val simply stood up and left without comment.

Those children are not worthless; no children are. Such a sweeping false judgment should never be made, particularly within the sacred walls of a temple. This experience Val shared appalled me and reminded me of the times my own children and those of other homeschool families in our area were judged in much the same way. I wish there was a way to shield homeschooled children against such uninformed bias.

I hope that with more families choosing to homeschool and their children doing well that some of the animosity and prejudice we experienced may disappear. Certainly, the educational changes being implemented as a result of Covid-19 are changing perspectives about education. Parents everywhere are now carrying more of the responsibility of educating their children, and they are discovering how challenging—and how rewarding—it is to interact with your children in this way day in and day out.

I see parents having the same desires for their children's educations that we had in our day. I also see a great deal of frustration as families try to ascertain what will work best for them. I tell these harried parents that filling in for the teacher temporarily is not the same as settling into homeschooling as a way of life and that it will get easier as they proceed. I feel a great deal of admiration for them as they take it on, adjusting and making the best of challenging situations.

Some of the families around me are welcoming the challenge and intend to keep having school at home even after this situation passes; others are giving up, finding the task of keeping their children occupied with worthwhile activities too hard. Many children are delighted by the change and the opportunity to pursue their own interests and objectives; others appear to be somewhat lost while out of their usual structured school environment.

Watching them reminds me of the first year after we brought our children home for their educations. One of the challenges I faced with my own children at first was getting them to read the instructions and get to work on their own—becoming self-directed and self-disciplined enough to go forward with their educations without constant nagging from me.

Every educational institution is feeling the challenges and changes being brought about by Covid-19 and our reactions to it. How we as a society cope with this season of change will have serious consequences to the future of education. What will work well; what will be the pros and cons of online versus classroom teaching, for example?

I fear that education will become even more of a one-size-fits-all affair when there is no interaction between students and teachers and even fewer opportunities for teachers to tailor their curriculums to each individual student. Will online classes become forums where the bias of the presentation—both political and religious—becomes the bias of the virtual teacher being the only viewpoint presented? Will the students be captive audiences, no longer having an opportunity to discuss or, if necessary or appropriate, refute the slant of information presented altogether and learn something more appropriate to their needs?

Will thoughtful consideration of what is truth—religious, scientific, and political—be curtailed or more easily manipulated without the diverse influence of many teachers and classroom interaction and discussion?

These are challenging times; may we have the discipline, foresight, and inspiration to deal with them properly and act, always, in the best interest of future generations.

> If you only read the books that everyone else is reading, you can only think what everyone else is thinking.
>
> —*C. S. Lewis*

CHAPTER FIFTEEN

God's Pharmacy

So many come to the sickroom thinking of themselves as men of science fighting disease and not as healers with a little knowledge helping nature to get a sick man well.

—*Sir Auckland Geddes*

The aim of medicine is to prevent disease and prolong life; the ideal of medicine is to eliminate the need of a physician.

—*James Earl Mayo, MD*

That emphatic childhood statement of mine, "I can do it myself," may also be a fitting title for this chapter. In our family, we consulted with healthcare professionals when needed, but as we gained experience we were able to deal with many issues at home using alternative modalities we learned about.

Following a particularly nasty accident to a family member, I consulted a doctor with whom I had cultivated a working relationship over several years. During the conversation, I stated that I "always bring situations and people to you when I think you can do something better than I can." He replied, "That is a very short list, isn't it?" I took his statement as a compliment, and I think he meant it that way.

Early in our child-rearing years, a relatively new doctor in town thanked me for keeping his family fed, as our children had frequent ear infections and we made regular visits to his office. But his joke upset me as our funds were very tight, and here I was in a doctor's office, again, when I thought I was becoming quite knowledgeable about herbal medicines and how to effectively use them.

So over the next few weeks I spent many hours researching treatments of ear infections, fevers, and childhood illnesses in general. I found herbal solutions that worked quickly and effectively. I believe after that we never went to a doctor for an ear infection or used acetaminophen for a fever.

Eye infections were another ailment that we found good herbal solutions for. Our children learned, after trial and error, that telling Mom about an eye infection earlier was a better choice than later. The longer an herbal treatment for an eye infection is delayed, the more painful that treatment becomes. We also learned to treat both eyes at the same time, even if the other eye wasn't showing signs of infection yet.

Once we had been herbal for a while, our children stopped catching common illnesses as often as their friends seemed to. For instance, year after year went by and none of our children got chicken pox, even when they were obviously exposed to it by cousins and friends at church and other activities. This was even true the year when, at a cousin's sleepover at Grandma's house, one of the cousins broke out in "spots." Grandma bet one of my sons money that he would get chicken pox from this exposure. He made good use of the money he won.

One summer, my dear Aunt Donna—more of a second mother to me, really—decided that our children were treat deprived. We did try to eat in healthy ways and "treats" were just that—meant for special occasions. Fruits such as apples, bananas, and berries were considered desserts at our house. Sometimes we made cakes, cookies, and pies with sweeteners we thought were more healthful than refined white sugar. At any rate, Aunt Donna decided she would provide the children with a large bag of Pepperidge Farm cookies and a gallon of ice cream, every week.

That fall, all our children—from eighteen-year-old Tony down to five-year-old Tara—got chicken pox, and pretty much at the same time. Was it coincidence that they were more susceptible to this illness after they started eating more refined sugar?

Grandpa and the Wild Horses

My father-in-law purchased several wild horses that were beautiful to watch as they ran. They were wild indeed; one of them smashed Grandpa up against the side of a large watering trough one day. Judging by the number of cuts and bruises he received, it probably smashed him more than once. I persuaded him to let me make several herbal poultices to apply to the worst of the injuries.

Herbal poultices and compresses are made by using the leaves and roots of plants known to ease pain, bruising, and inflammation and aid in the repair of tissues. Herbal poultices can be quite messy. A small one can easily be handled by placing some plastic wrap over the top of the poultice. Those used to cover large areas of the body, however, are much more difficult to contain. Little bits of herbs tend to go everywhere, especially as the moist poultice dries out.

I put the first poultices on the most damaged side of Grandpa's body because I wasn't confident how long he would tolerate my ministrations. By the time I finished placing poultices on the right side of his body, front and back, just as I had expected, poor Grandpa was not very happy with me. He refused to let me do his left side at all. I hung around so that the poultices would remain in place at least for a little while.

The next morning I returned to check on him and found just what I expected to find. The bruising and the pain were far less on the side where the poultices had been applied, and the hip joint and shoulder muscles were also much less stiff and painful. The difference amazed even me.

Today, we would also apply essential oils to the body and use homeopathy and herbs taken internally. The results would likely be even more impressive. At times, the healing capacities of the herbs would still be worth the mess.

Allergies

Allergies seem to be a family inheritance. My mother and some of her sisters suffered from allergies, as do both of my sisters and several cousins.

I was allergic to just about everything out-of-doors. Until I was well into my thirties, a lawn being mowed across the street could make me very sick. During Val's mission years, I went home from work more than once after hearing the big mower start up at the school across from the office.

I could not eat any sort of melons, and except for apples, any raw fruit I came in contact with made my throat itch and feel as if it were closing. Most nuts caused even worse reactions. Once, on a date to a formal dance, I reacted to eating bleu cheese dressing and broke out in hives from head to toe. Those painful and unsightly hives certainly spoiled that evening. I also couldn't tolerate a number of the chemicals found in hair products and makeup.

My father loved to camp, hike, hunt, and fish. Holidays such as the 4th of July were usually spent in the canyons of the mountains that surround our beautiful valley. Enjoying the great outdoors was a big thing for my family, despite the allergies that dampened the enthusiasm of some of us.

I have happy memories of most of these trips. Other trips required taking a lot of allergy pills, which meant that I fell asleep in the car on the way. I would be shaken awake to eat lunch and play for a while until the pills wore off. Then I would take more pills and fall asleep again until it was almost time to go home. Sometimes the entire trip felt like one groggy mess to me.

The site of a bee or wasp sting always became incredibly hot and swollen, and spider bites created similar reactions. So every time I saw either bees or spiders I panicked, until, as an adult, I discovered homeopathic remedies that alleviated these symptoms.

Visiting Val in Clifton, Idaho, when we were dating was a challenge for me, spring, summer, and fall. I didn't want to take allergy pills whenever I went there—after all, sleeping through dates is sort of frowned upon. But the other option was red, itchy eyes, lots of sneezing, and carrying a box of Kleenex tissues with me everywhere I went.

Val and I moved our little family to Clifton four years after we were married. Fortunately, we had started down the herbal road by then. I managed my allergies better, but not a lot better. If I stayed indoors when the wind was blowing, I could endure. But if you have ever been to Clifton, you know that the wind is nearly constant.

Little by little I was able to eliminate most of my simple allergies, but it took a conscientious effort. I began with liver and lymph cleansing herbs and learned how to combine these herbs in ways that were more effective than using them alone. I also researched and employed energetic/homeopathic remedies that eventually would become the standard allergy formulas of the Butterfly Express line. For me personally, Apis mellifica and Sepia succus made a big difference. Clay foot soaks and baths and the use of acupressure points completed my recovery.

It has been years since I have taken an allergy medication of any kind. I react to bee stings no more strongly than any nonallergic person. And I eat whatever I want. Except for reactions to a few lingering chemicals, as far as I know, I have no allergies remaining. I hike the hills surrounding our valley and gather herbs with no allergic reactions at all. This is such a nice way to live!

I credit herbs, homeopathics, essential oils, and energy work with this miracle in my life. Unless you have lived as I once lived and have been freed from it, you might have a hard time imagining the significant difference being allergy free makes in one's quality of life.

Severe Allergic Reactions to Drugs and Chemicals

I was seventeen years old when I experienced my first scary reaction to a medication. I had travelled with my parents to Oregon to meet my brother and bring him home from his two-year church mission. I had a mild sore throat, so I kept a lozenge in my mouth most of the time. As soon as we arrived back home I left for a date, still popping lozenges. By midnight, however, I knew I was in trouble because I had an incredibly painful headache and my vision was blurred. I felt disoriented and nearly walked through the large plate glass window of my parents' house at the end of the date.

From that time on, I started reacting to things that had never bothered me previously—such as antibiotics, dental anesthesia, some mouthwashes, throat sprays and lozenges, fly sprays and bug bombs, light yogurt, any food labeled "sugar-free," and a dozen or so other products. These newly acquired allergies were very confusing and annoying.

For a few years these reactions were limited to vision disturbances, followed by a nasty migraine headache and a feeling of confusion. As time passed, however, they began to affect my heart. Sometimes my pulse would race for several days, and other times my heart would feel as though it were skipping beats. With every new reaction, the symptoms became more intense, frightening, and debilitating.

It took years to discover the common denominator among the various substances to which I was reacting. It turned out to be a synthesized derivative, or amine, of the naturally occurring amino acid phenylalanine. Note the word *synthesized*. Only the synthesized, laboratory-produced version gives me problems. While this stuff is still a bit of a problem for me, my reactions are much milder than they once were.

Natural phenylalanine is found in dairy products, eggs, nuts, beans, and some meats such as poultry and fish. The only one of these foods that gave me problems when I was younger was certain types of nuts, but they are not a problem for me at all now.

The PKU test that is conducted on newborn babies tests the infant's ability to process phenylalanine. Phenylketonuria is doctor-speak for lacking the enzyme to process and utilize this essential amino acid. I do not know if the test detects the ability to process both the natural and the synthesized form. I am still trying to understand why some people, like me, react so strongly to the synthesized version while others do not.

Synthesized phenylalanine is found nearly everywhere. It is in "lite" beverages and foods, as well as cough syrups and cough drops, some brands of toothpastes, many types of mouthwashes, and just about any food product that boasts an incredibly long shelf life. (If the bugs won't eat it, we probably shouldn't either.) It is sometimes sold in health food stores as a supplement and is often misrepresented as a natural amino acid.

This chemical is also used to stabilize the formulas of fly sprays and bug repellents. While such products are not ingested, they still adversely affect many people, including me.

The synthesized version is given a variety of names, especially when used in artificial sweeteners. Since there are now many different types of artificial sweeteners on the market, it can be difficult to keep up with all the new names of this substance and its close relatives. Although the chemical makeup of each one seems to be notably different from synthesized phenylalanine, I feel they are all something I am better off leaving alone.

Despite being named for the natural amino acids they imitate, artificial sweeteners are chemical compounds. And as with all chemicals, there are potential dangers, often referred to as side effects.

Do herbs have side effects? There are medical authorities unfamiliar with the true nature of herbs who claim that they do. But they do not have side effects in the same way drugs do.

After nearly forty years of experience, I know that herbs can be very effective, predominantly because they provide key nutrients to our bodies that are often missing from our daily diets. If you analyze an herb that has been known for many years to be beneficial to nerves, for example, that herb will likely contain high concentrations of calcium and other nutrients that nourish and heal the nervous system. This is often true of many medicinal properties a certain herb is said to possess.

For instance, vitamin C is necessary for the creation of collagen, cartilage, muscle, and blood vessels. It aids in the absorption of iron, calcium, and other nutrients that support the adrenal glands, stress-fighting hormones, the health of bones and teeth, and cancer prevention. Massive amounts of vitamin C can be found in many common herbs and herbal preparations.

Dr. John Christopher, a great herbalist from the last century, claimed that everything you needed to know about curing gingivitis could be summed up in three words: white oak bark. Years ago, after making myself quite sick using a mouthwash that was recommended by a dentist and contained synthesized phenylalanine, I tried it. White oak bark is extremely bitter, but the results were spectacular. I now maintain my gum health by using either a tincture of white oak bark or making a tea to be used as a mouth rinse. Sometimes, I use it as essential oil well diluted in water.

Can a person overdose on an herb? Of course, but they can only overdose in the same sense that it is possible to eat too much of any nutritious food. I once saw a woman with a new fruit and vegetable juicer turn her skin and the whites of her eyes an interesting shade of orange by consuming too much carrot juice. Just like carotene, which is necessary to good health in many ways, nutrients in an herb can be overdone. But a person would have to ingest far more of that herb than is necessary or even sensible.

I cannot possibly teach as much here about herbal medicine, or any other alternative modality, as I might want to. I love to meet excited novices to the alternative healthcare world. It is fun to watch them learn and have amazing experiences. And it is satisfying to play even a small part in their educational journey.

> When the whole world is running towards a cliff,
> he who is running in the opposite direction
> appears to have lost his mind.
> *—Attributed to C. S. Lewis*

CHAPTER SIXTEEN

Valued Resources

A candle loses nothing by lighting another candle.
—*Father James Keller*

A man [or woman] only learns in two ways: one by reading, and the other by association with smarter people.
—*Will Rogers*

E*ven though we grew into using herbal remedies* almost exclusively, there were certain times when the expertise and counsel of professional medical personnel blessed our lives.

A book of scripture unique to The Church of Jesus Christ of Latter-day Saints is called the *Doctrine and Covenants*. One verse that I find both interesting and informative is section 42, verse 43: "And whosoever among you are sick, and have not faith to be healed, but believe, shall be nourished with all tenderness, with herbs and mild food, and that not by the hand of an enemy." It is self-evident why any person interested in herbalism might find this scripture appealing.

I want to discuss the phrase "not by the hand of an enemy." We do not consider the medical community to be the enemy. For years I have made a point to cultivate positive working relationships with capable women and men in the medical professions, as you never know when you will need such expertise. Because I have earned their respect, going to them with questions or for assistance is a meaningful experience and a great blessing.

One of our first experiences with hospitals and surgery occurred when our son Luke was about two years old. He developed a small hernia that required a surgery to repair—or so we thought at the time. I still remember Luke's reaction to the hospital because he was very unhappy and not afraid to let us know it.

My mother-in-law came with us to the hospital. She had bought Luke a two-headed purple plastic toy dragon that stood about a foot high. It looked quite mean. Luke sat it on the floor of his hospital room with one head facing the door, guarding it, and the other head facing his bed, guarding him. This arrangement calmed him completely. The first thing he did after emerging from anesthesia was check that the dragon was in place and on the job.

Grandma happened to fill out the paperwork for Luke's hospital stay. She wrote his birthday down as one day later than it really was—which was her own daughter's birthday. She also listed his name as Todd Lucas instead of Lucas Todd. She liked the name Todd better, and besides, it had been the name she had suggested we call him. Even though we called him Luke, she called him Todd for her entire life, and even put that name on his Christmas stocking that hung on her mantle. Was she confused or just stubborn? Who knows? Besides, Luke never minded the name change, but that incorrect birth date on the hospital record created a great deal of trouble when I later had to send a copy of it to the passport office.

At age fifteen, Luke had another surgery for a similar hernia. And a couple of years later he informed me that this problem was troubling him once again. He let me know in no uncertain terms that if he had to have another surgery in order to pass the physical to go on his church mission, he wouldn't go. He said that he was never going through that surgery again, no matter what.

I prayed often about his situation. Missions are wonderful growing experiences, and I wanted Luke to be able to serve one. In my prayers, I mentioned to the Lord over and over that herbal remedies could not heal the hernia as long as Luke would not stop running, jumping, and doing pull-ups. His brothers had rigged a chin-up pipe in our hallway, and doing a few pull-ups as they passed had become habitual for them all.

I am not exactly sure what I expected heaven to do about it, and I certainly didn't propose a solution; I just whined. After a short while, Luke burned his leg. (The story of this burn is found in the following chapter.) So, out of necessity, Luke had to stay still, and I was able to treat both the burn and the hernia. By the time the burn on his leg had healed, so had the hernia.

There may be some weakness in that area as, from time to time, Luke has experienced slight problems in the past. But with the aid of herbal remedies, he has avoided surgery or mesh and their attendant complications. He is now able to lift and carry heavy objects without pain or problems.

Our next surgery was to have pins inserted in Valaree's wrist after it was broken during a playtime accident. Years later, her younger brother Richard shattered his wrist when he fell off a horse. An extensive emergency room visit followed; fortunately, surgery was not required.

Luke once took a paintball to the eye, even though he thought he had played it safe by wearing protective eyewear and had removed it only after leaving the play area. Nevertheless, accidents happen, and he had to have surgery for an impact cataract.

More recently, Val had two eye surgeries to repair damage caused by a truck that ran a stop sign at high speed and collided with our car. Perhaps there is a nonsurgical way to deal with detached retinas and impact cataracts, but if there is, we don't know them yet.

This may seem like a lot of surgeries and emergency room visits for an herbal-focused family, until you consider that they took place over nearly forty years and cover some very active and apparently accident-prone family members.

Valaree was a precocious child, and by precocious, I mean that she was constantly in motion and often moved before considering the consequences of her actions. Too often she moved faster than I could get there to prevent trouble. It was surprising how many things she got into that her four older brothers had either failed to see or hadn't been interested in exploring. She now has two daughters of her own that are just like her.

As a very young child she would look up at me with a certain gleam in her eye that meant she had spotted something interesting, and she wanted to see if I had noticed her noticing it. I would look around quickly, hoping to discover what had caught her eye so I could get to it—or to her—before she reached for it and hurt herself. The fastest land mammal on earth may be a determined three-year-old.

One day, I saw that certain gleam in her eye while I was standing at the stove, so I looked around the room. The still-hot iron sat on the ironing board, the cord hanging down within reach, and Valaree was on the move. The race was on. I got there just in time to save her from a bad burn. There were similar instances nearly every day. It was never safe to take your eyes off Valaree even for a moment.

When Valaree was about four years old she broke her arm on the day of my sister's wedding, of all days. So Val took Valaree to the doctor while I finished decorating my sister's wedding cake, delivered it, and finished setting up for the reception that evening. When Valaree returned, I split the sleeve of her little pink dress so that her cast would fit into it. Getting brand new "Sunday best" clothes had been a big deal for all of our children, and Valaree didn't want to miss the festivities just because of a broken arm.

After my sister and her new husband returned from their honeymoon, Valaree and I went to see her on the Utah State University campus. There was a play area for children in front of their apartment. Valaree immediately ran off to play in the sand while my sister and I chatted. Suddenly we realized that Valaree had somehow climbed with one hand to the top of the spiral slide and was on her way down. Unable to slow herself because of her cast, she hit the cement pad at the bottom at full speed, where one leg crumpled under her, broken.

A four-year-old of Valaree's disposition, now in both an arm and a leg cast, was difficult to keep entertained. And our television had just died. We didn't feel we could afford another, and besides, the boys' schoolwork was coming along better without the draw of a TV. Day one of Valaree's convalescence was very long, and day two seemed even longer. On day three, one of Val's relatives showed up with their children, saw our situation, and held a family council, deciding that the best way they could help was bring us their only television for as long as we needed it. The children proudly carried in their VCR and every children's movie the family owned when the family came to deliver the TV. I have been on the receiving end of many wonderful acts of service, but nothing has touched my heart quite the way that family's unselfish act did.

When the cast was removed from Valaree's poor little arm, the arm was badly bowed. Yet the doctor assured me that it was a "green-willow" break and her arm would heal just fine. I could not persuade him to take another X-ray, so I took Valaree down the street to a chiropractor and had an X-ray taken. We then went back to the doctor's office and studied the X-ray, which clearly showed that the arm was even worse off than before the doctor had first cast it.

The doctor had wet-cast the original break, and then attempted to push the bones into place by applying pressure to the cast with his hands. But he had pushed in the wrong direction, further displacing the bones of Valaree's forearm. I suggested that he try again and that he dismiss any thought of sending me a bill. Our poor little girl was stuck in another cast for several more weeks, and the loaned TV remained at our house the entire time, even after the cast on her leg—but not her arm—had come off.

By that time, Valaree had grown accustomed to medical people poking and prodding her. Since it seemed odd to me that one little girl could be healing from two broken bones at such a young age, we decided to have some tests run to determine if there were nutritional issues or deficiencies that we needed to be aware of. The tests showed that everything was fine. To date, Valaree has had more broken bones than all her siblings and her father combined.

As Valaree continued her pattern of moving before thinking, I made the acquaintance of an orthopedic specialist who became both a valuable resource and a special friend, even though our first experience with him left much to be desired.

First Experience

When Valaree was nine years old, she was playing on our brand-new swing set, standing on one seat of a glider (a swing that has two seats), and her younger brother Richard was on the other. She was holding a stuffed bear in one arm and hanging on with the other. Richard did something she didn't like so she reached out to hit him, but to do that she had to either drop the teddy bear or let go of the swing. Being Valaree, and confident of her balancing ability, she let go of the swing, fell, and broke her arm.

The medics in the local emergency room of our rather small hospital recommended surgery in the larger hospital of a neighboring town and made the arrangements. We briefly stopped at my parents' house on the way so that my father and my husband could give Valaree a priesthood blessing before the surgery.

We slowly drove the thirty miles from my parents' house to the hospital as even the slightest bump caused Valaree to scream in pain. When we finally arrived, the surgeon was furious and chewed us out for inconveniencing the surgical team he had gathered by being slower than he thought we needed to be. All the while, he was roughly—in my opinion—unwrapping Valaree's arm, causing more pain than was necessary.

I wasn't sure who I was the angriest at—the doctor or Val for not putting a stop to it—so I took my worry-fueled anger out on the doctor. I got right in his face with a rather rude suggestion of where I was going to place my knee if he didn't let go of Valaree's and wait until he had calmed down. He calmed down. And I went into the bathroom and threw up, something I used to do after tense confrontations.

The surgery was successful. When I brought Valaree back in to have the pin removed, the doctor said he couldn't do it as his assistant had left for an emergency at home. Not wanting to drive the forty-five miles home only to come back again the next day, I asked if he would let me assist, and assured him the sight of blood was not a problem for me. He had me sign some papers, then we washed up and went to work.

He made a surgical cut so he could remove the pin, and I held the incision open with what looked like a pair of needle-nosed pliers. The pin had migrated slightly, so the procedure turned out to be more involved than expected. I hung in there, the pin was removed, and the opening stitched closed.

He took the time to explain why pins sometimes migrate in the bones of small children once the break has healed. I really appreciate it when doctors acknowledge that I have enough intelligence to understand what they are saying. I was smiling when we left his office, and it was not until we were well on the way home that what I had just done hit me, and I started to shake. We spent some time on the side of the road while I recovered my composure.

Second Experience

When our youngest daughter, Tara, was less than two years old, I became concerned about a slight inward turning of her toes as she walked. Family members and people in our community told me that it looked normal to them. But Tara was my seventh child, and it didn't look normal to me, so I made an appointment with this same doctor, as I wanted a professional opinion about what we were dealing with.

You might be asking why I would take Tara to the same doctor I had yelled at during our first meeting. The answer is simple: I had come to like and trust him as we worked together on Valaree's arm. I like confident people who know that they know what they know. This doctor knew he was good at what he did, and he had no reservations telling you that he *was* good. But he also respected intelligence and the desire to learn when he saw it in others. He had the heart of a teacher and educated those around him every time he spoke, treating them with respect. This, to me, is particularly important when choosing medical assistance.

This good man took the time to explain what was going on with Tara's body. Tara's feet were indeed pronating inward, just as I thought. But they were doing so because of the knees and not the hips. He informed me that he was aware of at least two Olympic runners who had similar issues and that it seemed to benefit them in speed and balance.

He further explained that if the rotation I had detected had come from the hip, it could create problems for her later in a pregnancy and that the outcome would be far better and less painful if such a problem is treated before the child turns two. He wished that more mothers were aware of the issue and knew to contact a doctor about the problem when the child was young. Because I was willing to listen, he gave me even more information that was of great value to me later in my role as a midwife.

Third Experience

A few years later when Richard broke his arm, the staff at our local hospital told me the break was into the growth plate and would require surgery. I had seen a few X-rays by then, and I had asked questions about what I was seeing each time. To me, it didn't appear that the break extended into the growth plate at all, so I took Richard to this same doctor at the larger hospital.

Was this overconfidence on my part? Maybe. Or perhaps it was a combination of experience and a mother's intuition. And maybe it was the sweet whisperings of the Spirit. At any rate, I had enough confidence to insist on seeking a second opinion before agreeing to surgery.

I took the X-rays and Richard to this specialist's office, where he cast the break, as the arm did not need surgery. He then asked if I could stay until he had finished with his last two patients of the day because he wanted to talk with me. I agreed because I loved learning from this man and because Richard did not seem to be in any pain at the moment.

After finishing his appointments, he taught me more about how to tell the difference between the appearance of a growth plate, an actual break, and a shadow on an X-ray created by technician error. I don't know that I have ever had any use for this information, but he loved to teach and I loved to learn. We had an occasion to work together one more time after that. I gladly referred everyone to him who needed his expertise. While he has long since retired, I still miss his advice and expertise, and I miss his wonderful attitude most of all.

CHAPTER SEVENTEEN

Burns and Blessings—Luke

What seems to us as bitter trials
are often blessings in disguise.
—*Oscar Wilde*

I*t was summer and our fifteen-year-old son Luke* had gone with his father to work in the salvage yard. Luke was carrying a small gas can to refuel a piece of equipment, but apparently the container had a small leak, and Luke's pant leg became soaked with gasoline as he walked.

Val was on the tractor, loading scrap metal onto a truck. Luke, being a Westover, became somewhat impatient with just standing around doing nothing, so he decided to prepare some scrap metal while he waited. While attempting to light a cutting torch for his own use, a spark fell on his gasoline-soaked pant leg and it burst into flame. Luke immediately dropped to the ground and rolled. Val jumped off the moving tractor and ran to his son, without even taking time to turn off the motor. The tractor continued moving until it hit a large enough pile of scrap metal to bring it to a halt.

Anyone who has experienced or seen a gasoline-fed fire involving clothing knows that rolling on the ground or attempting to pat the fire out with your hands doesn't work. Any tiny spark will ignite the next patch of clothing, and then the next. Gasoline-fed flames move quickly and burn extremely hot.

Fire is always a concern during the dry summer months in our area. Sparks from farm equipment can easily start a fire in the dry brush, and a small fire can turn into a major problem very quickly. When working during dry summer weather, Val and his boys always keep at least one fifty-five-gallon drum full of water in the salvage yard in case a fire should start. Val tipped a drum full of water, dumping out just enough so that he could carry the half-full drum to Luke. Val then dumped the remaining water in the drum on Luke, putting out the fire.

Luke's burning pant leg had also ignited a brush fire in the salvage yard. Val ignored the fire, put Luke in the truck, and headed to the house. With a bad burn like his, residual heat continues to damage muscles and flesh even after the fire has been put out. Luke needed to be placed in cold water immediately to halt further damage.

At home, Val placed Luke in a bathtub full of cool water, added some lavender oil, and gave him Rescue Remedy (a very effective homeopathic treatment for injuries and the onset of shock). After determining that Luke would be all right for a few minutes, he rushed back to the salvage yard on the north edge of our property to put out the brush fire. If it had been left to burn any longer, the fire would have spread to neighboring farms and homes.

Val believes he was gone for about fifteen minutes. When he returned, he found Luke on the front lawn with his leg in my large brown garbage can. Luke explained that he had gotten cold in the bathtub, and the tall garbage can seemed perfect for filling with water and a perfect fit for his leg. He had brought it outside where the sun could keep him delightfully warm.

Tara later said of this day: "I fetched a straw sombrero that Grandma had given us in Arizona. Luke's teeth were still chattering, so I also brought him a wool blanket. And there he stood, a sombrero on his head, a wool blanket around his shoulders, and his leg in a garbage can. He looked something between homeless and on vacation."

I had been gone for the day, and as I drove in I wondered why my son was standing on the front lawn, his leg in a garbage can, and so oddly dressed. And I knew I wasn't going to like the reason. Luke and Tara were playing a board game while they waited for their father to return. Oh, the sight that met my eyes as Luke lifted his leg out of the water.

I went next door to Grandma's house looking for something better than a garbage can. I knew that his leg needed to soak a little longer in water with some lavender oil in order to stop further destruction of the tissue and to manage the pain. I found two new garbage cans stacked inside one another sitting in Grandma's kitchen. What luck! I took the bottom one home and disinfected it properly. Having now put out the fire, Val returned while I was preparing this container, and together we moved Luke back into the house.

We were familiar with caring for minor burns using herbal remedies on a smaller scale than we were seeing here, and the treatments we devised had been very successful. The care given in the hospital, while intense and often successful, seems to violate many basic premises of herbal medicine and healing. We did not, however, choose to keep Luke home with this burn out of any fear of a hospital. We let faith rather than fear guide our decision that day, and we knew in our hearts that home was the right place to be this time.

We immediately began giving Luke certain remedies to prevent any infection from taking hold. We added essential oils to the water and soaked his leg again. I then made an herbal salve out of everything I had ever used for burns, including anodyne herbs, infection-fighting herbs, and herbs with tissue-regenerating properties. Because I had not yet developed the stomach for such things, Val changed most of the bandages. I would prepare fresh bandages and then leave, unless Val called for me. This was my son, and I hated causing him even a little bit of pain. The children did not help change bandages or sit up with Luke at night, as that was something I could do for him.

Luke never ran a fever or developed an infection. Just in case, and because it made him feel better to have something to do, I had my dad travel all over the valley to purchase tubes of Neosporin. While we were prepared to use them at the first sign of infection, we never opened any. In my experience, Neosporin is not nearly as effective at either healing or fighting infection as essential oils and herbal salves.

Luke did not seem to be in much pain that evening or throughout the night. Over the next few days, he said there was far less pain than he expected. Of course, with burns this serious, nerve endings do not send pain signals to the brain early on. It is the less-burned outer edges that cause the most discomfort, but lavender oil and cold water kept it to a minimum. After the salve is applied (we call it Miracle Salve), the pain subsides in about twenty minutes.

As night approached, we placed a pile of cushions on the couch so that Luke could be partially propped up with his leg still in the water. Val and I passed the night sitting on either side of him.

Luke's leg was burned on all sides from his hip to his ankle, and the burns were particularly bad behind his knee. The flesh of a burn softens when herbal Miracle Salve is applied and blood flow increases. Changing bandages was still a bloody job.

Over the next day or two, dead skin and flesh would pull away when the bandages were changed. Within just a few days, however, we could see little pink patches of *something* forming over the burned areas. At first, these patches worried us because we wondered if they were spots of infection. Within twenty-four hours of their first appearance, it was obvious that they were patches of new skin. I had seen such spontaneous generation of new cells before but with much smaller areas of burned skin.

Medical personnel told me that new skin would first regenerate from the outside edges of the burn, and that it would take a very long time for areas farther away from healthy skin to grow back. In fact, I was told that scar tissue would form in these areas and would not only be ugly but also stiff and rope-like forever.

We were also told that unless we frequently forced the leg into both straight and bent positions, the ability of the knee to bend would be permanently compromised. Yet, to me it made no sense to bend the leg and tear flesh that was healing so nicely and risk creating further scar tissue. So we were careful and moved his leg very little. As muscles and tendons rebuild, shrinkage occurs, and painful stretching is absolutely necessary to maintain mobility. We also understood that when muscle, tissue, and skin reach a certain level of healing, physical therapy becomes essential if mobility and flexibility is to be maintained.

Before school began again in August, Luke insisted on putting a plastic bag over his burned leg and joining his friends at an end-of-summer party at the lake. He knew they would be swinging off a rope tied to a tree branch and dropping into the lake and did not want to miss out. The bag, not surprisingly, did not stay on his leg after his first plunge into the lake.

Thankfully, Luke's leg healed thoroughly, and we give herbs and essential oils a great deal of credit for this blessing. For a time, he had one small scar where his boot top literally melted into his flesh, but he has no such scar today. The leg is exactly the same color as it used to be, and even tans the same. The knee bends as it should, without restriction.

Recently, a doctor in town sent a man with burned hands to see us. They were electrical burns, which can be particularly deep and nasty. The doctor had told this man he could go to the hospital burn center or to the Westovers and added that if he himself were in the same situation, he would go to the Westovers. Under our care, the man's hands healed quickly and thoroughly.

Luke's Words

I am Lucas Westover. When I was about sixteen or seventeen years old, I was working with my dad in our salvage yard. My father was loading scrap metal onto a semi-trailer to take to Nucor, a steel plant in Plymouth, Utah, that would buy his metal. I was pulling radiators, catalytic converters, and fuel tanks out of cars to get the cars ready to be crushed, when I had an accident. I will not give many details about what caused the accident, how I got burned, or about what I did wrong to get myself into a bad situation. Let's just say I did it to myself and leave it at that.

I remember smelling something burning, so I looked around to see what it was. I did not see anything burning, but then I felt pain in my leg and looked down to see almost my entire paint leg on fire. I immediately dropped to the ground and tried to put the fire out by using my hands to scrape dirt, gravel, and anything else that I could get my hands on to try to smother the fire. It did not work, and fear and panic begin to set in. I knew running would only make the fire worse, but dropping to the ground and trying to smother the fire out was not working either. I cast my eyes around the yard looking for my Dad. I saw him on the other end of the junkyard driving the tractor. I jumped up and ran toward him, calling out to him. When he saw me, he immediately jumped off the tractor and started running toward me. He just left the tractor driving off on its own. He didn't even take the time to stop the tractor. When he jumped off, he was hauling a bucketload of scrap metal to dump on the semi-trailer. He decided to let the semi-trailer stop the loader for him so that he would not have to waste a second shutting if off. He ran over to me and helped me put the fire out.

My pant leg was almost completely gone, and I was burned from the ankle to about 6 to 8 inches above the knee. My dad then helped me up and we started walking toward the truck. As I was walking, I was grabbing handfuls of the dead skin that was hanging from my leg and throwing them on the ground. I was amazed that I was in no pain.

Now, at this point in the story, I would like to jump back a few years earlier to tell of another story, because it is part of what led to my decision to not go to the doctor. My brother Tyler had burned his hand and then soaked it in ice water. I remember him not being in any pain at all despite having a bad burn. Even though I was not in any pain yet with my burn, I wanted to put my leg in cold water. Dad drove me down to the house. We went into the bathroom and filled the bathtub with cold water, and I put my leg in it. Sticking my leg in that cold water felt really similar to what it feels like to put really cold hands in hot water—only much more intense. That feeling only lasted for a few seconds and then went away completely. Once again, I felt no pain. But when I tried to pull my leg out of the water, it felt like my leg was on fire all over again. I could not handle the pain of having my leg out of the water.

My sister Tara and her friend walked in. Her friend's name, if I remember correctly, was Danielle, and she had spent the night at our house. When we had first arrived at the house, Tara and her friend were outside on the lawn with beach towels and swimming suits, running through the sprinklers and having a good time. You see, they were just kids at the time.

Somebody had left the swamp cooler on all night, and the house was really cold. With that, and with my leg in ice-cold water, I started to get cold, and even though I wasn't in any pain, I started going into shock. My dad brought me some Rescue Remedy, a homeopathic that helps with nausea and shock. I felt much better after taking a dose; my nausea and lightheadedness went away, but I was still very cold. I asked them to turn off the swamp cooler and turn on the heater. I wanted to go outside to be in the nice warm sun while the house warmed up. I ended up on the lawn, with my leg in a cold barrel of water. While I was sitting there, Tara and her friend started to play games with me to keep me company. My mom came home, and as she drove up the driveway, I pulled my leg out of the water. She took one look at my leg and began to try to convince me of the seriousness of my condition.

My mother made this really good healing salve, and seeing that I would not go to the doctor, she strongly suggested that we put this salve on my leg and use nonstick gauze to wrap my leg. You would not believe how much salve, nonstick gauze bandages, and ice they went through. The only pain that I felt during this whole ordeal was during the few minutes twice a day when my parents changed my bandages. Without having any skin on that leg, the air hitting it after they removed the bandages felt like a freight train.

What I noticed about the salve is that it did a very good job of helping my leg to heal. In fact, it seemed like my body was just absorbing the salve, and it seemed to me that the salve was actually becoming new skin. Now, my grandma really didn't believe in the natural healing methods and was seriously pro-doctor, but after seeing my injury and the way it eventually healed with hardly any scars, she told me that if I had gone to the hospital, they probably would have peeled the skin off my back and butt to cover my leg. To her, it looked like I was far better off doing what we did.

I do not want to come off sounding anti-doctor by any means—that's not the reason I chose to stay home and deal with this burn. I stayed home because I felt like it would be less painful to stay at home, as crazy as that might sound to some. And I knew my parents could deal with it; I felt like it would heal better if I stayed at home. I am actually very grateful for the hospitals and medical doctors and staff, as well as to my parents.

When I was a baby, I had a hernia surgery, and I had another such surgery when I was about 14. My parents have also taken me in to doctors for stitches, braces, cavities, and so on. I've even had eye surgery. My parents have done so much for me, and this burn is only one example of the time, money, love, and sacrifice that they put toward me. I'm sure even treating the burn at home was quite expensive, and it definitely took a lot of their time.

All in all, I would say that my burn was actually a really good experience, and I learned a lot. I am very happy with the way things turned out and with my decision and for having loving family and friends who are supportive and did everything in their power to help me.

CHAPTER EIGHTEEN

Living and Learning

I've learned that I still have a lot to learn.

—*Maya Angelou*

What we obtain too cheaply we esteem too lightly; it is dearness only that gives everything its value. Heaven knows how to put a proper price upon its goods; and it would be strange indeed if so celestial an article as freedom should not be highly rated.

—*Thomas Paine*

H*erbs were the first alternative modality* we became acquainted with, and homeopathy came next. To the uninformed, homeopathy may appear to be little more than voodoo or magic. Through experience, I found it to be far from that. We have also learned and incorporated other health care modalities into our lives.

Homeopathy

According to research, over 200 million people worldwide use homeopathy on a regular basis. It is included in the national health systems of several countries around the world, including India and Switzerland, and is practiced in forty European countries. Approximately 29% of European Union citizens use homeopathic remedies in their day-to-day health care. Even today in the United States, many people rely on homeopathy as an adjunct to their regular health care regimens.

One of my earliest experiences with homeopathic medicines was while I was pregnant with my youngest child, Tara. During the last weeks of gestation, she decided that being carried head down—the normal position—was not for her and instead persistently lay sideways. This is called a transverse lie, and if the baby is in this position when labor starts, a C-section is usually required.

During the final six weeks of this pregnancy, my midwife and her assistant manually turned Tara back to the proper position several times. She tended to turn easily, not hanging up as if the umbilical cord were wrapped around her in some way. But she would stay properly positioned for only a few days. Our hope was that when labor began, she would turn by herself or with a little bit of help, present properly, and be born in the normal manner.

I went to my previously scheduled appointment with my midwife. It was a forty-five-minute drive to her house, and by the time I arrived, I had started what we both believed was true labor. It was hard to tell for sure because I had experienced a lot of pre-labor as my body tried to coax this baby into a better position.

After the examination, the midwife handed me a small bottle and explained that this remedy—a homeopathic she called it—was supposed to cause babies to turn to a proper position. She had never used a homeopathic remedy before and neither had I. She told me to go home and wait an hour before taking the remedy. In the meantime, she would collect a couple of assistants and they would come to my house to turn the baby one more time. And if the baby could not be turned and kept in a proper position as labor progressed, we would be looking at a C-section.

With the midwife's mention of a possible C-section, my heart sank. It had been a long six weeks of intermittent labor as our little girl tried to decide which way was up and which way was down, and I was exhausted and discouraged. Yet I had a great deal of faith in the ability of my midwife, as she had easily turned the baby previously and we had been through the deliveries of four of my previous babies together. So I had some reason to hope that my baby could be persuaded to engage in the normal way. Nevertheless, the possibility of a C-section weighed heavily as I drove home.

Nearly an hour had passed by the time I reached home, so I placed the homeopathic pellets in my mouth and made myself a small bowl of chicken soup. Midwives, at least those I have worked with closely, don't believe that a mother should go into labor and delivery with her blood sugar low from hunger. Light, easily digested foods in small quantities are advised as labor progresses. I can tell you that this is much better than the hunger, blood sugar issues, unnecessary exhaustion, and lightheadedness many women experience during labor when they eat nothing. Having never had a surgery since a tonsillectomy in early childhood, it did not occur to me to avoid food because of the possibility of a C-section. And I had a great deal of faith in my midwife.

When I had finished my soup, I stood up to take my bowl to the sink, and felt my baby float in my belly, and then she rolled. I watched as her pointy little butt slowly moved from the left side of my belly to straight up under my breastbone. Then, with a soft thud she dropped into place, head down. Before I could even catch my breath, a very strong contraction hit. The downward pressure was intense, and the next contraction came just two minutes behind the first. I began to feel panicky.

Our children had stayed at Grandma's house while I went to the appointment with my midwife, so I was home alone. It was raining outside, our phone had been unreliable for several days, and repairmen weren't scheduled to come for another day or two.

From my front window, I could see my mother-in-law standing at her kitchen sink, so I grabbed a bright red blanket, stepped out on the front porch and began waving it, trying to get her attention. But when the next hard contraction hit, I threw the blanket over the outside light fixture and went back into the house.

Within a few minutes, my oldest son, Tony, came through the door with a note from Grandma. It said, "If you are in labor, I will do anything but come. What do you need?" I sent word back that the midwives were on their way and that someone needed to find Val, who was out and about on the property. Tony seemed to think this situation was a lot of fun and tore back to Grandma's house to relay the message and then went off to find his father.

My mother-in-law called a neighbor whose last two children had been born at home, both before the midwife arrived. She arrived quickly, and her calm attitude reassured me. About twenty minutes later the midwives arrived, and Val was only a few minutes behind them. Within a couple of hours, our precious little girl was safely delivered, and she arrived in a perfectly straightforward and proper position.

Some may believe that the homeopathic remedy was responsible, and others may consider it a coincidence, yet it is hard to argue with such dramatic results. During my years as a midwife, I saw homeopathic remedies help several babies to turn. None were as dramatic as my own experience, and their midwives also hadn't attempted to turn the babies manually before giving the homeopathic remedy.

It is difficult to describe the poignant feelings of my heart as I held my second precious little girl. Deep in my heart, I had secretly longed for Valaree to have a little sister to share girl things with.

As I looked at this precious baby girl, my heart melted. It was obvious that she was going to be fair-haired and light-skinned, very unlike Valaree's dark hair and eyes. My mind went back a few years to my two oldest boys. Mother used to call dark-haired, dark-eyed Tony and his blond, blue-eyed younger brother her "chocolate cake and vanilla ice cream" grandchildren. History, with little girls this time around, was repeating itself as I had only dared to hope.

Tara was a delight as she grew up. She was intelligent, talented, beautiful, and *all girl*. When she was very young, she insisted on only wearing dresses or skirts—no pants or Levi jeans. I made her several sets of skirts and tops out of easy-to-care-for polyester fabrics, and her favorite set was aqua blue with white polka dots. I can still picture her whirling around the front lawn, skirt swirling about her legs, and our beloved big white dog whirling with her.

As a child, our son Richard had severe allergies. Like his mother, he reacted dramatically to bee stings and to pollen and dust on windy days. We learned which of the homeopathic remedies relieved symptoms of specific allergic reactions. There was one for pollen and bee stings (Apis mellifica), and another for reactions to mold spores (Allium cepa) that worked effectively for Richard.

One afternoon when a young cousin of mine was visiting, Richard, who was about four years old, came out of his bedroom wheezing and struggling to breathe. My cousin began looking for my shoes and the car keys. I squirted some homeopathic drops into Richard's mouth and waited a few seconds. Nothing seemed to be happening, so I grabbed the other bottle and gave him a few drops of that. This time the results were as immediate as I expected them to be.

Eventually, we mixed both remedies in the same bottle. At the potency we were using, and in accordance with homeopathic protocols, this was a perfectly acceptable thing to do. Many people have found significant relief from their own allergic reactions by using these two remedies in combination.

Arnica is a local herb that, as a poultice, has proven very effective for bumps and bruises. The herbal literature states that arnica cannot be applied to open wounds and cuts, but this does not apply to the homeopathic version of arnica. Soreness, swelling, and bruising are always greatly reduced when homeopathic arnica is applied to the tissue as quickly after an injury as possible.

Eventually, arnica oil began to be used at home births that I attended. It is positively astonishing how much less swelling and soreness a woman experiences when arnica oil is used whenever an internal evaluation is conducted. I wish I had known about the use of arnica during the season I was having my own children.

Another summer, Richard fell off his horse and broke his wrist. The horse ran off and Richard was forced to walk back from the hills above our home. By the time he got home, he looked white and nearly in shock. We quickly treated him homeopathically for the impending shock and called our favorite orthopedic doctor and told him we were on our way to the hospital. We arrived there about forty-five minutes later.

While getting the arm ready to be set, Richard's fingers were placed in what looked like finger traps to hold the arm in place. They then raised his fingers until his elbow was bent at a ninety-degree angle, perpendicular to the cot on which he was lying. The nurse started hanging weights from his elbow joint. This was intended to pull the bones back into their proper alignment and was painful, to say the least. Richard's eyes rolled up as he started into shock. The doctor turned to call for assistance, and while his head was turned, I squirted some homeopathic Rescue Remedy into Richard's mouth. By the time the doctor had turned back, Richard was looking back at him quite normally. Homeopathics really can work this effectively and quickly, which is one of the reasons I love them.

When the doctor looked back down at Richard and saw he was no longer going into shock, he turned to the nurse and said, "Never mind, this is the Westovers." He had seen what could be done with my little bottles long before this took place, and he simply reminded me that I should be careful not to put too much liquid into my son's mouth as he might be going into surgery. So I put the remedy on my hand and placed my hand on the back of Richard's neck instead. Homeopathics often work this way as well.

When the doctor was finished with Richard, he asked me some insightful questions about homeopathy. Now it was my opportunity to do a little educating. He never did use any of my "magic juice" (his term) in the hospital, however, as he valued his surgical privileges too much to risk it.

Before we were exposed to homeopathy, we had made some progress with Val's health issues by applying what we had learned about herbal medicine and nutrition. But there was still such a long way to go. I give homeopathy a good measure of the credit for Val's eventual recovery from the issues that plagued him for years.

I came across a book in which a medical doctor who used homeopathy in his practice told of his friend's recovery from serious health issues, a story that sounded much like what Val had been experiencing. At the end of the book there was a section labeled "For the Practitioner," full of advice on the use of homeopathic remedies. I began looking for those remedies, but since homeopathy was not yet well-known in our part of the United States, I couldn't find them in the potencies the book called for.

So I placed a call to a world-renowned homeopathic manufacturing company in England. I told them my troubles and the man asked me a range of questions. The call stretched so long that in my head I was calculating the likely cost of this overseas phone call. He ended the conversation by asking for my address, which seemed odd since I hadn't ordered anything. I wanted to ponder the things he had told me before I placed an order. At any rate, I gave him my address and hung up the phone. Homeopathy was still new to me, and I felt quite confused about it all.

In a short time a small package arrived at the house with a return address in the UK. Inside were the remedies I had discussed with this man, along with instructions. No bill was enclosed. There is little doubt these remedies aided Val's healing process.

Foot Zone Therapy

It was around this same time that I learned about foot zone therapy. One of our earliest experiences with this modality occurred shortly after I learned the technique. I will let Val share this story in his own words:

> *A neighbor had a fire get away, and so Travis and I hurried over to help. The main fire control effort by the professionals was up on the mountain, above my neighbor's house. One small fire truck was down below, where other neighbors were trying to save local buildings, but this truck seemed to be guarding the road rather than being of any help to the fire.*

We almost had the lower fire contained several times when the wind would pick up and we would lose ground again. In the end, the fire got away and burned a friend's hay shed and other buildings. By the time all the fires were finally under control, Travis and I had spent most of the day on the smoky hillside.

When I got home, I suddenly felt very tired and sat down in an easy chair to rest before I cleaned up. The combination of not moving and residual smoke in my lungs overcame me in just a few minutes, and I started fighting for breath. I could not get up out of the chair. I couldn't even yell for help.

LaRee happened by shortly, and I could barely whisper that I really needed help. She had just finished learning to foot zone and offered me a treatment. When she worked the areas on my feet connected to the lungs, it hurt like the dickens! She had practiced on me many times before and it had never hurt like that. As she zoned my feet it felt as though a very heavy blanket was being lifted off my chest, and I started breathing normally again.

As we were finishing Travis came through, and I told him to sit down and let his mother work his lungs. He scoffed and left. When he came home later, he was coughing and spent the next day in bed. It seems the damage was done from the smoke inhalation, as the foot zoning did not work for him at this point as it had done earlier for me. But the "old man" got up the next morning and went back to work!

Essential Oils

The day before Thanksgiving, Val and his sons were working on a small project. Richard was on a ladder that was perched precariously on an unstable mound of dirt, and Val was trying to hold the ladder steady. Somehow, Richard slipped off the ladder, landing on his father. Val then fell, and his lower back landed across a chunk of cinder block. He was quite sure he had broken a couple of ribs. He didn't want to move because of the pain but was eventually able to slowly roll over and, with a little help, stand up.

Being the sort of man he is, Val decided that, if he moved carefully, he could still measure, mark, and cut the metal sheeting until the crew finished their work for the day, as that would not require him to bend over much. Sitting still on the ride home resulted in enough soreness and stiffness that Val had to be helped into the house. I immediately applied essential oils and arnica, and in a few hours, he seemed to feel much better. He rested over the holiday weekend and within a few days had completely forgotten about the injury.

A week or so after this injury, Val lifted something too quickly and vigorously while twisting his upper back. There was a snapping sound loud enough for me to hear from nearby. The ribs had snapped. They did not stay in place as they had before, and there was a large bump on one side of his lower back. When I pressed on the rib signals, as outlined in foot zone therapy, I could feel the displacement of the ribs.

Val then carefully climbed into the tub, and I added a Butterfly essential oil blend that I had formulated years before to the water. The blend, called LeMillenia, was designed to assist broken bones to move back into place, and we had seen it done many times.

Within a few minutes, the front and back muscles of Val's upper body were visibly and strongly contracting, enough to make all the muscles too sore to even touch. It took most of the night and a priesthood blessing before the contractions and the pain subsided. The ribs appeared to be back in place by morning, and the rib signals on his feet were also now perfectly aligned. The bump on Val's back was gone, and the ribs healed very nicely. We applied LeMillenia and pain-relieving essential oils on the area, just in case, for a few days afterward.

TCM and Other Modalities

I eventually studied traditional Chinese medicine (TCM), focusing on basic theory and the use of acupressure points. Eastern cultures have been using some of these health care principles for centuries, and modern science is beginning to validate some of the concepts through research and analysis.

I took classes in health kinesiology, a fascinating modality that originated in England. The things I learned have been a huge blessing in our lives over many years. I also became acquainted with several people who worked in a variety of other alternative modalities. I studied them as well and found them interesting, thought-provoking, and useful.

All this was followed by classes in craniosacral therapy. I very much enjoyed taking these classes with my daughter Valaree, a daughter-in-law (I am so blessed by my daughters-in-law), and a close friend. I enjoyed being the student rather than the teacher for a change.

Currently, I teach my own combination of many of these principles, including foot zone techniques, because I have used them and they have blessed our lives.

I am happy to say that at sixty-eight years of age, I am in very good health. My heart works well, and people often remark that I seem to have the energy of ten women. They exaggerate—possibly on the low side. Take this morning, for example. I got up at 5:00 a.m., lifted weights for forty-five minutes, and then worked out, fast and hard, on my elliptical machine for another forty-five minutes. Then I put in a full day of work.

This is a typical daily schedule. I am blessed—or cursed, depending on my mood—that my home and my work are currently pretty much one and the same. Sometimes this means that I don't know how to quit and "go home" at the end of a long day.

Although Val was diagnosed with diabetes as a young man, he has not suffered from this ailment for many years. His digestion functions well, he has excellent balance and reflexes, and he has far more strength than most men his age. As he says, "I jump and run where few my age can follow. Nearly everyone I grew up with is getting shorter, or else I am getting taller. What do you think? I can lift a hundred pounds with ease. I could lift a lot more, but it is not fun anymore. I eat chocolate."

Val and I both know that herbs are effective and that they work because they are nutritional powerhouses. They are neither magic nor voodoo; they are food. Since we have a deep and abiding faith in a

Heavenly Father who loves us, we do thank Him for the wonderful blessing of herbs. We wonder at people who would rather poison themselves with drugs rather than use herbal preparations to rectify the nutritional deficiencies that may be contributing to their ill health.

I firmly believe that the lives of each of our children have been blessed by the knowledge we have gained and applied using alternative healing modalities.

It is often a source of frustration that many people will give their doctor and their drugs months, weeks—even years—to alleviate their suffering but become discouraged or even disparaging if an herbal remedy doesn't set things right in a few hours or, at most, a few days. And if there is any slight bump in the road to healing, the herb is likely to get the blame.

Healing practices, by definition, are meant to "do no harm." Nutritional herbal remedies are far less likely to do harm than ingesting certain toxic or poisonous substances administered under the guise of healing. Often, such drugs only mask the symptoms, and we have found no valid statistical or logical arguments to the contrary.

The Master Healer

We absolutely believe in God's power to heal. I myself have experienced this miracle of healing on more than one occasion. There have also been times when I have been very happy to seek traditional medical care. Nevertheless, there have been far more instances when I have been grateful for the knowledge we have acquired and for having had the faith, the confidence, and the patience to stay at home and do things right.

CHAPTER NINETEEN

The Midwife

The greatest joy is to become a mother;
the second greatest is to be a midwife.
—*Norwegian Proverb*

The word midwife derives from Old English, *mid* meaning "with" and *wife* referring to "woman." Thus, originally, this term meant "with-woman." Being *with* the woman during her pregnancy, labor, and delivery is the standard midwives strive for.

I was a midwife or a midwife assistant for several years. It might take an entire book to tell the stories of all these amazing women, their families, and our birthing experiences together. Working so closely with women and their families was a great privilege. I thank them, each and every one.

Helping other women have meaningful birth experiences, like the ones I had at home, was a longtime dream of mine, but to achieve that dream didn't necessarily mean I wanted the responsibility of being the primary midwife at births. The thought of that much responsibility was quite daunting. I did know that, at least, I wanted to become the best midwife *assistant* the world had ever seen.

I attended four or five births with the midwife who delivered my own babies. I was mostly an extra pair of hands and a pair of younger feet to fetch things when they were needed. These experiences were very precious to me.

Val and I counseled together about my pursuing this dream of helping women. When the timing was right, I contacted the midwife who had been the partner of this wonderful woman who had delivered my own children, as she was no longer practicing due to age and health concerns. The midwife I contacted had attended one of my own births during her training days.

The training of a midwife is rigorous and lengthy. I thought that I had studied a lot and was well prepared to begin training, but as I soon discovered what becoming a midwife under the tutelage of this midwife would really entail, I began to study more in earnest. I also attended every conference and class offered by professional organizations that I could.

I began to get hands-on experience, one birth at a time, by accompanying this knowledgeable woman to as many births as I could. I soon realized that I was very fortunate in my choice of a trainer, as she was, and is, both an excellent midwife and a teacher at heart. She has an impeccable reputation throughout several states, and, thanks to her training, I am also well respected.

During my years serving as a midwife, I always asked couples to pre-arrange for medical backup should we find ourselves in need of assistance or advice. If they were unwilling to do so because of the cost, it was okay with me, as I knew several doctors with whom I had cultivated working relationships who were willing to help if and when it might be needed.

Midwives are trained to be hands-on and follow the baby's progress and positions, as well as the mother's status, through each stage of labor. Being there early to observe the labor process and the baby's progress is an important part of ensuring the mother's and the baby's safety. There is no mad rushing into the room at the last minute and catching a baby that the doctor *hopes* is positioned properly for a safe delivery.

Good midwives pride themselves on their palpation skills and on their understanding of female anatomy. They develop and rely on their ability to listen to a baby's heart tones and understand what this intelligent language is communicating to them. The ability to foresee a problem developing during prenatal visits or during early labor is a crucial skill.

Midwives are thoroughly trained in the mechanics of birth and would be embarrassed if they had to transport the mother for an emergency C-section in anything but the most unusual circumstances. They may do a trial of labor at home, but the possibility of a C-section should have been foreseen and prepared for long before it is needed. A C-section team should have sufficient time for preparation so that proper procedures, not accomplished in haste, will ensure that the mother and baby will be safe throughout. Usually, a doctor has been consulted and is standing by.

After the birth of her third child, our daughter Valaree was injured in a rollover car accident that damaged her pelvic structure, ribs, and liver. During her subsequent pregnancy, we discussed the possibility, even the likelihood, that she would need a C-section due to these injuries. So when her water broke and no labor began after a typical length of time, we moved her to the hospital and to the care of a physician.

After two rounds of Pitocin, contractions still had not started. A full thirty-six hours after our arrival, a C-section was ordered, with my blessing. But there was no emergency, no police escort, no baby under stress—only midwives, doctors, and family working together in the best interests of both mother and child, and all went well and according to plan.

Valaree was able to have two more children, and both were delivered at home and normally—no C-section—but the deliveries were difficult and not at all like the births of her first three children before the accident.

Home birth typically follows a certain rhythm. Ideally, the prospective mother will call the midwife at the first sign that she *might* be in labor. All the midwives I worked with encouraged their patients to do this. Sometimes the midwife will advise the mother to relax for a few minutes in a warm bath that includes either a little bit of ginger root or lavender essential oil, as such a relaxing bath will usually halt *false* labor.

This bath also tends to help settle early labor contractions into a consistent pattern. So within a few minutes, the mother should have a clearer picture of whether this is true labor. Of course, the midwife would instruct the mother to call back with any concerns, since we would rather respond to a false alarm than miss getting to a birth in time. Once I received such a call, I could usually leave my home in under two minutes, even if it was in the middle of the night.

A home birth allows a relaxed mother to move around her own home during the labor. Her husband is present, calmly breathing with her and holding specific pressure points through each contraction. It is an amazing thing to watch a husband and wife labor together for the good of their baby.

The senior midwife keeps a close watch on the mother. Assistants are to be seen rarely and heard even less. There are few things more annoying for a mother in labor than a gaggle of women gabbing away while she is trying to concentrate during a contraction. Concentration aids pain control and the baby's journey.

The baby's heart tones are monitored as needed. For the mother, relaxing baths, light nourishment, and a minimum of stress and intervention is the norm. Serenity, support, and encouragement surround the mother every second of this momentous journey. It is as different from a typical hospital birth as night is from day.

I have come to trust that all my training, study, and experience will be available to my mind and to my hands right when it is needed most. I have had certain information come to my mind that I didn't know I knew, only to go home later and find that information in a book I had read several times.

I would like to share one such experience. I was midwifing for a mother who was a very small woman. The baby, like its father, had large shoulders and failed to make the proper rotations in utero, and a shoulder dystocia developed. This birth was well past the point of safety for a C-section when I was called. This was the most intimidating birth complication I had yet been present for.

A shoulder dystocia means that the baby's shoulders are presenting at the wrong angle and are at risk of becoming firmly stuck against either the mother's sacrum or pubic bone. This situation is difficult to detect, and every midwife and doctor I have known has a justifiable fear of encountering such a situation. Even performing a C-section becomes extremely dangerous if the situation is allowed to proceed beyond a certain point. Retracting a baby who is far down the birth canal runs a high risk of damaging the baby's neck and shoulders or possibly causing the baby's death. Using several special maneuvers and techniques, this baby was brought into the world safely and without serious injury. The mother did well also.

When I arrived back home I was too keyed-up to sleep, so I pulled out every reference I had ever seen on coping with shoulder dystocia. While reading one comprehensive article by a very experienced midwife, I kept saying to myself, *I did that*, and *I did that also,* at each suggested technique. Every worthwhile maneuver and intervention mentioned had come to my mind right when I needed it most. I turned the page only to learn that the baby she was describing had died. I began to cry, uncontrollably, as hard as I have ever wept in my life. I cried so intensely that Val, who was sleeping in the room directly below, heard my sobs and came to see what was the matter.

When I finally started to calm down, a deep feeling of gratitude came over me, an appreciation for all those who had trained me, and for the countless hours of study I had put in. I was even more grateful that the Holy Ghost, just as promised in scripture, had brought to my remembrance those things I needed to know at the very moment they were needed.

Often, my mind has been filled with thoughts beyond my own, only to find that the other attendants received the same impressions at the same time. I have seen midwives and assistants work together almost as though they were one person, operating with a singleness of mind.

One such experience involved a mother who was giving birth leaning forward on an Amish birthing stool. She had previously expressed a deep desire to hold her baby as soon as it was born. While this is typical at a home birth, this mother was particularly adamant. Her previous births had occurred in hospitals where she had not been able to hold her newborns until quite some time after their births.

As her baby emerged, we saw that the umbilical cord was looped around the child's neck and around its torso, and an additional loop was passing between the baby's legs, making an injury to the little boy's scrotum a possibility. There were at least three areas of serious danger for the child if the cord tightened any further.

The mother, not able to see the trouble from her position, reached down and began lifting the baby upward. She lifted her child fiercely, exultantly, and with amazing strength. Six hands, those of the midwife and her two assistants, each reached for a different place of possible trauma. The baby's father reached forward and prevented his wife from lifting the baby any further until the problems could be resolved. Stopping the baby's upward motion and preventing the tightening of the cord wraps required both his strength and his soft words. Like each of us, the father was right there, doing what needed to be done in a timely and effective manner.

My own hands went between the cord and the baby's trachea. Why there and not somewhere else? I do not know, except to say that I have seen this sort of thing play out many times and in many different situations. No two attendants ever reach for the same thing, whether it is a cord or a piece of equipment, nor do we get in each other's way. And often, just as in this instance, no words are spoken.

More times than I can possibly relate here, I have known things that I could not possibly intuit from what I was observing or had previously been told. I call such impressions "walking in a shaft of white light." It must be experienced to be understood and, perhaps, believed.

Another such experience involved yet another umbilical cord wrapped around an infant's neck. The baby was not yet far enough into the world for the cord wrap to be seen, and the wrap wasn't tight enough yet to alter the baby's heart tones. But somehow, I knew we were headed for trouble. It was as though I could see in my mind's eye where the cord lay and when it would become problematic.

At just the right time, I reached past the baby's head to clamp the cord in two places. The cord, which I could now feel but still not see, truly was wrapped around the baby's neck. I managed to cut the cord between the two clamps without harming the baby or causing the mother a single tear. Midwives usually prefer to leave the cord pulsing as long as possible before cutting it, for many good reasons, but it was not possible in this situation.

This wondrous spiritual gift—this *walking in the light*—has been present at virtually every home birth I have ever attended if the family and the midwives were well-prepared, well-trained, and emotionally and spiritually ready to receive such a blessing. Nonetheless, it was never intended to be a substitute for knowledge and training. I don't believe it could be present if it were expected to be used in this way. Such special intuitions and inspirations are a blessing for all present.

On occasion, I have felt the presence of ministering angels and have sensed that departed family members were not only attending but were offering real support. Their presence can be so tangible that it's almost as if they are within the visible, physical realm alongside us.

One dear woman and her husband expressed well what I am trying to describe. This mother suffered from severe endometriosis, which was impeding the baby's progress into the world. It had been a long and difficult labor. The pushing stage was also unusually long, and the mother was exhausted.

I helped her into a sitting position, with her husband behind her to lend her strength and give her something to brace against as she pushed. Suddenly, as they both shared with me later, they felt "someone" slide in between them and assume the hard work of pushing that baby out.

It was incredible as I watched the mother relax just as the baby made a rather abrupt and forceful entry into the world. Everyone in the room who witnessed it had tears in our eyes. I have tears of gratitude welling up just remembering this sacred experience.

Of great significance is what develops in the mind and heart of the mother and, often, the father as well. A successful home birth creates and emotionally unites the parents at the same time a new life is safely brought into the world. One young father broadcast live video so that his mother could witness the birth. The baby's grandmother voiced what I had observed: with tears in her eyes she said that she had watched her son grow from a boy to a man during this labor.

I have witnessed the deep strength of women and the power of a loving relationship between husband and wife magnify that strength. No matter how good their bond was before the birth, a woman and her husband emerge from their birthing experience stronger, more mature, and more in love with each other.

Most birthing women would do anything to keep their babies safe. I have seen women reach deep into their souls for one more ounce of strength when it seemed impossible. A woman who has given birth has a strength and an attachment to her child and to her husband that is nothing short of miraculous. Bonds for eternity are formed at such times.

Legality

During the time that I was practicing, midwifery was not illegal in any of the states where I delivered babies. It is still not "outside the law" in Utah. Idaho passed licensing requirements a few years ago, about the same time I retired. Even under the new law, being present for and delivering my own grandchildren is still legal. And responding to an emergency when called upon is also legal. Nevertheless, the present legal environment would make me extremely nervous in responding to a call. Who would determine if the situation was an emergency under the law's vague wording? In such a situation, and since I would not have assisted the woman previously during her pregnancy, I would be facing many unknowns. And if it was a real emergency, there would be a good chance of something being seriously wrong, things I might not be able to turn around at this late stage and with so little information. I would rather not have a bureaucrat, or a jury, determine if I will watch my grandchildren grow up from a jail cell. Nevertheless, how could I *not* respond to such a woman in distress and possibly in serious trouble?

Certified Nurse Midwives

The new law in Idaho requires a woman to be a Certified Nurse Midwife (CNM) in order to practice. CNM training is very medically oriented, and a nurse midwife must work under the supervision of a medical doctor. While this may sound good in theory, it does not seem to be working so well in practice.

A CNM, by virtue of her training and supervision, creates the same conditions and makes the same errors that hospitals sometimes do. Such training does not include the unique aspects that set home birth midwives apart and that allow us to create an ideal birthing experience that is safe, calm, and as comfortable as possible. CNMs are still rare in Idaho, and I do not know any who are delivering babies in my area.

What a dilemma this law creates for trained and experienced women like me. The law also creates a difficult and dangerous situation for women who live at a distance from regular medical help. In rural areas, it is not always possible for medical personnel to respond rapidly enough to save a life. A hemorrhage in conjunction with a miscarriage is just one example of a possible tragic scenario.

Because of the unfortunate way this law is written, a trained midwife like myself must choose either to ignore a woman who is in need and is unattended by competent help or to assist and risk legal consequences. This is not what women like me signed up for when we invested the effort and the expense to learn how to improve women's lives.

Even though they may lack proper training, more parents are opting to have their babies at home—unaccompanied by a trained midwife. While I personally find this terrifying, I must admit that it might be a better alternative to *some* of the hospital births at which I have been present.

Shortly after this law was passed in Idaho but before it went into effect, I had an experience that illustrates the dilemma families and trained midwives may now face. I answered the phone early one morning to hear the very frightened voice of a six-year-old boy. I knew him well as I was the teacher for his class at church, and I had worked with his mother as a midwife. I was touched that he trusted me enough to call for help. He told me he had just found his mother, semiconscious, in a pool of blood on the bathroom floor.

I had learned just a few days before that this woman was pregnant. They had not informed me earlier because they knew about the passage of the new law but did not realize it had not yet gone into effect. I was glad I knew that she was pregnant, as at least it gave me an idea of what might be going on. I grabbed my bag, told my family to call my assistant, and was out the door.

When I arrived, I found the situation exactly as this boy had described; he had not exaggerated in the least. He had returned to his mother's side and was stroking her face. What a scene: blood nearly everywhere, in the toilet and all around the woman, and this precious little man in the middle of it. There was no time to lose.

I opened my bag and went to work, giving him instructions: "Please hand me the little bottle, top row, fourth from the left," rapid-fire, one after another. He was phenomenal. I have rarely seen grown men behave with such calm and focus while under such intense stress.

After stabilizing the mother's bleeding and vital signs, I assessed the situation more fully. There had been a miscarriage, that much was certain. The afterbirth, meaning the placenta and accompanying membranes, had not yet passed. *Would they pass naturally?* I asked myself. *Would I need to take measures to assist the completion of the miscarriage? And how severe would the hemorrhage be then?* When a miscarriage causes such severe bleeding at an early stage, it is likely that there will be further problems later as well.

We were too far from the nearest hospital and the woman was in too fragile a condition to move her even a little. Fortunately, the boy's grandmother and my assistant had arrived by this time, and her husband was on his way. Many hands are always better than just two in emergencies, and the grandma was available to comfort this little grandson and his younger siblings.

We waited. Eventually, with patience and with the use of difficult maneuvers that aren't fun for either mother or midwife, the afterbirth came. I thanked heaven for my detailed and comprehensive training. Finally, with the mother as stable as possible, we prepared her for transport to a hospital for assessment and a necessary blood transfusion.

Once the ambulance had departed the scene, I pulled this brave little boy onto my lap, as he was still shaking from head to foot. Through tears and trembling lips he asked, "Is my mommy going to be okay? Is she going to come home some day?" I have tears in my eyes, these many years later, just recalling the moment. I softly took his face in my hands and waited briefly for him to look me in the eye and asked, "Have I ever, ever lied to you?" He shook his head no. "Do you trust me?" He gave an emphatic nod. "Your mommy will be fine," I said. "She may be in the hospital for a day or two and when she comes home, she may be very tired and will need to rest a lot for a few days. So you will need to get things for her and help her by playing quietly with your younger sister and brother. Can you do that?" "I can do that!" he declared and went off to find his siblings to get started on his important task. That brave little boy has since grown into a very capable and impressive young man.

I then got in my own vehicle and followed the ambulance to the hospital emergency room. When I arrived the doctor asked me, "What did you have to do to get that placenta out?" I smiled and answered, "Is the answer pertinent to your medical treatment here?" I work well with doctors and had worked with this good man before. A competent midwife always gives doctors all pertinent information, clearly and concisely and using medical terminology, but she tends not to provide extraneous information.

The doctor answered no, it wasn't pertinent. But given that he was already fairly certain what I had needed to do, he was extremely curious where I had obtained such training and capabilities. We did not discuss it much further as there was still work to be done, and I was glad that it was his work to do and not mine. He completed a thorough internal examination and determined that I had left nothing behind that would cause problems. "An impressive feat," he added.

He then asked, "Why did you wait so long to call for an ambulance?" Thoughtfully, I replied, "What would the ambulance crew have been able to do in this situation?" He acknowledged that they would not have had the skill set or the legal standing to do what we both knew had needed to be done and done quickly. He then added, "It is fortunate that there are women like you in rural America, with the necessary training and skills to respond in these situations. If you had not been there, this beautiful young wife and mother would have died today."

"Doctor," I responded, "the state of Idaho has just passed legislation making what I do illegal, starting in July of this year. I will likely be the last generation of my kind in this state." He was appalled, as he had been previously unaware of this news.

> There is a greater gift than the trust of others, and that is trust in oneself. Some might call it confidence, others name it faith, but if it makes us brave, the label doesn't matter, for it's the thing that frees us to embrace life itself.
>
> —*Jennifer Worth*

I miss my midwife days, but I do not miss the heavy responsibilities that come with it. Nor do I miss being the first responder in these types of emergency situations. But I would do it again in a heartbeat and wish it were still a legal option in the state of Idaho.

Obtaining a License

Considering the number of births I had attended and birth certificates I had filed before the law went into effect, the Idaho state registrar's office suggested that I complete a short medical course and obtain a license. I declined. One of many important reasons was that I knew the alternative treatments I used were more effective than the medical treatments I would be required to use after my training. For example, I was not interested in having to use drugs to stop bleeding rather than herbal remedies, which I had seen work without side effects many times.

Grandbabies

I treasure all the times I was present for the births of my grandchildren. If I had not barely missed the births of my last two granddaughters, I would be able to say that I was present for more of my grandchildren's births than I have missed. What a joy this has been to me!

Retirement

Even though I was privileged to have been part of many inspiring and just plain wonderful births, I reluctantly retired in 2006, as Val and our growing company needed me. My capable midwife assistant stepped right up and shepherded our remaining expectant mothers through to delivery.

For some time, I greatly missed being a midwife, but for whatever reason, I seem to have finally moved on. I still love being present for the births of my grandchildren, but I no longer have any desire to be the primary midwife. Now I am not responsible for being anything but Grandma. While it feels odd, it is nice in its own way.

I love sharing these precious moments with families. I love being part of a baby's first acquaintance with this mortal world. Being a home birth midwife is a sacred experience. I will forever be grateful that I was allowed these opportunities. I came to love Val even more deeply during these years, and I appreciated my family even more, especially my oldest daughter, who often carried the lion's share of the tasks at home when I was away.

CHAPTER TWENTY

Midwifery Specifics

We have a secret in our culture, and it's not that birth is painful. It's that women are strong.
—*Laura Stavoe Harm*

E*ven though this memoir* is not a midwife manual, I would like to share my thoughts on a few subjects in the spirit of teaching—something which, as a midwife, I cannot bring myself to resist.

Choosing a Birth Attendant

A birth attendant, whether a doctor or a midwife, should be chosen with great care. There is no substitute for experience and training. What your midwife (or doctor) requires of you during the gestational period (the pregnancy) is a very good indication as to how seriously she (or he) is taking the responsibility of your health and the well-being of the baby.

Another important marker, in my opinion, is whether or not the midwife insists on having medical backup available. While transporting a mother in an emergency situation during a midwife-attended birth is extremely rare, when it occurs it may be that a few extra minutes to find a medical team will be important. Such arrangements are best made in advance.

I had *hoped* to deliver at least some of my grandbabies, and it has been my great privilege to do so. However, the thought of pressuring my own daughters or daughters-in-law regarding who attends their births and where those births take place offends my very soul. A woman's right to deliver her babies where and how she desires is a cause I have fought for since my own first birth. It offends Val also, as he demonstrated when he supported my decision to deliver our third child in the hospital rather than at home because that was what I wanted. I hope that no member of my family has ever felt any kind of pressure from me in this regard.

A woman's comfort and trust in her attendant cannot be overemphasized. I once traveled a great distance to help with my daughter-in-law's planned home birth. And when she expressed her desire to go to a hospital, I immediately supported her. Laboring and delivering in the hospital was right for her and for this birth and within her comfort zone, and it was her choice to make.

While I loved attending home births, and home births were right for me, I will fight for every woman's right to bring her child into the world where, how, and with the help of whatever caregiver she chooses.

Midwives—a Unique Breed

> Midwives have skilled hands—and know how to sit on them.

Our attitudes toward birth and birthing women set us apart. I have had more than one doctor tell me they wished they could be a fly on the wall at a midwife-attended birth. Among their reasons are that "midwives somehow deliver over-intact perineums." I have had doctors want to discuss and witness delivery accomplished in a better position than with the woman flat on her back.

Doctors have also asked me how excessive bleeding is handled at home. During one of my own pregnancies, one doctor asked me what I would do if I experienced a hemorrhage. I asked him, "Where am

I having this hemorrhage?" He jokingly replied, "In the hospital." So I replied, "Run for the door!" Since I obviously inferred that I would prefer to have excessive bleeding handled at home rather than in the hospital, he asked no further questions that day.

Birthing practices in hospital settings have come a long way since the days of "twilight sleep." I give credit to the persistent efforts of midwives to teach the skills of being "with women" for these changes.

Delivery without Cutting and Stitching

One of the first things midwives learn is how to "deliver over an intact perineum." Intact perineum means that we do not cut women in order to get the baby out, and we don't allow them to tear either.

I could write a treatise on why episiotomies (cutting) increase the woman's likelihood of further tearing and creates pelvic floor issues for the rest of her life. I could also compare midwife and local hospital statistics on tears and repairs, but that is not my purpose today. You can, if you are interested, research and study it for yourself.

More than once I have heard doctors comment that not only are midwives somehow able to prevent tears but that we get "unreasonably upset" with ourselves if we "allow even so much as a skid-mark."

I went many years in training and in my own practice without seeing a woman tear enough to require even a single stitch. The one time I did was a very special circumstance involving a very short umbilical cord, a very tall woman, and no way to turn the baby into a position that would protect the mother's delicate tissues. Even so, the suturing doctor commented that "no tissues that would not heal nicely" had been compromised. He told his attending nurse, who was being rather disrespectful to me, that "neither you nor I could have accomplished such a thing."

On the other hand, I have never seen a woman's delicate parts protected any better than by a local doctor one day. Two "gloved up" midwives were present, including me, with permission to assist if we saw a need. Not once did either of our hands reach for a stressed area of tissue with oil or massage before the doctor's own hands were there. I have worked with some of the best midwives around, and this doctor is up there with the best of them in my experience and estimation.

Suturing

Midwives, depending on their training, are taught how to suture, and in the states in which I practiced, suturing by midwives was legal. I was somewhat trained in this fine art, but I have never stitched a woman following a birth. Since we rarely see tears and never cut a woman, we seldom have the opportunity to get experience. Doctors have much more experience with this than midwives. Midwives, myself included, have no qualms about bringing people to doctors when we feel that they can do something better than we can.

Sepsis and Other Infections

Some may bring up the risk of infection as a reason not to birth at home. I have never seen infection after a home birth. Hygiene, cleanliness, and sterility is a point of pride with midwives. Our overall statistics on this are as good as, if not better than, hospitals.

A part of this clean record may be that the woman has already established an immunity to most of the bacteria present in her home. Midwives are careful not to bring any contaminants with them. Yet another part of this may be that herbal remedies used both during and after the birth fight infections effectively.

Birthing in Water

There are both pros and cons to this birth trend. Warm water can provide relaxation and pain relief during labor. In addition, adding the right essential oils or herbs promotes an effective and efficient labor. That said, it is more difficult to assess the amount of bleeding when the blood is diluted by water. And it can sometimes be challenging to get the woman out of the tub and tucked into bed once the birth is finished.

My most recent granddaughter, Luke and Samberly's baby, was born in a bathtub with ginger powder added to the water. Samberly's labor was so pain free—different from her previous six labors, five of which were at home—that she did not feel the need to call anyone to come and assist until the baby's head began to crown. All the assistants, including myself, missed the baby's arrival, and there was nothing left to do when we arrived but clean up. My son and daughter-in-law knew what they were doing, were well-prepared, and they had a marvelous experience with the birth of this child. They were quite proud of themselves and content with the way things turned out.

Postpartum Depression

Postpartum depression is an unfortunate and debilitating situation. Statistically, rates of developing postpartum depression are slightly lower for those who opt for home births compared to those who deliver in a hospital.

What causes a woman to experience postpartum depression? Sometimes it seems to result from a nutritional shortage. A good diet, combined with proper herbs and essential oils, can help correct this condition quickly. Good nutrition may even be an effective preventative measure.

Other times, when complications have occurred or the birth didn't go along as smoothly as the parents envisioned, disappointment may undeservedly translate into guilt, which then slips into depression. Or perhaps the trigger is hormonal as the woman's body adjusts from a pregnant state to that of a nursing—or not nursing—mother. Too often, however, fatigue may be all the trigger that is needed. A new baby in the house is an exhausting situation under the best of conditions.

Suffering from postpartum depression never means that the woman has failed in some way. Neither does it mean she is not a good mother or a good person. Such feelings are depression talking. Supportive family and discussion are often helpful, and experience has taught us that essential oils can be a great benefit as well. But professional counseling should be sought whenever needed.

There is one other thing I have seen: many depressed mothers, possibly because of the guilt they feel about not being overjoyed at the arrival of their new baby, will go to great lengths to hide negative feelings from both family and birth attendants. Family and friends need to pay close attention to new mothers and look for the subtle signs that are being hidden from caregivers.

Rh-negative Mothers

Being Rh-negative is a problem only when the mother's blood type is negative and the father's is positive. Val and I are such a couple. With the births of each of our children, and all such births that I attended, a blood sample from the baby's cord was collected right after the cord was cut and sent to the local hospital for immediate testing. If my new baby's blood was positive, I made sure I got another shot of Rhogam myself, and I insisted that the mothers I delivered do the same.

Some in the herbal community believe there are alternative ways to handle this situation other than taking the mother in for a Rhogam shot. I disagree. In my opinion, there is not enough evidence—either statistical, scientific, or even empirical—to not getting a Rhogam shot. The baby's health outweighs the inconvenience, cost, and any other issue. Rh-negative blood type is a genetic inheritance in my family line, and prior to the development of this treatment, there were some heartbreaking tragedies.

Occiput Posterior

A local doctor referred a woman to me who was less than two weeks away from her due date. Money was tight in their home and they had no insurance to help with the expense of a hospital birth. I immediately went to conduct a prenatal examination, since arriving at a birth before meeting a woman and ascertaining a few details is never a good idea.

When I entered her home, the woman said to me from across the room, "Please don't tell me this baby is sunny-side up." By this she meant a position where the baby is lying with its back against the mother's back and its face pointing toward the front of her belly. So I didn't, even though it was obvious from the concave shape of her abdomen that the baby was lying in that very position. I believe she knew but didn't want to know, so I didn't talk about it.

I was aware she had delivered a previous baby that had presented in this position. She had labored and delivered this previous baby while lying on her back, and it had been a long labor and the pain had been intense.

With a posterior presentation, the back of the baby's hard little head presses against some very sensitive nerves as it passes the mother's sacrum and lower back. Excruciating pain is the natural result, especially if the mother is lying on her back where her own body weight and the weight of the water and baby-filled uterus will prevent the sacrum from moving out of the way as it would if she was in an upright or kneeling position.

Less than a week after our first visit this mother went into labor. I encouraged her to walk during the labor and at one point had her sit, leaning forward in a tub of warm water with a few drops of essential oil. The labor went quickly, and the pain was far less than she had expected. She delivered sitting on the very edge of her bed, with her husband behind her holding her. The baby emerged with its sweet little face looking right up at its mother. It was a precious moment. Then the mother exclaimed, "Why didn't you tell me this baby was posterior?" I replied, "I didn't tell you because you told me not to!" Because of the different way we handled labor and birth—and without the fear that might have been expected because of her previous painful experience—everything had gone very well.

Thanks for listening.

> Working hard for something we don't care about is called stress. Working hard for something we love is called passion.

CHAPTER TWENTY-ONE

Miracle Baby

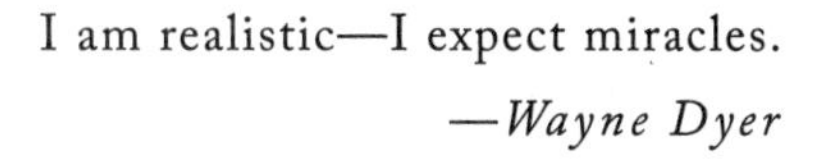

I am realistic—I expect miracles.

—*Wayne Dyer*

Where there is great love, there are always miracles.

—*Willa Cather*

A person's a person, no matter how small.

—*Dr. Seuss*

O*ur son Travis and his wife, Megan*, announced that they were pregnant. In my world, *they* are pregnant, not just the woman. I believe the expectant father should fully participate in this experience, skipping the morning sickness if he wants to. The expectant mother is welcome to skip that part also. At least most of the women I worked with were happy to do this.

Travis and Megan asked if I would be willing to midwife for them. I was more than willing; I was thrilled. This was Megan's first pregnancy, but she was not unfamiliar with pregnancy, as she had older siblings with children of their own. Travis, having grown up in my home, probably knew more than he wanted to about pregnancy, labor, and birth. We began prenatal visits immediately.

We waited, expectantly (pun intended), for the fundus to rise above the pubic bone. I use this particular development as a benchmark for when Mom and Dad will be able to hear the baby's heart tones through my Doppler equipment. But the fundus came up too early based on the projected due date. It also came up higher on one side of Megan's abdomen than the other. I could not think of any good reason for such a scenario except if she were having twins. We had just had two sets of twin grandchildren born quite recently, so this did not seem like a valid probability, statistically speaking. Other indications for twins that I would have expected to see were also missing.

So we arranged through Megan's backup doctor to have an ultrasound done at the local hospital. Megan, her mother, and I went to the appointment as a team. Travis was not present, as he was working away from home at the time. With the situation being somewhat worrisome to me, we decided to go ahead without waiting for Travis to return.

Technicians tend to speak quite freely during an ultrasound unless something looks wrong. If they see something they don't like, they will talk about heart tones or just about anything else except the one thing that is worrying them. Then they advise the mother to see her doctor on her way home. Or, if the doctor is available, the technician may invite the doctor to join them to discuss the ultrasound.

Megan's backup doctor arrived shortly after we did. I had previously told him that I was concerned, and for me to order an ultrasound this early in a pregnancy added weight to my concerns. I was grateful he had taken the time to meet with us. Because of the doctor's presence, the ultrasound technician said very little.

Once the technician finished the ultrasound, Megan sat up, adjusted her clothing, swung her feet to the floor, and we waited. As I had fearfully anticipated, the doctor informed us that Megan had a large mass growing in her uterus. My heart sank through the floor because I knew that such a mass might be fibroid or something even more serious. While fibroid tumors are rather common in women, a mass growing during pregnancy has a high likelihood of being an aggressive and potentially life-threatening tumor.

The doctor recommended an immediate abortion, followed by surgery to remove the mass. He warned that there was "every possibility" that a complete hysterectomy would be needed.

I watched this young woman absorb those few short sentences and the recommendation that she sacrifice her baby for the *possibility* of saving her own life. And that even if she sacrificed her child and survived herself, there was "every possibility" that she would never be able to bear children again. Megan slipped on her shoes and walked out the door without a word to anyone, tears streaming down her face. I knew how much Megan wanted to be a mother, and my heart was breaking for her.

I turned to her mother, a woman I had loved and respected for years, and said, "What are you thinking?" She answered, "She was better taught than that." I will never forget the pain on her face as she followed her daughter out the door.

I stayed behind to visit with the doctor. The only remote hope he offered was that it might be only a fibroid. But even then, he said, a woman could not carry a baby to term with a large fibroid tumor growing alongside the baby. It was his firm opinion that if Megan refused immediate abortion and surgery, she would be risking her life for nothing because the baby would not survive no matter what.

The only option offered to us by the medical community was the immediate death of the baby Megan was carrying. Walking out of the hospital had made her rejection of that option crystal clear. She never wavered in her faith or love for her unborn child, so we all hunkered down to fight for her life and her baby's life.

There are few herbal options that control the growth of a fibroid during a pregnancy that do not pose a risk to the child. Most herbs that restrict tumor growth are far too strong to be used during pregnancy. We continued to search for more information from everyone we knew.

Because we had little reason to expect this pregnancy to go to term, we took steps to support fetal lung development. We tried everything we could think of for both Megan and her baby. Before long, I could palpate both the size of the baby and the mass, but it required extreme gentleness, limiting what my hands would otherwise have been able to determine. We could also feel the mass in the uterine foot zone signals on Megan's feet.

Whether in response to our efforts or through the grace of God's intervention, the fibroid stopped growing. That was the good news. The bad news was that from time to time Megan would cramp and bleed, sometimes a little and sometimes enough to frighten us. Once it was bad enough that I called her doctor, even though Megan was hesitant to do so. While I don't usually ignore a mother's expressed wishes, this was my daughter-in-law and my grandchild. I asked the doctor if he could give Megan something to slow the cramping, as I knew there were certain drugs, with potential side effects, that could slow premature labor. The doctor refused, reiterating his opinion that fighting to maintain the pregnancy was not in Megan's best interest.

I was aware that nearly all tumors do not spontaneously bleed off or stop growing, so I was cautiously hopeful. A fibroid, however dangerous, sounded better than a life-threatening tumor. There was no way to know whether the bleeding and cramping were caused by the mass/fibroid pulling away, or if the placenta was detaching from the uterine wall, which would cause a miscarriage and the death of the baby. It was a trying time, and both Megan and our son stayed strong through it all.

The Faith of a Mother

Megan is a woman who steps up to challenges. At my request, she stayed on careful bed rest. She read. She sang. She buoyed us all with her faith. As each crisis passed, we began to be cautiously optimistic. Megan asked if we would hold a baby shower for her, which seemed to express her faith in a positive outcome, so we happily complied. The Friday evening of the shower was a big celebration. We had come so far, and, despite everything, we were so hopeful.

Megan began cramping again late the following Sunday afternoon, just two days after the baby shower. It was February and the beginning of the worst storm of that year's winter season. Val and I were in town, fifteen miles away, on assignment at one of the local nursing homes. When I remember that we nearly stayed in town because of the weather, it frightens me still.

When Travis and Megan arrived at our house, they began the same steps we had successfully used before to stop the bleeding and cramping—in other words, to stop the impending miscarriage. They had some success and it seemed as though this crisis, like the previous ones, might pass.

Megan was only twenty-six weeks along in her pregnancy. No midwife and few doctors—except in specialty units at very large hospitals—have the training to cope with a baby born this prematurely. The possibility of a baby surviving should he be born at this early gestational age was terribly remote.

Even though Megan had been given several blessings during this pregnancy, Val offered one more, in which she was promised that her baby would live and grow up to be a healthy adult. Megan was then able to sleep for a while.

Travis and I went into another room and quietly discussed possibilities. He asked me what I thought the baby's chances would be if it were to be born now. I considered them to be very, very slim because we were so far from full term and the baby was extra small due to the stress placed on its growth by the mass and the periodic bleeding.

I was concerned because I knew that according to law, hospitals are not required to take extraordinary measures to keep babies alive when they are born before a certain number of weeks or under a certain weight. This precious baby would not meet mandatory resuscitation standards, according to policy, in some hospitals. The only thing we could do was try and stop the cramping and keep the pregnancy viable for a few more weeks.

Fortunately, great strides have been made in the last few years in the care of very premature babies, even though not all hospital policies have been updated to take advantage of these new technologies, but there is hope. And such tiny little preemies can not only survive but quite often they thrive and go on to enjoy a long and high quality of life.

Because Preston, Idaho's hospital is a relatively small one, there is a lack of experience with extreme situations. This is not a criticism, just a fact. Amazing and capable people work there, and they have been there for us and performed wonders many times.

With the near-blizzard weather conditions, traveling to the hospital while the baby was being born would be far from ideal, yet staying at home didn't make sense either. There seemed to be no good options for the baby should he be born at this time.

If Megan hemorrhaged in the car on the way, there would be much less that I could do in the cramped space of a vehicle compared to being at home with proper equipment and the ability to move around as needed. Hemorrhage was a distinct possibility with a fibroid or a placenta that had been trying to pull away for weeks.

Megan continued to sleep, and I continued to worry. But the situation seemed to be stabilizing, so although I was worried I was also hopeful. We had seen cramping and bleeding several times before during this pregnancy and had been able to stop it successfully each time.

When Megan woke up, she said that there was a great deal of pressure "down there," more than she had ever felt before. I did a vaginal check and a tiny little head was right there, at the tip of my fingers. And in the space of a few seconds, I was holding a tiny, almost transparent, little boy in my hands. His parents were crying and holding on to each other, and I was crying too, knowing that they would both be brokenhearted at the loss of this child. There are some things in life for which you simply cannot prepare yourself.

As I held this little boy, a myriad of thoughts raced through my mind: *Should I hand him to his parents so they can feel the life that is in him? But what if that also means watching their baby boy struggle for breath and then stop breathing altogether?* I was trying to find my faith and didn't know what to do. I wanted so badly to hear direction given by heaven.

My heart was mourning as I considered the possibility of never getting to know this precious grandson in this life. I had heard promises pronounced in multiple priesthood blessings that I expected would be fulfilled—but he was so very tiny! I was at a complete loss to know what was best or what part I was expected to play in the fulfillment of those promises. While my thoughts may have been conflicted, this incredibly small bundle of humanity in my hands was so much alive and so very *present*.

I have held both life and impending death in my hands, and the difference between them is pronounced and profound. This tiny little boy was ALIVE! He was making little mewling sounds, and even in those first few traumatic moments, it was obvious that he intended to stay with us if he could. Right then, I heard a quiet voice over my right shoulder say, "I could use a little help here, Grandma." You may explain it any way you choose, but that voice in my ear put me right to work.

I immediately tipped my hands downward so that any mucous in his tiny throat could drain out. The length of his body was shorter than a can of soda. He was so fragile. But I could see the beating of his heart, pumping away, moving his tiny ribs. And he was breathing.

The baby was completely covered with vernix, God's waxy protection for skin when inside the womb, and which also becomes a wonderful lubricant after birth if no one scrubs it off. I had never felt vernix so thick, but then, I had never held a baby that was so far from term, either.

I laid him against his mother's chest, covered him ever so gently with a clean, soft cloth, and folded her shirt around him. We then quickly prepared for transport to the hospital. If the baby survived long enough to reach the hospital, he would then be past any nonresuscitation window, so every possible effort would be taken to keep him alive.

I was in love with this tiny little boy and his valiant spirit already and prayed as hard as I have ever prayed, before or since.

After warming up the van, Travis carried Megan to the middle seat; the baby was still snuggled against Megan's chest with her clothing and a quilt folded around them both. Lying on mother's chest and skin to skin gives the baby the reassurance of the familiar sound of her heartbeat, as well as the warmth of her body acting as an incubator for him.

Travis climbed into the very back row, behind Megan, and rode hanging over the seat, holding his wife around her shoulders and talking softly to his tiny son. I have rarely heard more tender or loving words spoken.

He looked so tiny snuggled there and, tiny as he was, he did snuggle. Snuggling a baby onto its mother's chest skin-to-skin is a technique for preemies called kangaroo care. I understand it was pioneered in the United States at Johns Hopkins University. It was the best method to keep the baby alive regardless of where he had come into the world.

Driving in an Idaho blizzard is not for the faint of heart. Snow was blowing heavily against the windshield and across the road, creating almost white-out conditions and making it nearly impossible to see the dividing lines or the edges of the road. It was to our advantage that Val had driven this thirteen-mile stretch of road in just about every sort of weather imaginable over many years.

If the interior lights were turned on so I could check Megan and the baby, Val could not see the road at all. So my sense of touch was all I had to assess mom and baby. Thirteen miles had never seemed so far.

As we traveled, I placed one hand gently on the baby's neck to check for a pulse. His amazing little heart just kept on beating. My other hand was under Megan, as that was the only way I would be able to tell if the placenta separated or hemorrhage occurred.

The pencil-thin umbilical cord was still attached to both baby and mother, and it kept pulsing merrily, bringing the baby oxygen, nutrients, and important final antibodies. I did not attempt to perform any type of procedure except for very gentle, almost nonexistent, pulsing pressure on his back when my fingers were not on his neck. Sometimes I did this, sometimes Megan did, and we hoped this might assist his heart and lungs a little. Babies this size are impossibly delicate, and it is easy to rub their skin off just by touching it, so all that vernix was a blessing.

If you haven't seen a child this premature, it is difficult to imagine how fragile he was. It would be easy to unintentionally cause internal damage as well as damage to those tiny little arms and legs.

Although I had an infant-sized mask in my kit, I didn't get it out, as even gently breathing for a baby this small could potentially "blow" the lungs. As the question of oxygen passed through my mind, "no" was pronounced clearly. Throughout the entire ride the Spirit of the Lord was close to us, such that I knew what to do—and what not to do.

The lining of preemie lungs often sticks together, preventing full inflation. Doctors sometimes need to administer a surfactant to correct this problem. Apparently, the things we had given Megan for the prevention of this stickiness had worked as this little guy was breathing just fine on his own. I had seen this same outcome previously when using the same remedies, but never in a baby so small.

We stayed moving and on the road despite the storm. The umbilical cord kept pulsing and the baby kept breathing. Megan did not hemorrhage. We reached the hospital safely where medical personnel took over, and we watched and waited. I can't speak for the others, but my own emotions vacillated between hope—we had come so far—and despair, but somehow, hope kept winning. We all loved this little boy so much already. Our hearts sank a little when we were told that he weighed only twenty ounces—one pound, four ounces. Could he possibly survive and have any chance for a good quality of life? The words of the several priesthood blessings kept replaying in my mind.

It turned out the anesthesiologist working in our small local hospital that night had done his residency in a neonatal preemie unit, and he was amazing. Once the baby was hooked up to the machines, he kept his oxygen levels and blood values stable.

I had requested response from McKay-Dee Hospital in Ogden, Utah. That hospital's resuscitation policies would cover this baby and its newborn intensive care unit (NICU) is internationally ranked. But the hospital could not send a helicopter because of the severity of the weather, so instead they sent two ambulances. One of the drivers later told me this was done to increase the odds of one of them getting through safely. The drive takes about an hour and a half in good weather, and the ambulances took far longer that night because of the extreme weather. Everyone, including the anesthesiologist (judging by the look on his face) was relieved to see the "experts" arrive.

Val gave the baby a priesthood blessing at the hospital after he was as stable as could be hoped for. Val had asked for the baby's name for this blessing and our son told him, "His name is Thomas." I don't know if that was a name Travis and Megan had agreed on beforehand, but it felt right for this little boy, and I felt joy to know him by name.

This priesthood blessing, like others before it, clearly stated that Thomas would live and grow to adulthood. I will not describe other details in this blessing or the effect it had on Val, who felt privileged to pronounce it. Looking at that tiny little boy, it was almost impossible to imagine the promises given even coming true. But standing there beside this spunky little boy and feeling the feelings that we were feeling, these blessings felt assured.

Travis went with his new son in the ambulance and Megan stayed behind because the placenta had not yet passed. In the morning, I would take her to join her husband and her son in Ogden. Val recalls with reverence the events of that night and the following day.

Val's Experience

My thumb felt bigger than his head when I gave Thomas a blessing. He was promised in the blessing that he would thrive and grow up normally. I have been humbled a few times in my life, and this was certainly one of them.

The storm was letting up enough that McKay-Dee Hospital decided they could send an ambulance that would have all the specialized equipment Thomas needed. We prayed that the ambulance would make it through the storm, and it did. Travis traveled with Thomas in the ambulance to Ogden, and LaRee and I stayed with Megan. The next morning, after Megan had stabilized, the three of us drove to the house, where I picked up the extra car so Travis and Megan would have a car available in Ogden, and both cars traveled to McKay-Dee Hospital in Ogden, Megan riding with LaRee.

It was about 10:00 a.m. when I passed Cornish, and I could suddenly feel Thomas giving me a hug that seemed to say, "Thank you." At first, I thought that meant he had died, but then I felt peace and that somehow it would be all right.

When we arrived at the hospital, Travis told me that his tiny son's heart had stopped about an hour earlier, and all attempts to restart it had failed. A doctor was soon found who could give a blessing, and miraculously, Thomas's heart started beating again and he was stabilized.

From My Own Journal

After I arrived home from the hospital after little Thomas was born, I sat up into the wee hours of the morning to find some peace in prayer and in the scriptures. I recorded what I read and felt in my personal journal:

> *Scriptures I read from the Book of Mormon this morning:*
>
> *Jacob 4:6 "Our faith becometh unshaken, insomuch that we truly can command in the name of Jesus and the very trees obey us, or the mountains, or the waves of the sea."* This is what I saw in Val. Looking at the tiny little boy, there was no reason for hope, but words were spoken, commands given, faith exercised.
>
> *Verse 7 continues, "Nevertheless, the Lord God showeth us our weakness that we may know that it is by his grace, and his great condescensions unto the children of men, that we have power to do these things."*
>
> *Jacob 4:10: "Wherefore, brethren, seek not to counsel the Lord, but to take counsel from his hand. For behold, ye yourselves know that he counseleth in wisdom, and in justice, and in great mercy, over all his works."*

Jacob 3:2 "Feast upon his love; for ye may, if your minds are firm, forever." A wake-up call to me to stop wallowing in self-pity and find my faith!

And, finally, the clincher. *Parts of Jacob 2:13 "And the hand of providence hath smiled upon you most pleasingly"*—I'll say! "*. . . [yet] ye are lifted up in pride of your heart.*"

I came to know—it was one of those "taught in whole sentences" experiences— that it is my pride that makes me think that anything *I* do or fail to do directly causes certain outcomes in another's life. *God* is in charge, and *His* purposes will unfold.

If I am in tune with the Spirit, and willing, it can be my privilege to be part of His process, but if I am not, the privilege will be given to someone else. I find the phrase "God has no hands but our hands to do His work today" rather ridiculous, as God is all-powerful. His purposes will not be frustrated by my shortcomings. Little Thomas will have exactly the life he and God agreed on, and it has been my great blessing to be a tiny part of its beginning.

Promises Fulfilled

Even though Thomas was still tiny, after he had been in the NICU awhile he wanted to be up and observing, not just lying there in his clear plastic unit. He was so very alive and so glad to be alive, and he wanted to become better acquainted with this new world.

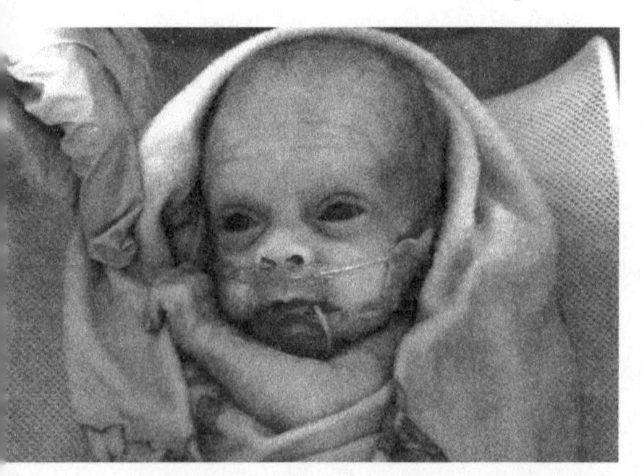

LaRees's grandson, Thomas, in the hospital (note size of gloved hand)

I was teaching a series of classes in the Ogden area at the time, so I would go by the hospital in the evenings, scrub up, and hold my precious grandson. "Oh, good," one of the nurses said one day, "Grandma is here to hold

Thomas!" My arrival allowed her to catch up on other duties for as long as I could stay. Toward the end of the hospital stay I was told I could hold him up so he could see the world. This was a remarkable thing for such a tiny preemie.

This was a tender season for the entire family. When I was home between visits to Ogden, my other grandchildren almost constantly talked about "Baby Thomas." I could not give any one of them anything to eat without all of them folding their hands in a prayer over the food and asking heaven to bless "Baby Thomas" one more time. If there were four or five of them present, each one wanted to have a turn. I believe the prayers of children are received in heaven in a very special way.

Thomas was eventually discharged from the hospital and came home. He was still tiny and was on oxygen, but he was feisty and determined. At his first follow-up appointment, the doctor was surprised at how few drugs Thomas had been given during his stay at McKay-Dee. The list of drugs looked long to me, but I guess such things are relative.

Thomas remained on oxygen for what became a very long time. When he was learning to crawl, he would drag his small oxygen tank behind him. The hoses would stretch across his face with his effort to move forward if someone was not close by to fetch whatever he was trying to reach.

Almost a year to the day after his birth and with their little son no longer on oxygen and doing well, his parents left him with us for a few days for a much-needed mini vacation. They had planned to take Thomas with them, but I had felt uneasy about it. After some persuasion on my part and prayer on everybody's part, they left him home with me.

A few days later it seemed as though he was becoming less alert and active, and that morning he did not seem to play and splash in his bath as much as he had done the day before. I was involved in teaching a four-day class to students in my home so I called a friend to sit with Thomas in a rocking chair right next to me, where I could keep an eye on him.

He had been sleeping and seemed to be doing fine, but when I glanced down at him again I *knew* he was in trouble. I called my employee and the three of us headed to the hospital. By the time we arrived, Thomas's chest and abdomen were retracting with each breath, a sure sign that an infant is having serious trouble breathing. The first thing the nurse asked was, "How long has he been breathing with chest retractions?" I answered, "About half as long as it took us to get here!" She was obviously relieved to hear it had not been very long.

The medical team ran tests and attempted to put a breathing tube down his throat, but Thomas fought them with determination. I tried to comfort and reassure him, and I will never forget the look in his eyes. It was as though he was saying, "Grandma, help me! Make them stop, Grandma!" My heart broke. My eyes are filling with tears again just thinking about it.

The lab technician stepped back into the room with the test results and, seeing the fight Thomas was putting up, said, "I will run these tests again. There is too much fight in that child for these results to be right." The doctor replied, "You forget whose son this is." Was he referring to Travis or Megan? They are both very determined people. Thomas had already demonstrated in his short life a very strong determination of his own.

We contacted Travis and Megan on their trip and gave them an update. The situation was serious enough that they could not be out of touch in case the attending doctors needed to speak with them. They returned home on separate flights so that one of them would always be available by phone.

I returned home to my patiently waiting students, hating every minute of being away from Thomas. An ambulance was taking Thomas to a larger hospital with more specialized facilities, and Val followed. I joined them the following day after my class had graciously departed a day earlier than scheduled. Val and I stayed with Thomas until both Megan and Travis arrived. Within a few days Thomas was released. He stayed on oxygen, but only for a short period.

Today, Thomas may be a little small for his age, but he is healthy, highly intelligent, and quick-witted, and his wide smile is infectious. He has every chance of living a normal or even an extraordinary life. I cannot look at him without recalling the host of miracles that accompanied his birth.

Megan not only successfully survived the pregnancy and the "mass" but went on to have three more children, and another is on the way as of this writing. Thomas is a terrific big brother to his three sisters. Megan developed small fibroids but has been able to rid herself of them using herbal remedies.

Grandson Thomas

Miracles

I have been part of or a witness to many miracles, some of which came suddenly, just when and how they were needed. Others were a series of serendipitous events over a long time that combined to make a miraculous whole.

Serendipity. I love that word. To me it means *miraculous*. The dictionary definition is "the occurrence and development of events by chance in a beneficial and happy way." *By chance*? I think *by heaven* is a better way of describing it.

> Miracles happen every day. Not just in remote country villages or at holy sites halfway across the globe, but here, in our own lives.
>
> —*Deepak Chopra*

I have had people, events, and bits of knowledge come along just when I needed them. This was especially the case prior to Megan's pregnancy and Thomas's birth when I first learned about fibroids and extreme preemies. Interestingly, I also learned what *not* to do, as well as what to do. Tiny preemies are very different from full-term, or even slightly premature, babies. Normal resuscitation protocols could easily damage both their lungs and their skin.

Miracles come in many forms. Sometimes, because they come about so gradually, we only recognize how much we have been blessed *after* the entire series of events has played out. With every bit of healing any member of this family has ever experienced, the tender mercies of God have been abundantly present. This is certainly true of Megan's pregnancy with Thomas, his birth and survival, and his heart problems at one year old. Thomas experienced every kind of miracle imaginable.

> Believe in miracles. I have seen so many of them come when every other indication would say that hope was lost. Hope is never lost.
>
> —*Jeffrey R. Holland*

CHAPTER TWENTY-TWO

Family, Faith, and Forgiving

You will find it necessary to let things go, simply for the reason that they are too heavy to carry.
—*Corrie ten Boom*

T*he "middle of the middle"* is how Val refers to people who tend to follow the crowd. While there may be advantages to walking your own unique path, there can be downsides and difficulties as well. This is especially true when doing things differently from your family.

Val and I are regularly the recipients of gracious support from both family members and neighbors. We have also been the target of a fair amount of gossip, judgment, and persecution, as were our children. Looking back with more wisdom and perspective, I can see that interactions with family sometimes caused trouble between Val and me and led to our children being exposed to slanderous stories about their father.

Pondering the Imponderable

Chickens will literally peck to death an injured member of their flock. Sometimes the chick needs only to be smaller or different from the rest in some way to be a target. My father explained this to me when I was a little girl questioning this behavior among the chickens. It seems that people, even families, are sometimes not so different.

Val often tries to soften the pain I feel when members of my family act this way. He points out that when I left the "middle of the road," it was the tendency of my family to blame him for my choices rather than to blame their own sister or daughter. This explanation makes some sense, but it doesn't change the painful consequences from the behavior of members of my family.

> I didn't set out to be different. I set out to be the very best me I could be.
> *—Author Unknown*

My mother-in-law could embellish a story as well as anyone, and sometimes she would tell the most outlandish stories about her son Val to both me and our children. Long before the end of her life, however, she came to see the damage these tirades were causing and stopped—absolutely stopped—after acknowledging the poisonous effect of her words. This was a poignant lesson to me about repentance and change.

Even before this change, she was often our greatest defender. Because of the choices we were making, such as homeschool and home birth, we were taking hits from nearly all sides. The mother bear in her rose up and defended us, usually just as loudly as she chewed us out sometimes. She supposed she could light into us for something, but the rest of the world better not.

I usually responded better to her tirades than I did to my family's criticisms. Because her stories were often so in-my-face and exaggerated, they brought out my own mother bear instincts and I would get angry, and then I would get stubborn. With nearly everyone but my own family, that is how I usually respond to such nonsense.

Her stories did not cause me to doubt myself or Val and did not trigger the resentment I felt or the bad behavior I displayed when manipulated by my family. Rather than creating friction between Val and me, her outrageous behavior tended to make me even more grateful to be married to the "real" Val Westover. I hope at least some of her stories have had the same positive counter-effect on our children, and I believe they often did. There were times when her words caused lasting harm.

A Parable of the Master Teacher

> *The kingdom of heaven is likened unto a man which sowed good seed in his field: But while men slept, his enemy came and sowed tares among the wheat, and went his way. But when the blade was sprung up, and brought forth fruit, then appeared the tares also. So the servants of the householder came and said unto him, Sir, didst not thou sow good seed in thy field? From whence then hath it tares? He said unto them,* an enemy hath done this *(Matthew 13:24–28).*

We have learned how to tell our friends from our enemies. A friend is one who encourages you and builds you up, helping you be more of what you need and want to be. A friend defends you. A friend loves your family almost as much as you do. An enemy, however, deliberately and repeatedly does you harm, by word or by deed. An enemy continually sows tares among the wheat of your family life. Even today, the tares sewn in our family by storytelling and gossip keep springing up as destructive weeds.

One of our children apologized to me a few days ago for spending too much time listening to these sorts of stories as a teenager. Some of our children protect their own children from these destructive seeds by limiting their contact with certain family members, as they continue to gossip and tell untrue stories. Protecting one's family is every person's duty.

Why, you may ask, am I sharing this unfortunate side of my life? It is because I hope that our children and grandchildren may read these words someday and consider their own behaviors as I have had to consider mine. I have asked myself what I might have done—perhaps, should have done—differently. I have also asked myself if I participated in this family trait of criticism and backbiting.

As a young wife and mother, I responded poorly to this near constant onslaught of gossip, and a great deal of damage had been done before I saw it for what it was. Even then, when I began to see it, I failed to step up and put a stop to it. I failed to show full loyalty to Val, just as some of my family was failing to show their loyalty to me and to the man who joined their family through marriage. I should have been as loyal to Val as he has always been to me.

Am I able to justify my behavior? I tried to explain, as I wanted my family to see the reality of the good man I married. I wanted them to see that we were "walking our own walk" together, the one we felt heaven wanted us to walk. I wanted them to know of our dreams, to understand and support us. In all this I thought I was defending Val, but a person does not need defending when among true friends.

There were times when my family's near constant censure triggered discouragement, nastiness, and whining in me. I would become unfairly annoyed at Val and more frustrated, sometimes vocally, by his health issues. "Murmuring" it is called in scripture, and I hate it when I see it in myself.

Following a visit or phone call from members of my family, meaning my parents and siblings, I often treated Val less kindly than he deserved. And at times I expressed my discontent to our children. Did such complaining create issues with their father that neither he nor they deserved?

One thing I came to dislike about spending much time with some family members was their almost constant emphasis on money and some little thing I was "doing without" that they implied Val should have been providing.

According to my family, if I was tired or discouraged, if we were short on money or didn't make it to a family gathering, it was Val's fault. On the other hand, if we went on a family vacation or bought a new vehicle, they saw it as Val's extravagance or his inability to put his family's needs in proper order. A no-win situation.

I came to dread spring as I would be reminded that I might not have a new dress for Easter while other women would. But if I did wear a new dress, I would be told that other men bought their wives corsages. And if I had a new dress and a corsage, I would be told that other men bought their wives amazing presents.

Such comments usually began with "So-and-so said … ," placing the blame for saying it on someone else. I would think that everybody must be thinking the same things, and I would direct my anger at the so-and-so person and not at the person telling me these things. My teenage boyfriend had played this nasty game against me and it took too long to walk away. But this time it was family, and walking away didn't seem possible, since families are supposed to be forever.

Val's illness was not seen by them as a personal tragedy or a family struggle, merely further proof that Val was less of a man than he should be—and lazy to boot. Even accidents were said to demonstrate that Val was too careless to take proper care of his family.

In their minds, almost anything I did that was different was *Val's* idea: herbalism, homeschooling, even my years as a midwife. They were examples of Val expecting too much of me. And they made sure that others, including our children, heard their opinions. It didn't matter that these endeavors fulfilled my own dreams, were done at great cost, and required great sacrifice on Val's part.

If Val displayed any discouragement because of his poor health and its impact on our family, some—who somehow considered themselves experts—saw signs of mental illness. And if Val had good days and began to resemble his former enthusiastic self, such ups and downs were touted as further proof of mental instability. Regrettably, hearing such comments bred a measure of discontent and ingratitude in our children.

Val's mother was beautiful and smart. Both of Val's parents held good jobs, and they owned a farm. Since Val's mother worked "outside the home," however, she was a target for judging and gossip.

Eventually, one of my sisters began analyzing me and our children, relating her "findings" to extended family, neighbors, and people in our community. I have heard almost countless tales from many people over the years, tales that can be traced back to members of my own family.

Our children have been told varying stories about our courtship over the years. Even though my sister was only four years old when I first met Val, her version of events is often accepted as the gospel truth.

When young children are bombarded with such biased nonsense, it is bound to color their perceptions and damage familial relationships. There ought to be more loyalty and love within a family, in spite of shortcomings, for a house divided against itself cannot stand. So I have since adopted the attitude of "please love us both, or leave us both alone." But the potential estrangement this may bring breaks my heart. This display of backbone may add fuel to the stories that Val is trying to isolate me from my family. And once again, those stories will be far from reality.

If Val has sometimes expressed negative feelings about my family's treatment of him, he has had great cause to do so. He has sometimes been angry—especially when he could see the damage their commentaries were causing to our marriage and our relationship with our children. But then he would catch himself, and because of who he is, Val would try to treat my family even better. Loving and forgiving family is not only a tenet of our religion, it is Val's personal code. He tries very hard to live up to this high standard.

Val sometimes found himself with a wife who was out of sorts with her family. He would give me a day or two to cool off, then he would do his best to persuade me to go visit my family whether I wanted to or not.

Families: Joy and Pain

In spite of these challenging family dynamics, and until recently, we were in and out of our parents' lives and homes, as they were ours, for many years. Mom and I sometimes shopped together, and often she would offer to watch children at her house while I shopped. She recognized a busy homeschool mother's need for a little peace and solitude from time to time.

My mother also believed that one-on-one time between mother

and child was important, and shopping with only one or two children provided me with an opportunity for positive interactions with each child. She may not have approved of our homeschooling, but she did what she could to facilitate it.

Mom and I talked almost every day, and sometimes several times a day. We shared recipes; she helped me with sewing projects and taught my oldest daughter to sew. We quilted together, and she stayed with me when my babies were born. If my dad was helping with a project at our house, she came too, just to help out. During our homeschool years, she invited any of our children who finished their assignments early to come spend the day with her and Grandpa. It was a wonderful incentive to work hard. I got to know my mother even better while typing up many of her journal notes and church talks.

Val and the boys would use their equipment and skills on projects at my parents' house. Both of my parents lived with us during the final months of my mother's life, and it was a privilege to watch my father patiently care for my mother during a time she needed him most.

We lived next door to Val's parents most of our married life and visited them nearly every year at their winter home in Arizona. During the leaner times, visiting them in Arizona was the best vacation we could afford, and we hold wonderful memories of these vacations.

I suspect some may wonder if our in-laws love and appreciate us as much as they do their own children. My in-laws were very good at making me feel as much a part of the family as their own two daughters. Sometimes it meant that I got a chewing-out, which was fine with me if I deserved it. I loved them very much for the way they treated me from the moment Val and I talked about becoming engaged. They didn't think we should get engaged before his mission, but they accepted me with open arms anyway. I was already their daughter in their hearts, and they treated me as such.

When Val's mother arrived home from work, she would often honk her car horn furiously, a signal that her grandchildren should come running. If she knew I had a project going, such as decorating a wedding cake, she would invite the little ones to her house. She would also invite them over to "help" if she were making something yummy, such as hand-dipped chocolates.

After Val's mother's death, Val's father spent a lot of time with us. He often went with us on vacations and to visit our adult children. These were delightful times, and I am so glad we had those memorable years with him. Even though there were some conflicts, I am so glad we made the choice to raise our children next door to their grandparents in Clifton, Idaho.

I had a rather unique relationship with Val's mother. For example, when our farm animals would get out and annoy her, she wouldn't call right away. Rather, she would wait until she saw me pass her house on my way somewhere else. Then she would call and leave an exasperated message on my answering machine. For my part, I would wait to call her back until after she had left for work the next morning! Sometimes my messages were apologetic, and other times they were not much sweeter than hers had been. Sometime between those two phone calls, our children would have rounded up the escapees and dealt with whatever mess they may have made.

This phone call system seemed to work well for us when we needed a chance to express a certain annoyance, but we also remembered to share nice and appreciative things on the recording machine. If we forgot, we could always call back again. Just think of all the in-person arguments we avoided!

Val's parents were *definite* people and held strong opinions, which they didn't mind expressing, often at length. But they were also exactly who you wanted in your corner when things got rough. I loved them dearly when they were with us and miss them every day.

Forgiving

I love my sisters, my brothers, and my father. And I love and admire my mother, miss her dearly, and often wish I were more like her. I miss interactions with these family members more and more. Nevertheless, family members are supposed to be your best friends and be counted on to defend you when you are under attack. They shouldn't be the ones attacking you and reveling in your distress. It is tragic when some of the worst trials in one's life are brought on by the deliberate actions of close family members.

Stress in family relationships can cause deep pain and is deeper than any other physical or emotional suffering I have experienced. I have often wondered if the death of a loved one could be more painful than their loss by estrangement. I have been blessed not to have experienced the death of a child or sibling yet, but I do know the pain of losing relationships with people I love dearly. I also know the pain that comes from choosing to protect myself, Val, and our children by distancing ourselves from deeply loved family members. It is frustrating and hurts abominably.

In a recent conference held by our church, a speaker related that the prophet Joseph Smith freely forgave a person whenever they asked his pardon—even if he knew that the person would likely attack him again. Why would he forgive? I believe it was because he knew that forgiving someone, even when we think they will likely continue their hurtful actions, not only heals our hearts but allows us to think rationally about the future. But forgiving someone—even loving someone—does not also mean that we have to *trust* them and allow them back into our lives.

As I pondered the example of Joseph Smith, I recalled a recent reprimand from a member of my family, when I was told that I should not be angry at the gossips in our family (at least they acknowledged there were gossips!). Instead, I should be grateful that such gossips were providing me the kind of trials that would build character.

This bizarre admonition made me angry all over again about the years of gossiping I had endured. I wondered if this marked the beginning of a new kind of manipulation. My character, and that of Val and our family, may have been strengthened by these "trials," but our reputations have been diminished by them, and the success of our business ventures has been seriously impacted more than once.

The Bible story of Joseph in Egypt, who was sold into slavery by his brothers, was brought to my attention that same day. It was pointed out to me that Joseph magnanimously told his brethren years later, "Be not grieved, nor angry with yourselves, that ye sold me hither; for God did send me before you to preserve life."

I read and reread this long story in the Old Testament. I pondered why Joseph would say something that seemed so inappropriate since his brothers had done him a great wrong. Surely, I thought, they should hold themselves responsible and feel deep regret, whether God had worked things out for the faithful Joseph or not. Owning up to one's errors is an absolute requirement when seeking forgiveness. What his older brothers had done to him, and might do again, could not be dismissed so easily. But as I read, understanding started to grow.

During the great drought in Egypt when Joseph's brothers came seeking food for their families, Joseph overheard them talking amongst themselves when the brothers did not know that Joseph could both hear and understand their language. Joseph heard them express how terribly sorry—to the depths of their souls—they were for dirty deed they had done to their younger brother Joseph so many years ago.

Joseph's response to hearing their sorrow was to test the depth of their regret. So Joseph put Benjamin, their youngest brother—as he had once been—at risk. Joseph challenged his brothers' integrity and made them choose if they would sacrifice their brother to buy food and their own security.

Does this mean that Joseph did not forgive his brothers until he knew that they had *earned* it? Forgiveness is not earned, so that is not the point, and as the scriptures say, "the Lord was with Joseph," to such an extent, in fact, that "his master [Pharaoh] could plainly see that the Lord was with him." Joseph could not have had the Spirit of the Lord with him and become the noble man he was without ridding his soul of darkness and forgiving his brothers long ago.

Even though he had already forgiven them, Joseph still tested his brothers, ascertaining who they were now and how they would act in the present circumstances when life and death was again on the line. Once he knew their hearts and could trust them, only then did he offer words of comfort and tell them not to grieve or be angry with themselves *any longer* about events for which they had fully repented of. He reminded them that God is omnipotent and had a plan to turn bad into good all along.

Would Joseph's responses to his brothers have been the same if his brothers had shown themselves to be untrustworthy and unrepentant, willing to again risk their younger brother's safety if they were forced to return to their aging father without his dear son Benjamin? I believe Joseph's responses would have been different, and that he would have protected himself and gone to great lengths to protect Benjamin and his father, Jacob (Israel), as well. Fortunately, their repentance and their love for their younger brother was sincere.

From carefully studying this story, I came to see that while Joseph had forgiven his brothers years earlier, he did not hold them blameless for the havoc their actions had caused. He proffered consolation for their own sorrow only *after* his brothers had demonstrated a change of heart and could reasonably be trusted.

Forgiveness freed Joseph's soul, and forgiveness frees each of us as soon as we are able to offer it. Joseph grew up in Egypt with the peace of conscience that forgiveness brings. Holding back *trust* until it has been earned, however, protects us.

As I understand this principle, when seeking forgiveness from another, confessing the wrong you have done is required, but one shouldn't wait for an apology to forgive. It may be necessary for the offender to acknowledge their error in order for trust to be reestablished, but it is not necessary for forgiveness to occur in one's own heart.

Forgiveness does *not* require that we ignore certain facts and that we have to accept continued destructive behaviors. Perhaps forgiveness has more facets than just the letting go of anger. The strategy of "keep your friends close and your enemies closer" is not just crazy; it can destroy your peace of mind, personal safety, and odds of success. In my opinion, it is an important facet of forgiveness to be clear enough in our minds to know when to protect ourselves from further danger. We should be willing to trust that God will answer our prayers and tell us when we can trust them again.

Keeping dangerous or destructive people at a distance—while still loving them and wishing them well and doing good for them—can be another facet of a forgiving heart. It may not look like forgiveness to others, but they don't know your heart. This is only between you and your God. God knows our hearts and God can heal our hearts—that much I can promise you.

Sometimes, as new stories are told by old members of my family, I once again feel something close to anger. But perhaps anger is not the right word; it is more a feeling of despair, a renewed sense of vulnerability, and a further depletion of trust. Feeling hurt and vulnerable does not automatically mean that our forgiveness wasn't real. But it does call for some introspection, where we may ask ourselves, *Have I truly forgiven this person? Or have I only moved on, accepting the way things are, and despairing that the situation will ever improve? Am I linking forgiveness with despair and resignation?*

During one of those seasons when my family's treatment of Val had me particularly upset, I came across an old "Dear Abby" column, where someone had asked, "How does a person tell when they have finally matured?" Abby answered, "When they have forgiven their parents for *real and imagined* faults."

I have tried to do that, to truly forgive my parents and my sisters for real and imaged faults. Val may not *trust* them any more than I do, but he also has sought diligently to *forgive* them. He once held some hard feelings toward his outspoken mother, but those feelings are no longer with either of us. Patience, forgiveness, and compassion are the high price required for feelings of peace of conscience and joy.

None of us have control over the actions of others, but we have some say as to how those actions may be allowed to impact our lives. Yet feeling completely helpless can also be damaging, as victimhood is a sorry emotional state where there is little growth.

How does one rise above a victim mentality when faced with prolonged destructive behavior like gossip? It has taken me far too long to acknowledge that this behavior and its source is destructive, just as it did in that unhealthy relationship during my teen years. But once I recognize unhealthy behavior and come to understand its consequences, I can no longer allow myself to walk down that same destructive road.

I have learned that the path to emotional freedom from dishonesty, manipulation, and victimhood is the same today as it was when I was seventeen. The first step on the road to personal peace is to take responsibility for one's own actions. The second step is to make prayerful and purposeful choices. I am trying very hard to do that, and as always, Val is my greatest support.

Val, the Wind Beneath My Wings

I can be stubborn. I can be determined to the point of being obsessed, some say. Most see me as a self-confident person, but underneath these more noticeable traits lies a good measure of fear and uncertainty and a lingering need to be well thought of. This has passed down through the generations and was reemphasized in my childhood. These traits have sometimes caused me to hesitate instead of moving forward with my dreams.

"Courage is fear that has said its prayers," describes me. Val has put my dreams first and helped me reach my goals. Sometimes that meant helping me embrace my faith instead of my fears, pushing me a little to be who he knew I could be and who he knew I wanted to be. Val encourages me to figure out what I want to do and what I think is right and then to pray for guidance. Then together, we embrace heaven's vision and act on it.

When I wanted to learn to foot zone, Val helped make it happen. When I wanted to become a midwife, Val somehow scraped together the money I needed to buy the supplies and learning materials. He did the same when I wanted to learn about herbs, homeopathics, essential oils, and craniosacral techniques. He sacrificed and worked hard to add first one and then another room onto our house to give me room to teach bigger classes. He has literally given my dreams room to grow. Even during the worst of his health issues and times when money was the scarcest, the things that I wanted so badly to do were priorities for my husband.

When I am in the middle of writing a book and he is "seeing nothing but the top of my head" for weeks on end, he fixes his own meals—and often mine too—so that I can keep working. I have asked myself what sort of books he might have written, what sort of dreams he might have fulfilled, if I had made the same space for his dreams as he made for mine.

Val has a brilliant mind and an ability to understand and remember things that he studies. He sees the big picture, whether it's a religious principle, political theory, building project, or mathematical equation. This can be annoying when I may have failed to see certain important aspects of a situation myself.

Several years ago, I decided that it was time to improve my health and take off some weight, so I purchased a used treadmill. But my regular workouts began to exacerbate an old sciatic issue. Tara suggested that I get an elliptical machine instead, which was a good idea, but the nice ones are expensive.

I found the perfect machine while teaching a series of classes in Layton, Utah. Each night while talking to Val on the phone, I would sing the praises of this elliptical equipment and moan about how expensive it was. In the end I decided that I could do without it. On the last night of class, I called Val to tell him I was leaving for home and when to expect me. He replied that he had arranged for me to pick up this machine and that he had already paid for it.

He did a similar thoughtful thing a few years later when I had found another piece of exercise equipment I wanted badly. But it was outrageously expensive. I told him that he was absolutely not to buy it, but he replied, "It is being delivered on Tuesday." I love using this particular machine, as do my class members and employees.

Once I mentioned that I had found the most beautiful dress and a jumper that I liked, but I couldn't decide which one to buy. He said I should buy them both.

While Val is my greatest supporter, I must also acknowledge the dedicated efforts of our daughter Valaree. So often her contribution of assuming some of my work responsibilities has made Val's support of my dreams a reality, and our family and our company would flounder without her. We have been the beneficiaries of wonderful support from our other children as well.

Did Val, as my family claims, drag me against my will out of the middle of the road? No, but sometimes he had to run to keep up. Val often enthusiastically brought home new ideas—for his family, for his business, for just about anything. Sometimes, though not nearly as often, it was me coming home with a new idea and a new dream. It is also true that once a new idea is presented to me and I have studied it and found it interesting, a team of wild horses, financial concerns, lack of time, or any other factor cannot hold me back from pursuing it, usually somewhat obsessively.

Not long after we obtained our first personal computer, I had stayed home from church with a headache and Val, while at church, had heard about new software programs by the Family History Library in Salt Lake City. He was excited to share what he had learned, but I was less enthused, not having heard the original presentation. "You are getting all excited about this," I said, "but you know it is me who will be put to work!" "But you can do it with your new computer," he said. Well, I have been hooked on researching family history ever since.

This seems to be typical of my personality, almost obsessively taking hold of new things and running with them. It is also the pattern that when Val is the first one to discover an exciting new thing, it quickly becomes "my thing." My family was bent on seeing such things as me following Val's lead or, even worse, me being pushed into certain endeavors against my will. The truth was that most of the time both of us just happened to be interested in (and possibly overly enthusiastic about) the same things.

Val Westover values and honors freedom of choice and personal responsibility more than anyone I know. Force is not in his nature, although he has what can only be described as a *forceful* and exuberant personality, which is one of the things I love about him. His enthusiasm is contagious and helps him gets things going and get things done.

Val expects other people to have opinions and to have thought them through enough to defend them or act upon them. He has rarely crossed an opinion that I have taken time to think through. In times when we have differed on a proposed course of action, Val (or I) will wait until we are both in agreement or until we have hashed out a compromise. Our children may not understand this about us because such discussions are purposely held in private.

Val expects a lot from people, just as he expects a lot from himself, including clear thinking and high moral and ethical standards. He expects people to work hard, strive upward, and live their dreams no matter the cost. And he expects kindness and compassion. Too often, however, he has been disappointed, but that has changed neither his outlook nor his lofty expectations.

Val hopes that people—especially his children—will pray about decisions and proposed courses of action, just as he tries to do. And he expects us to live by the answers received. Val and I have prayed a great deal over family relationships. He feels he can no longer trust those in my family, nor does he encourage me to reconcile with them. His heart aches for himself and for me, as there is so much more we hoped to have experienced as an extended family. Nevertheless, if my aging father needs something done, Val is right there doing it.

We are now focused on preserving and protecting those family relationships that remain, which includes our own marriage. We cannot allow the tares that have been sown previously, and are still being sown, to overrun the wheat that is our immediate family—our children, their spouses, and our grandchildren.

One of our children asked us recently if we are happy. Val replied, with a chuckle in his voice, "Happy with each other!" That is so true, and for now, that is enough. And what adds to our happiness are the family relationships we cherish, the grandchildren who love us, the friends we enjoy, and the gospel we love.

During our engagement years, I came across a poem by Sara Teasdale called "The Beloved" and have kept a copy among my personal papers. It describes a portion of my feelings toward Val.

It is enough of honor for one lifetime
To have known you better than the rest have known.
The shadows and the colors of your voice,
Your will, immutable and still as stone.

The wild heart, so lonely and so gay,
The sad laughter and the pride of pride,
The tenderness, the depth of tenderness,
Rich as the earth, and wide as heaven is wide.

It has been my privilege to be the recipient of that depth of tenderness for all these years.

> Never lose hope. The butterfly is proof that beauty can emerge from something completely falling apart.
> —*Jane Lee Logan*

CHAPTER TWENTY-THREE

Butterfly Express & Butterfly Expressions

How does one become a butterfly? You must want to fly so much that you are willing to give up being a caterpillar.
—*Trina Paulus*

Don't quit before the miracle happens.
—*Unknown*

Hope Renewed

A *detailed manual I wrote* and published about essential oils begins with a section titled *Hope Renewed.* Even though it is quite long, it is precisely how I feel about essential oils and herbal remedies and explains why our company came to be. A small excerpt may serve as an apt introduction to our company Butterfly Express, LLC.

> *Essential oils are sensitive by their very nature. Our sensitivities are the vehicle through which we can touch others emotionally for good. It follows, then, that if essential oils are to heal our hearts, calm our nerves, revive our hopes, and ground our fears, they must also be sensitive.*

THEY ARE!

There may be tears in your eyes and a lump in your throat about now if you have used essential oils with faith and gratitude. I do not know how, but I know that essential oils have sensitive natures.

Love your oils, pray for and with your oils, and use them with gratitude. If you do this, they will bless you abundantly.

Butterflies

This memoir begins with the story of my grandmother, her love for her husband, and her love for me. I explained why I love butterflies and what they represent—a beacon of hope for the future. So it was only natural that our companies should be named for butterflies, to remind me of the ability of essential oils to help us see the path we are meant to walk and who we are meant to become. Butterfly Express is our way of passing on the hope we feel to others. And Butterfly Expressions is my way of teaching people how to find their own path and carry this hope in their hearts.

Alternative modalities such as essential oils, along with taking responsibility for our own well-being, can help us find our own chrysalis or place of safety and peace, where we can then remake ourselves into what we were meant to be all along.

In its earliest days, our efforts to do good were very small, and I sold herbs and vitamins only as part of my foot zone practice. I arranged to buy products at wholesale so that my clients would be able to afford what they needed. My entire inventory fit in the living room closet that was 34 inches wide and 22 inches deep. Val had built shelves in the closet from cheese-mold boxes he purchased when a plant in the area went out of business. It was a very humble beginning compared to the thousands of products we offer now.

Later I began making larger quantities of the herbal tinctures I used for my own family for those who asked about them. Even at this nascent stage, Val had starry eyes regarding my little venture.

We were using herbal remedies and homeopathics, I had learned to foot zone, and we had built a small clientele before I came across my first essential oil. The creation of Butterfly Express as an essential oil company was another milepost in our family's walk with alternative healing modalities.

In spite of everything we thought we knew, we still encountered a health problem we could not solve as quickly or as thoroughly as we wanted to. Luke was experiencing hip pain and misalignment, and it didn't respond to chiropractic care or anything else I tried. It wasn't slowing him down much yet, but I was beginning to worry.

A friend, knowing of my frustration, brought me a bottle with a few drops of a certain essential oil blend. I had never heard of essential oils, so as instructed, I applied a few drops to Luke's hip that evening and again the following morning and also that afternoon. The morning after that Luke reported that his hip was feeling much better, so I called my friend back to ask where I might get some more of that "magic" liquid.

The next weekend we attended an expo in Salt Lake City where we had a booth set up and were selling some of the shelving made from the cheese boxes—the same thing I was using in my herb closet. I noted on the schedule that Dr. Gary Young was to teach a class on essential oils. The only thing I knew so far about essential oils was that the one I had used was blue, it had worked, it was sold by Dr. Young's company, and that I wanted to know more.

Dr. Young is a talented presenter and showman and had a great subject. He also had at least one extremely interested student—me. I came away from that one-hour class feeling that I absolutely had to learn more. I also had to get some of those essential oils and get better acquainted with them at home.

I walked out of the classroom and straight to Dr. Young's booth, but a throng had already gathered. After standing in what seemed like a never-ending line, I finally reached the table and reviewed my very short list of essential oils I hoped to purchase. At the top was frankincense. We didn't have a lot of money in those days, but surely I could afford at least that, I thought. That one oil, in what seemed to be a very small bottle, was $75.00 before tax! $75.00 was a large portion of my monthly grocery budget, so I consoled myself by buying a book about essential oils instead.

I read that book, and then purchased another and then another. I felt capable of learning about this healing modality, as I had learned about several other modalities and a host of other new things.

I scheduled extra foot zone appointments and set aside the money to purchase some essential oils. I learned that Dr. Young's essential oils were some of the highest-priced on the market, but they were also supposed to be the very best. I started researching some more.

Dr. Gary Young was a pioneer and quite likely the main driving force behind essential oils becoming known as a healing modality in America. His study of the benefits of essential oils and his enthusiasm for sharing what he learned impacted many lives, including those of my family.

I learned that his company, Young Living, was a multilevel marketing (MLM) organization. Multilevel marketing is an effective way to get recognition for your product, but it was a deal-breaker for me, and the structure of some MLMs tends to increase the price of the products.

I wanted to learn everything I could about essential oils, including how I could become adept at recognizing quality or lack of quality when I saw it. I read many books, including some translated into English but originally authored by old-world masters, about the use of essential oils for therapeutic purposes. I soon learned that perfumery-grade essential oils were not at all the same as essential oils used for therapeutic purposes.

I began purchasing samples from various companies. Val's mother, who was wintering in Arizona each year, sent me samples of nearly every essential oil she came across, but many were either too old or had been sitting out in the hot sun too long. It was helpful to have different grades of essential oils to play with and learn from. A friend also gave me several samples of oils from Young Living. It was getting easier to tell the high quality from the low-quality oils. I was learning that one sure way to judge quality in essential oils is to gain experience with the aroma and energy of a wide variety.

I tried to see into the minds of the oil blenders and asked myself, *Why are they putting these certain oils together? Does the order in which the oils are placed in the blend matter as much as the books insisted?* It was a marvelous adventure full of learning and experimenting.

I think that learning how to blend essential oils may be more fun than learning how to cook, except working with essential oils can be far more expensive. I had to take on more foot zone clients to finance my research and development.

I wondered if I could develop a nose for essential oils without traveling to France and spending a fortune, as some books indicated was necessary. I determined that if it could be done, I would do it. There were books that contained recipes for blending oils, but I found that many of their suggestions did not produce worthwhile oil blends. With effort and experience, the blends I made were getting more effective, and I felt like I was developing an increasingly sophisticated nose for aroma and quality.

After Butterfly Express had grown enough to add several employees, I discovered that those who worked with the oils every day developed a nose for quality. When a batch of new oils arrived, we would pass them around for evaluation, where each employee would identify which they thought were lower quality and which samples they preferred. Their opinions were often unanimous. An important exception was with hormonal oils and our female employees. Preferences could be influenced by menstrual cycles or menopause.

I like to encourage customers to "use essential oils every day, but then trust your instincts. If an essential oil 'hangs up in your head' or feels buzzy and weird, it is likely it includes some man-made chemicals. Trust your own opinion, sometimes in spite of what the laboratory tests may say about a certain essential oil."

Once I had created a few blends to achieve certain outcomes, I began passing them out to my foot zone friends. Some had experience with essential oils; others didn't. I also began using them on our children.

We had discovered another alternative healing modality that was effective and could be both physically and emotionally beneficial. A well-crafted blend of essential oils can have a profoundly positive effect on the emotional drivers of physical illness.

Before long I was supplying enough friends and clients with products that I began to think of us as an essential oil company, and the results we experienced were often phenomenal. The money I earned from both foot zones and product sales was invested right back into inventory and education.

Valaree came home from her schooling to join the company when there was only me and one other part-time employee (hardly a company at all, really). Val was supporting me every step of the way. He offered financial support as well, when we needed to buy a company van and when we didn't have the up-front cash to buy the essential oils we needed to keep up with growing demand.

We found ourselves in need of a website. I hired two different people to build us one, but the results didn't meet our needs. So I asked Valaree to learn how. She knew the business and our product line, and she understood what our website needed to do. Even though her college education had been in horticulture, she took on the task. Valaree now writes code and oversees all aspects of the tech department of Butterfly Express. As a child, Valaree had learned how to learn, and that capacity continues to serve her well every day.

Our vision for the Butterfly companies is to share what we have learned about maintaining and improving health. We want to provide our customers with the best products available, and we want to help them achieve good health and successfully deal with any crisis that may arise.

Val says that a company should do their best to provide a better product at a lower price than their competitors; doing this is one of the few justifications for being in business. He felt the same way about the construction company that was our living for many years. We value being able to provide excellent products for the lowest possible price, as a product that is meant to improve one's health is of no value if the price is so high they can't afford to buy it.

From the beginning, I felt that this modest company had a destiny to fulfill, and Val and Valaree agreed. We felt that we were meant to change lives by sharing the things we had learned. However, I had no idea that our humble beginnings would eventually grow to touch thousands of lives, but Val knew. Val always knew where we were going. Valaree may also have had a good idea of what this company could become and the future we were building together. Some of our other children may have foreseen what Val and Valaree saw as well.

Even though the initial interest in these modalities and the early dreams were mine, many of our family and associates added their own determination to lead our humble beginnings into a bright future. Together we mustered the strength to keep going during the difficult patches, as there were days when my ability to see this company's future wavered. Yet there were other days when I said to the burgeoning company, "Please don't grow, don't grow—you will consume my life!" Never mind that all the while I would be obsessively working (or was it playing?) to reach as many people as possible.

Val had no such vacillations and kept telling me that *when* the company got bigger, I would be able to hire people to do the things I didn't want to do any longer. Out of necessity I have taken his advice the past couple of years and hired a large number of helpers. While I may still be in the thick of it too often, I am able to choose on most days to focus on what I really want to do.

The most important factor in Butterfly's growth has always been word-of-mouth advertising by those who have used our products and have come to love them and the people at the company who assist them. This grassroots type of advertising strategy continues to provide us with a steady flow of new customers. Best of all, they are very happy to have found us.

We also reach a wider audience by publishing quality educational materials and providing opportunities to learn. When there are students who want to learn, I become the teacher who wants to teach. Teaching continues to play an immense role in my life, and answering questions often takes up a large part of our days in the Butterfly companies. Above all, we feel that God has blessed us! There is simply no other explanation for some of the miracles we have experienced.

Family members are often involved in the company. Our son Tony is adept at all things computer technology related. He spent many months helping Butterfly Express meet the challenges of operating a web-based business, accommodating smartphones, inventory, and accounting software to the needs of our expanding company. He ascertained changes happening in the marketing world, moving us in the appropriate directions.

Our son Travis has a genius for construction with an incredible ability to visualize a mechanical or structural problem and quickly see the easiest and best way to make necessary modifications. His daring exploits on the Last Chance Canal project were, without a doubt, the difference between success and failure. Val admits Travis is better at steel fabrication than he ever was. Travis works with us, when not completing construction projects, by handling the purchasing of essential oils. At one time his wife, Megan, worked here as well; she is an angel.

Today, Luke inventories and inputs into the inventory system the data on almost all the oil coming into Butterfly Express. He does this because he is one of the very few who never makes mistakes with numbers! Luke lives close by, along with his wife and eight children. His older boys are helping Val and him get the farm back up and running, and some of the younger ones are a great help to me, as are Valaree's children. I often think that Luke's wife may be more like me than any of my own children.

We have never put any obligation on any of our children to work with us, and they know they are free to make their way in the world separate from us or our company. We feel great joy when some of them choose to come back to work with us here, in the world of our dreams. What a joy it has been to work side-by-side with some of our children and with Val. This is especially true of working with Valaree these many years. Her husband, Daniel, now works with us; how I love this dear man and the place that he has in our hearts.

In Val's Words

LaRee and Valaree are very close and share most everything. Valaree anticipates her mother's needs. By the time LaRee is aware that she needs something, Valaree will often have it ready and waiting. She is very supportive of us.

Most, perhaps all, of our children love us and would do anything for us if we really needed it. Valaree is watching out for us every day, and she does the little things that encourage, bring peace, and remind you that you are not just loved, you are worth loving. That is precious.

The professional level of competence Valaree has brought to this company is astonishing. It is a complex world Valaree lives in, and she is an integral part of this company. We have not found anyone with a master's degree in computer science who can keep up with her.

One of the most gratifying parts of my life is teaching children. I love that so many of our grandchildren are present in our daily lives. Following the pattern we set decades ago, they have usually completed their day's schoolwork by the time they arrive, but not always. I am grateful to be involved—even if only a small degree—in educating the rising generation.

Day-to-Day Operations

One of the most challenging aspects about running a company may be the hiring, and the occasional firing, of employees. I tend to take it personally when an employee moves on, even if for personal or family reasons. I am relieved that decisions about employees are not, for the most part, my responsibility anymore.

We hire employees with specialized skills when needed, and their work ethic is always an important factor. Over the years, however, we have also hired people just because they needed a job. For several years one of Val's responsibilities within our local church organization has been to match people who need a job with jobs that are available in our area. Long before Val was asked to serve in that official way, he had a habit of hiring people in need when our company had an opening.

When making a hiring decision, Val has shared with me more than once this principle: "Skills can be taught; character, not so much. And we want employees with character. We can teach them whatever else they need to know."

Being down on your luck or badly needing a job does not necessarily indicate a lack of character. Neither does having made a mistake or falling into less-than-desirable habits. It is the direction a person is going right now and the desires of their heart that often indicate character.

Stress and hurt feelings, whether between fellow employees or employees and management, exist in any company from time to time. And the logistics of family-owned-and-operated businesses such as the Butterfly companies present another set of challenges.

Suppose, for example, an employee decides that they would rather do something other than their assigned task. They may then set about doing what they want to do until their supervisor approaches them, or they go to their supervisor first. Either way, they explain with a bald-faced lie that Val or I or another family member or person in a management position asked them to do this certain task—the one they wanted to do—instead of their original assignment or normal duty. The supervisor then has to ask one of us why work assignments had been changed without their knowledge, and, of course, we deny that any such reassignment has really taken place.

The supervisor is faced with two alternatives, both likely to turn out badly. He can ignore the employee's lie and accept the consequences of leaving important tasks undone, or other employees will have to fill in, causing resentment to build up.

Alternatively, the supervisor and the family member may speak with the employee together to set things straight. But then the story changes: "It wasn't really Val; it was LaRee who said that Val said that." The person who is supposed to have said . . . is, of course, whoever is not present at this meeting. The whole thing pits Val and LaRee, or other family members, against each other, leaving the supervisor and everyone else trying to determine what is true. This game wastes time, needed tasks are not completed on time, supervisors and employees are unhappy, and ill feelings creep in in nearly every department.

This he said/she said game may be leveraged to arrange an extra day off, to get someone into trouble with management, or for other reasons. If this type of scenario starts occurring often, the work environment can become tense. A supervisor can feel slighted, complaining they are not being allowed to run their department how they see fit. They may begin to resent those who are involved and may even start to express their discontent to others, spreading ill feelings even more.

When family and extended family members work together as we do, these sorts of behaviors can become particularly devastating. The he said/she said game can create a rift between marriage partners and in other family relationships as well. The gossip can spread, disrupting otherwise strong family ties.

Val decided to hire one of my sisters—keeping her close, in other words. He reasoned that if she could see how we really are as a couple and as business partners, it might bring an end to her gossip portraying him as a nasty and controlling man. Instead, it gave her more access to both of us, our children, and our employees and allowed her to raise havoc in our business. Whenever she could get either Val or me alone, she would tell twisted stories about the other. Our grown children became easy targets, and I wondered if our grandchildren were next.

We tried without success to resolve the situation and eventually had to let her go, which caused additional stress within the family. My biggest regret—other than the loss of the companionship of my sister—is that I did not find my backbone and handle her dismissal myself. This would have saved Val from taking yet another undeserved hit from my family.

> My loyalty belongs to those who never made me question theirs.
> —*Riya Pathock*

We have many loyal and wonderful employees at Butterfly Express, and they feel like family. We care about them and are committed to their welfare. We appreciate their kindness and support and their efforts on behalf of this company.

My husband, daughter, son, and son-in-law manage most of the day-to-day details of the essential oil company that buys and sells internationally. Some of our grandchildren work for Grandpa and Grandma part-time, which is an indescribable joy to us. We are able to be involved in their lives and teach them some of the lessons that are important to us.

Butterfly Expressions, LLC

Around 2004, following the advice of our accountant and our lawyer, we formed a second Butterfly company. My teaching, writing, and eventually live broadcasts and YouTube videos came under this new company's umbrella. I would still consult with Butterfly Express as needed, but I would, at last, be free to concentrate on teaching others through classes and the written word.

I racked my brain for an appropriate name for this new company, knowing it should be Butterfly something-or-other to be recognizable as a companion to Butterfly Express. Express was the perfect name for a company committed to shipping helpful products as efficiently as possible. I settled on "Expressions" as the perfect appellation for a company dedicated to teaching. I would be expressing truths that I so badly wanted others to know, principles that I wished I had known sooner, and lessons I had only learned through hard experience. Butterfly Expressions was born.

> Teaching is demonstrating that it is possible.
> Learning is making it possible for yourself.
> *—Paulo Coelho*

My goal in teaching is to acquaint others with the modalities and techniques that my family has benefited from over the years. I want to teach them well enough that class members can go home and, by continuing to learn one experience at a time, find healing for themselves and their families. I want to help each person gain confidence in their ability to care for themselves and their families and walk their own walk.

The teaching facility that Val built includes several bedrooms and a kitchen, as well as a large teaching area. As groups of people come together for classes, which mostly consist of women, several things tend to consistently happen. For example, multiday classes sometimes feel like big sleepovers, where we form friendships that last long after the class has ended. Class members become support groups for one another and sometimes share their joys and pains. By building up one another and lending each other strength, they become better wives and mothers and improved versions of themselves.

The environment seems to be a key part of what makes these classes special times of healing and growth. In the words of C. S. Lewis, "I have learned that while those who speak about one's miseries usually hurt, those who keep silent hurt more."

I have learned that nearly every group will have at least one person who is suffering from panic attacks, depression, anger management, or other serious issues. Every person, no matter how perfect their lives may appear, knows what it is like to suffer, be treated unfairly, or to have made mistakes. In every group, there will always be one or more persons who have lived through serious abuse of some kind or another.

I often watch in amazement as students benefit from the modalities we teach and practice during class, including essential oils, herbal remedies, homeopathics, acupressure points, various energy and Chinese medicine techniques, foot zoning, and craniosacral techniques. Being in a safe environment where these modalities are applied with love and acceptance assists people in making changes for the better.

We have witnessed panic attacks subside and then go away altogether. We have seen emotional triggers laid to rest, never to return. Energy work can have a tremendous effect. There are those who believe that trauma creates "glitches" in the energy and electrical patterns of the body, but with time and effort, these rough spots can be smoothed out.

Time and time again, we watch attitudes change, relationships heal, and physical health improve. I had witnessed such positive outcomes previously when working with people individually, but I did not expect to see it unfold in a classroom setting. Please understand, we do not pretend to be psychiatrists or social workers. Class members merely love one another and learn together, and we enable them to be more proactive and better care for themselves and their families.

We often feel the healing balm of the Savior's love during these wonderful hours of compassion and healing. I have been blessed to be a part of this for many years and have said many times, "I am the most spoiled woman you know!"

For some time now, very capable people I have trained have been blending the oils that Butterfly Express offers. And Valaree and Daniel have recently created some wonderful blends of their own, and the only part I played was to pat them on the back. The one downside to splitting the business as we have done is that I miss working with oils. I hope someday, before I totter into my grave, to "play" at blending oils more than I am currently able.

My focus now is to educate and answer questions. My life tends to be hectic, where I find only rare moments of peace and quiet, but I wouldn't have it any other way. I love what we do here, and there never seems to be enough time to do the things we love for the people we love.

The most effective kind of teaching, of course, is by example. That may be one of the biggest reasons why so many people take my classes, read my books, and follow our blog and newsletter: because we have lived and are trying to live the things we teach—to walk the walk.

Teaching itself is not that profitable at the modest rates I charge. Will my teaching ever collect enough money to pay for the teaching room, kitchen, and bedrooms that Val added on to the house? It doesn't matter, since if the classes do not quite pay their way, Val makes up the difference and supports me as he has always done. Whenever I tell Val how spoiled I am, he replies, "I hope so!" I certainly have been spoiled—especially if you define it as being married to a man who does his best to provide you with both the time and the money to follow your dreams.

I love to teach and am never so energized as when I am in front of a group, learning with them. I do not look forward to the time when this part of my life must draw to a close. And while I am not getting any younger, I sometimes feel I am heading in that direction through teaching, making me younger at sixty-eight than I was at fifty-eight.

However, as I learned when I walked away from midwifery, whatever God has in mind for me will be a wonderful place to be. For the first time in my life I have books in my house that I have not read. I even have books I want to read again. Perhaps that may happen in the next stage of my life—that, and service in the temple or serving a mission for my church and the God I love. I can hardly wait to see what the tomorrows of my life may bring.

CHAPTER TWENTY-FOUR

Burns and Blessings—Val

There is no panic in Heaven!
God has no problems, only plans.
—*Corrie ten Boom*

I*t was just before lunchtime* on a warm day in June of 2006. Val was spending the day working in our salvage yard, about a quarter of a mile from the house. He was cutting the gas tank off an old truck, a task he had performed many times previously. But in a hurry to get home for lunch, he might have pushed safety protocols somewhat as he is used to heaven's protection.

An errant spark landed and the gas tank exploded, throwing him back several feet and covering him with burning gasoline. The clothes on his upper body ignited and began to burn. Welding leathers protected his lower body. His fire shield and gloves literally melted. Val knew help wasn't coming; he had to get himself home.

His pickup truck was blocked in by the semi-truck and trailer parked in the salvage yard, so he couldn't drive home in the pickup without first moving the semi. But his hands were too badly burned to manage the gears on the semi, even if he could have somehow climbed into the cab. So he walked home. On the way, Val plunged his hands into some mud to ease the pain. It was the first of many miracles that Val remained conscious long enough to walk the quarter of a mile home.

When he arrived at the back door, he kicked it a couple of times with his feet. I glanced over as my niece opened the door. The sight that met our eyes was horrific, and from across the large room, I shouted, "Are you okay, Hon?" He answered, calmly, "I believe that is the dumbest thing you have ever said to me." And I suppose it was.

Our daughter Valaree was there with her three small children, and we immediately went to work using homeopathic remedies known to be helpful for shock and for burns. We soaked towels in cold water into which we placed lavender and other essential oils. We wrapped these around Val's head, upper body, and hands. The residual heat in his body made the towels hot very quickly, and we had to change them frequently in an attempt to cool his flesh.

Nearly 70% of his upper body was badly burned, and the clothes were completely burned off. And the more dangerous consequence—which we realized only later—was that he had inhaled when the explosion occurred, meaning he had literally gasped in flames and fumes. We had dealt with burns before, but certainly nothing this serious and extensive. And the internal injuries meant this was going to be a very different experience.

A second miracle unfolded in those critical first minutes, as Valaree's one-, two-, and four-year-old children played contentedly and required very little attention from us. From the story the oldest boy shared later, I have thanked heaven for the "pretty ladies" who played with them and kept them safe while we were attending to Val. I cannot speculate who these "pretty ladies" may have been, but I am profoundly grateful for their presence. Other members of our family have felt the close presence of deceased family members at particularly stressful times, and I can only imagine that this was one of those very special times.

Val's burns were horrendous, but we had been herbal for many years and had successfully treated Luke's burns using herbs and essential oils several years before. So it simply did not occur to Valaree or me to take Val to the hospital. We began assessing the damage with an eye to cutting away the most badly-charred pieces of flesh and muscle while the nerves were still deadened from shock and the burns themselves.

Val's hands were so badly burned that at first I thought I was looking at the remnants of his welding gloves. I soon realized that there was no trace of the gloves left. His fingers looked like thick-cut bacon, charred black and curling up at the edges.

His face was also a terrible sight, and I worried particularly about his right eye, lips, nose, and ears. A few days later, medical personnel would tell me that there was no way *anyone* could save his hands or his ears. After a couple of hours, we felt we had him reasonably stable. All the burns were covered, but they were still so hot and so deep that they were heating through our cold towels in less than ten minutes. It was a constant challenge for three of us to keep them changed and cooled.

Eventually, although his flesh was still hot and burning internally, the combination of the cold cloths and the severity of the injuries brought on renewed shock symptoms. We had several heaters going, and it was a hot day, so the rest of us were miserably hot, but Val was beginning to shiver and shake. Once again, we used homeopathic remedies for shock that were blessedly effective.

By evening, Val seemed to be doing quite well. We were adding pain-relieving and nervine herbs to the water we soaked the towels in. Val did not ask for, or seem to require, any drugs for pain, not even an aspirin.

I thought to myself, *Okay, we can do this. It won't be fun, but he is a strong man with a strong will!* I had worried about losing him so many times during the years of his illnesses. Although this was very bad, I had a quiet confidence—call it faith, if you will—that we could get through this too. That optimism didn't last long.

The first day or two went relatively well, but then the swelling began in earnest. I have never seen anything so awful: Val's face, neck, and shoulders were one huge, swollen mass. Internal swelling had begun as well, and I feared he would soon be unable to breathe. Without homeopathic arnica, I don't know how he could have survived.

I had previously studied aspects of Eastern healing philosophies, and both Valaree and I had taken classes in various energy modalities. We began holding acupressure and other points said to be helpful with trauma, shock, and breathing difficulties. At one point, during the second or third night when Valaree was having trouble staying awake, her hands would drop away from the points and her father would begin again to struggle breathing. So she taped her fingers to these points and spent the night sleeping, sitting upright with her hands taped in place.

For several days, at least, we did energy procedures on his chest and abdomen night and day. When we stopped he would start to hiccup, and minutes later he would begin coughing or throwing up pieces of burnt flesh from his damaged esophagus and trachea.

We were continually praying, since by now we had a pretty clear picture of how seriously injured he was internally. In the wake of the previous burns in the family, I had done a considerable amount of research on burns and thought I understood what could be accomplished with alternative remedies. I also had a pretty clear idea what a burn center would offer if we went there. Neither option looked good enough, but the only peace I could find was in continuing our efforts at home.

I vacillated between hope and despair and worried that I didn't have enough knowledge or skill. But I also knew that we had to do it, and the Spirit whispered reassurances and peace. These feelings are markedly different from overconfidence or conceit. Even though I didn't know how much recovery he might achieve, and I wasn't sure that he would survive, I was at peace. By definition, it is impossible to describe this peace "which passeth all understanding." We simply had to keep on trying as we felt we were being directed.

Val was given at least two priesthood blessings that first couple of days, which brought us untold comfort. A dear neighbor who was a humble yet great man gave one; he has since passed, and we miss him. Our friend who is also our lawyer and owns a ranch nearby gave the other blessing.

The first blessing was brief and to the point. The second, in lawyer fashion, was lengthier, with lots of phrases to cling to. But the messages of both blessings were essentially the same and even used the same rather unusual phrasing in places. On the whole, we learned that we were caring for Val as the Lord wished us to.

Val was also promised in both blessings that he would survive and "direct his own healing," which was fulfilled in some unusual ways. While I thought I was the expert, as sick as Val was, he often shared insights and made suggestions regarding his care. These special insights sometimes set my feet on a different, but very effective, path.

We felt the love of our Heavenly Parents and our older brother—our Savior, Jesus Christ—very strongly over the next several weeks. We also felt the presence of caring family members from both sides of the veil separating this and the next life.

In the middle of the third night, the house was dark and quiet and Val seemed half-asleep, it being sometimes hard to tell. I was trying to let both him and Valaree get more sleep, as Valaree was still recovering from the before-mentioned accident that damaged her pelvic structures. Suddenly, I was aware of the presence of two people not of this earthly realm. It wasn't so much that I could see these figures as I could sense them. Because of what was included in the two blessings previously given to Val, I later looked for photos of these two people in family histories. The moment I saw their pictures I recognized them and later discovered that both had been badly burned in their lifetimes.

When I first sensed their presence, however, I feared they had come to take Val "home" with them. I felt profound grief as I was not ready to let him go and I did not want to carry on without him as we still had many dreams to fulfill together.

For a moment I thought, *My neighbors will never understand and will think this crazy herb lady killed her husband by keeping him at home!* I soon felt peace with it all, however, and there was a measure of relief that if he were to leave me, his suffering would not have been as prolonged and intense as I had feared it might become. These thoughts came and passed in an instant, and I felt a profound reassurance. My mind filled with the words, "We have only come to watch with you. You are so very tired." From that time on, I loved the nights, as the feeling of peace and of presence was so profound that I knew everything would be okay. We had the strength and the guidance to go on in the manner that heaven wanted us to.

Two of our sons and our son-in-law were working on a project away from home and returned home as quickly as they could. Tyler soon flew in from Indiana, where he was completing post-graduate courses toward a PhD. Richard also came home to help. It was the day after my nighttime visitors came that my sons and son-in-law arrived, and Val was coherent enough that evening to request everyone to gather for family prayer. Each of our children took a turn voicing a prayer, then Val pointed his foot at our son-in-law, Daniel, and asked him to express his views about whether we should take him to the hospital or continue caring for him at home.

Daniel stood and said, "We have *it* to do, Mom. We will be here as long as you need us." Each one expressed similar feelings that treating Val at home was best. Valaree and I could not stop weeping, and we both knew that this was right. The Spirit was strong, and the family unity was positively tangible. I am not sure the others really knew what we were up against, but Valaree and I were aware, and we were already exhausted. Each one pledged their support and came through in wonderful ways over the following weeks.

Much later, Val disclosed that he knew if he went to the hospital, he would not come home alive, but he was willing to do whatever his children counseled and agreed upon. What Val wanted most was for his family to be united in their decision.

Tara also came home immediately after being informed of Val's accident but sadly, because she thought she might have strep throat, she was not present for this prayer and discussion. She drove back to Provo, Utah, the following day and did, in fact, develop a serious strep infection. No one had a problem with Tara's absence during this time as she was attending BYU, it was an intense time in her own life, and she would probably have appreciated some help herself. Had we not been overwhelmed by Val's constant need for care, we would have been more available and happy to support her. The next time Tara came home, her father was using even his more seriously burned right hand to feed himself.

I have wondered if her presence during these memorable and sacred times would have influenced future family relationships. It was a difficult yet unifying time as the family worked and prayed together to save Val's hands, nose, ears, and his life. Sadly, she missed a special time of family bonding.

Months after the accident, Val showed me the will he had drawn up only a week before the explosion. As part of the will he had left his personal journals and other writings to Tara. Maybe he was feeling that out of all of his children, the two of them might have understood each other the least. She does not know her father's heart yet. This is the true tragedy and heartbreak of our lives today.

Val's parents assisted every day. The flies and grasshoppers were very bad that year, yet I was still highly reactive to insecticide. Those flies buzzing around Val nearly drove him crazy, so Grandpa would spend hours swatting them, and Grandma controlled the grasshopper population that kept jumping against the windows.

Val's sister would come by and play the piano for hours, which calmed Val's spirit as well as mine.

My parents also visited and pulled me aside to ask how I was going to support myself. I understood their concern, but this upset me terribly. Val was also their son and he was in terrible trouble. I returned to Val's side and cried; they did not speak to Val at all that day.

Their less-than-loving and sympathetic behavior reminded me of a story my mother told me. While Mom was in the hospital recovering from cancer surgery, her sister visited and shared what she had included in the letter to her missionary. Telling her son of his aunt's cancer, she added, "Not everyone is going to still be here when you get home."

We laughed much later about how inappropriate this aunt could sometimes be, but at the time we did not laugh about how her remarks had hurt my mother. I felt much the same about this interaction with my parents, as I needed them to love Val and be as hopeful for his welfare and his future as they were for mine.

If they really wanted to be of assistance, all they had to do was ask; the dishes, the laundry, and the flies were all calling out. Or they could sit with Val while I took a shower or a desperately needed nap. I wish that I had found a way to involve them in the miracles we would experience in the coming months.

Between the time of Val's accident and my mother's onset of dementia, Val felt that Mom had found a measure of acceptance of him and our choices. He felt that she finally recognized how much damage gossip had done to the family and was now doing all she could to make up for it.

Those years before Mom's mind left us were precious, and we had some lovely times together. I wish we could have had more time to get to know each other better before her mind reverted to the past and confusion set in. She was a beautiful and gracious woman, and, if you are somehow listening Mom, I love you.

Once the internal swelling set in, Val was unable to orally take any fluids or nourishment. A doctor in town said he would arrange to get Val a home IV, but it never happened. Instead, he insisted that I bring Val to town for blood work and evaluation before he would arrange for an IV at home. I later found out that he had arranged for a Life Flight helicopter to be on site when we arrived even though we had not given him any indication that we were coming in. A friend who is a hospice nurse also tried to secure an IV for us, but to no avail.

Dehydration became a chronic problem that we fought every way possible. We made herbal teas using vitamin and nutrient herbs, and since Val could not swallow these teas normally, I administered them as enemas, once every hour, for the first three days and nights after the swelling set in. I recall stumbling into the bedroom and falling onto the bed, exhausted, when within what felt like only minutes, someone would wake me. At first, I would panic, thinking there must be a serious crisis for them to be waking me so soon. They were waking me on my orders, as I insisted on doing every enema myself because I knew I could do it without damaging the rectal wall.

A doctor later asked how we managed to avoid complications from dehydration. I told him what we had done, and how long and how often we had done it, causing him to say, "You must have sliced his poor rectum up something awful!" I replied the same as I had with this doctor several times before: "Did someone write 'stupid' across my forehead recently?" I had training and experience, and I certainly had the motivation to do it right. Even though I was scared to death, my can-do attitude helped get me through.

Herbs are very nutritious, and the last section of the colon absorbs nutrients well. It wasn't a perfect solution, however, as the better solution would have been to administer an IV, but it was the only option we had available. Valaree feared her father was slowly starving to death; he lost so much weight so quickly it was almost as though he was melting away before our eyes.

We would prepare dressings by smearing large blue hospital pads with herbal salve and essential oils. Then we would layer nonstick pads on top of that, and that would be covered with yet another layer of salve. We went through seventeen gallons of salve the first few days.

Changing the dressings on Val's chest and back, arms and hands, and face and neck was a horrendous experience. Our equipment included a large overstuffed recliner the boys purchased in town and several large Lovesac beanbag chairs that we called "puff balls." The grandchildren loved them, but they were assigned medical status now. The boys would stack the puff balls and then lay their father forward on them. For the first several days, Val would lose consciousness, and we would then change the dressings on his back. When we were finished, the boys would ease Val back into the recliner and we would change the dressings on the front. After giving him a moment to gather more strength and courage, I would change the dressings on both hands and on his face and neck. I did not think Val knew I was going into the bathroom to vomit after dressing his hands.

"I am not in as much pain as you think," Val told me at the time, which is similar to what Luke had said about his leg burns. Only recently did they both admit that they were saying that to spare my feelings. I remember only one instance when Val admitted to feeling pain during his ordeal, and that was in the middle of the night when I stumbled over the blankets I had been sleeping on that were near his feet. I fell on his badly burned right hand and he whimpered, but only for a moment or two before regaining control and composing himself.

On another day, while observing new symptoms, I began to worry about renal failure and researched possible homeopathic remedies for this condition. I knew which one I needed, but I didn't have it and ordering it would not get it to us in time. In despair, I told my good friend and employee about the problem and asked her to research other potential remedies we did have. She simply gave me a hug and said, "Do not count out your friends. Betty just dropped off a small bag of homeopathic remedies, so let's see if the one you need is there." I thought, *This is a very unique remedy I need, and she would have no reason to have it.* But when we looked in the bag, there it was. She had ordered it before Val got burned, for no reason except that she always listens and responds to promptings. This good woman has been a part of many such miracles over the years, and this one literally saved Val's life.

Such tender mercies were almost daily occurrences for weeks, and we were grateful for each one. Similar to what I had experienced as a midwife, what I needed and needed to know would be made available when the need arose.

We had previously amassed a supply of nonstick pads and other medical items. With Luke's burn, we had learned the hard way that all of Utah's Cache Valley does not have enough medical supplies for a non-hospital to handle even one serious burn. Even though we were well supplied, we appreciated every thoughtful item our neighbors brought by.

One neighbor who was a nurse brought me some expensive burn salve. The herbal salve I had made was working well, but it was a challenge keeping the salve on Val's nose and ears. I discovered that if I layered this expensive salve over our herbal one, it formed a crust that kept the herbal salve in place.

Luke's wife, Samberly, faithfully came up every night for weeks and worked the foot zone signals on Val's feet to help him breathe. She had three small children, including a set of twins. I don't worry about getting old and needing help because help lives close by and can be counted on. Another neighbor who was totally unacquainted with energy work took one of the midnight shifts and merely did what he was told, running the signals on Val's chest and abdomen as instructed. He soon realized that if he stopped, Val would be in serious trouble within minutes.

Val's recovery came slowly, and we have some fond memories of that time. There is nothing like a great deal of stress to either make or break a couple and a family. I remember changing some dressings one day, then going to the kitchen and eating half a chocolate cake a neighbor had brought. It tasted heavenly. Then I changed the dressings on Val's hands and went back and ate the other half of the cake. Oddly, I didn't gain any weight during this ordeal, which may be one of the blessings of stress, I suppose.

As the area's garden crops began coming in, a neighbor brought over a large bag full of freshly picked corn. Val's mother, who answered the door, thanked him for his kindness and asked who in the world had time to husk all this corn. She then handed him a chair and some totes to put the corn in when he was finished husking it. He husked it all and even came back with other produce from his garden.

The first time Val got out of his recliner to go to the bathroom was a Sunday, nearly two months after the explosion. The family had gone to church, leaving Val and me home by ourselves. He decided that he wanted to take his first bath and could not be dissuaded. So I ran him a bath and helped him carefully get in. The look of joy on his face was priceless, as he has always loved what he calls long "soaky" baths.

When it was time to get out of the tub, however, he could not lift himself into a standing position, and I couldn't get any leverage while standing outside the tub. So I rolled up my pant legs, straddled him in the water, and lifted. By the time we succeeded, I was almost as wet as he was, and he was completely exhausted by the effort it took.

We had taken Val on a couple of short rides around the neighborhood in the back seat of his mother's car, and one day he decided it was time for a longer trip, to Logan. We went to a parts store. His right hand was bandaged, and his left hand wasn't strong enough to open the door. Once inside, he stepped up on the small platform and sat on one of the stools in front of the parts counter. Even from this higher vantage point, he could not lift his head enough to look the clerk in the eyes, and I wondered if he would ever be able to, as the muscles of his chest, neck, back, and arms had been so badly damaged.

It was many more months before he could raise either arm high enough to comb his own hair. And it was even longer before he was able to button his own shirt. Val had always been proud of and grateful for the dexterity of his fingers, an essential skill in his line of work.

The boys were finishing a large construction project for our neighbor that Val had been in the middle of before the accident. As soon as he was able, Val insisted that I drive him down our driveway and up the neighbor's driveway so that he could check on progress. He really didn't need to as he had taught his boys well, but I still drove him over to keep him happy. I had surmised that if I didn't help him get dressed he would have to stay in the car, but I was wrong. In my mind's eye I can still see him standing in the middle of the half-built horse arena with his bathrobe flapping in the breeze and his embarrassed sons insisting that he go back home.

I am so grateful to have shared so many years with my good man. During his previous illnesses, I tried to wrap my mind around the possibility of finishing my life out alone. I am so grateful that I was not called upon to do that, as Val is and has been my dearest friend, ever since our first date when we sat in a restaurant, laughing and talking past my curfew without realizing it.

The story surrounding Val's accident and recovery was taken, for the most part, from my journal entries. At first, I scribbled notes that were jotted down under stress and in a hurry, some of which included remedies we were using. A little over a year after the accident, I consolidated my jumbled notes into a coherent and lengthy narrative and added to that as Val and I shared recollections and feelings. We consider some experiences too sacred and private to be shared in this memoir. Not long ago, Val said there are parts of this story he has never shared, not even with me. That made me curious, but I will not ask about them. He will share them when, and if, he is ready to. After all, it is *his* story.

Val's Recollections

Many are the critics who scoffed when I did not go to the hospital to treat my burns. My cousin Jim was burned and spent nearly three months in the burn center. Jim brought the sacrament [similar to the Eucharist] to me the second day after my burns. After seeing me, he was so disturbed that he said he could not come back. And he did not. Years later, after a frank discussion, he said I was lucky to not have gone to the hospital. Also, he had insurance, and his portion of the bill was enough to scare you. It would have bankrupted us. Jim has marveled at how well I healed.

I have a neighbor who did an internship at a burn center who told me that I would lose my ears and my right hand if I survived. We have a successful track record of treating burns, and maybe we could show the world a thing or three if they would listen. I recovered. No lost hands, no lost ears.

My arms were burned all the way around. I have a spot under my wrist where the hair is normal, and the rest of my arms have only light fuzz. Only a careful examination of my arms reveal trauma; you have to look very closely.

My back and chest are similar. There are large areas on my abdomen and back where the burns went into the muscle, and they are scarred badly. [This is Val's perspective, even though we printed a poster with a picture of Val getting a back massage, taken about a year after the explosion, and there just a few patches of redness.]

I had many areas that were still in bandages months later. I did not have any skin grafts. I have not had any plastic surgery. LaRee is the only one that has treated my burns.

I wear a T-shirt to go swimming, but I do not go often as the chlorine bothers my skin. I have served in the LDS temple and am sometimes assigned to work in the baptistry. My turn assisting patrons in the font can last up to two hours. The chlorine irritated me, and I would turn bright pink from the tip of my head to my waist. After the chemicals were changed, I no longer had a problem.

Yes, my face is different: my lips are not as full, and my nose and ears are slightly different. I think I look younger, not older, as a result of my burns as my new skin has very few wrinkles. Doctors and even surgeons have asked how I smashed my right hand, as it does not look like a burn, and the skin is soft and smooth. It is plastic-like except where it has calloused over my knuckles. Some of the fingers on that hand, where tendons were damaged, are pulled a little bit out of normal positioning.

Doctors and surgeons have been amazed to learn I was burned. They touch my face and ask, "Who was your surgeon?" I reply, "LaRee." Silence.

On my first visit back to church, I was invited to stand and share my feelings and testimony. After that, the stake president [a religious leader that oversees several congregations] stood and bore testimony that I had been attended to by angels. I thought he was referring to LaRee.

Val's Testimony

Miracles: I think I am a miracle. You may think what you like. I would like to explain what I think it takes to receive a miracle. First, you need a broken heart and a contrite spirit. That much is easy when you are up against it. Then you just need a little faith. That is all. The Lord does all the rest, according to His will.

CHAPTER TWENTY-FIVE

Head Injury

I'm sorry to say so
but, sadly, it's true
that Bang-ups
and Hang-ups
can happen to you.
—*Dr. Seuss*

I*t was my birthday,* and Valaree and I were celebrating at a local restaurant when my cell phone rang. It was the secretary at the grain mill in Malad, Idaho, where Val and his crew were working. She said there had been a bad accident, but that they believed "he" would be fine. I remember the sinking feeling in the pit of my stomach as she spoke, as I had a husband, two sons, and one son-in-law on that job site that day.

Travis and his brother were attaching trim to an overhead door, with Travis working about fifteen feet above the ground. Val was inside the building at the time and felt sick as he heard the sound of Trav's coat sliding down the wall outside. He ran out to find his son lying on the ground in a heap. He appeared to be conscious but groggy, and his eyes were closed.

As they were trying to assess how badly hurt he was, Trav's eyes flew open. He threw his father and brother-in-law off, jumped to his feet, and started running. Before either of them could reach him, he toppled over backward, smacking the back of his head on the pavement. Val and Daniel, our son-in-law, said the sound of his head hitting the pavement was sickening, describing it as something like the thudding sound a watermelon makes when it's dropped on the floor and smashes to pieces. The doctor told me later that, as bad as the first fall had been, it was the second fall that did the most damage.

I have pictured what the doctor described in my mind and looked at illustrations online and in anatomy books many times since that day. As the back of Travis's head hit the pavement, the brain rebounded forward into the front of the skull, bruising the brain and causing bleeding in fragile tissues. The odds of permanent damage from such a fall are very high and the odds of achieving a full recovery are very low.

An ambulance was dispatched to take him to the hospital in Malad, and a Life Flight helicopter was notified to meet them at the hospital for transport to a larger hospital in Pocatello. Travis was kept as still as possible as they waited for medical personnel to arrive, and a priesthood blessing was given. A short while after the ambulance arrived at the hospital, Life Flight also landed. The Life Flight crew grew anxious, trying to get the doctor in Malad to release Travis to them, as time is critical with head injuries.

Val wrote later:

> *I was in awe of the help I felt was being assembled on the other side of the veil. I was mostly quiet. I had given my son a blessing. And I knew that he would be okay. The wind had gone from my sails, and I needed my wife. I needed LaRee.*

I wish I had been there to hear that blessing, as I could have used such an assurance. By the time I arrived, Travis had been sedated and was being loaded into the helicopter. As I looked at him, I wondered if it might be the last time I would see him alive. He was so very still, and still is *not* Travis.

Travis had recently been to the temple for the first time and had been attending regularly since. For members of our church, the first temple experience is an important milestone in a person's life. His having had this experience brought a measure of comfort to this mother's heart. He was planning on serving a mission, as his girlfriend of several years had recently left to serve one herself. Not long before, Travis had received a special blessing, and I recalled the words while waiting for the helicopter to take him up and away from me. They included the thought that Travis "would be known far and wide as a *gentle man.*" I thought of his Aunt ReNee, whose brain damage as a child has made her the gentlest of souls. I pled with heaven that this injury would not be the road to that sort of gentleness for Travis.

While Val and I were driving to Pocatello, I received my own witness that Travis would be okay. We entered the hospital through the emergency room doors and couldn't tell which way to go to find our son. My memory is that I could hear him bellowing from quite a distance away, "Are you going to find my mother, or have I got to do it myself?" Val does not recall this, so it's possible it was only in my mind. When we found him, he was unconscious, and we were only allowed to glance through the door for a short moment.

Travis was moved to intensive care, where the next few hours were touch and go. No one was allowed in his room but hospital staff, so we used the time to call family and tell them what we knew, which was practically nothing. Since no one would be allowed to see Travis until he was stabilized, there was no point in their coming yet.

Eventually, a doctor came and informed us that Travis had suffered a severe enough blow to the head to cause bleeding in the frontal lobe. Since the bleeding seemed to be diminishing, they wanted to wait before doing any procedure and see if the bleeding would stop completely on its own.

Both Val and I perceived that the doctor was watching us closely as he spoke with us, and I remember thinking, *I wonder if he is expecting me to pass out, or become hysterical or something?* Even in a crisis that isn't in my nature, and Val is unlikely to behave in such a way under any circumstances. Apparently, the doctor concluded that we could both be trusted to be in the room with the victim of a head injury. Val's description of this matches mine in all particulars:

> *After our "interview" with the doctor—he had been watching us closely—he decided we could be trusted to go and see our son. But only one of us at a time would be permitted in, and only for a couple of minutes each. The doctor went with us, and I could tell he was still checking us out, so I stayed on my very best behavior. A few minutes later he met us again in the waiting room and told us that since it was almost Thanksgiving, and since they had an unusually high number of patients, we would be allowed to help. But only one at a time, he stressed again. He wanted someone in the room monitoring Travis at all times. If he moved, the doctor wanted to know, and Travis could not be allowed to pull out any of the tubes. The hospital simply did not have sufficient staff to do the job.*
>
> *LaRee and I took turns; we had to stay alert, so we traded every hour or so. It was a long night. Travis is a formidable man, and a mother might control him if he awoke; the nurses, maybe not. Our role in this capacity was only to last until morning.*
>
> *We did not ask to stay on, nor did anyone explain, but our duty tour was extended indefinitely. Maybe when the next shift started, they thought we had already been approved. When the doctor made his rounds the following morning, he asked for an update on our observations, and then we were asked to leave for a few minutes. We were called back in and our vigil began again. Another day, another night.*

During the second day of our vigil at our son's bedside, Val was asked to give a priesthood blessing to a man's wife, who was also in the ICU. She had been declared brain dead and her family was struggling, trying to decide whether to unhook her from the machines that were keeping her alive. Since there had been no opportunity to go home,

Val was still in his dirty work clothes. Normally, a man dresses up to speak the words of a blessing, but Val accepted the invitation anyway. The Lord called the woman home, and she peacefully slipped from this life a short while later, without medical intervention and no need for the family to make such a difficult decision. This was a traumatic experience for Val, but I felt, as did their family, gratitude to heaven for sparing them this hard decision.

When I was in the room with Travis, although he was not fully conscious, he was extremely restless. Sometimes he became quite agitated, just as we had been warned he might become, and he badly wanted to remove the tubes. He seemed to want to get out of bed and go somewhere; knowing Travis, probably home, or maybe even back to work. When he was in an agitated state, I had only to put my hand on his chest and encourage him to lie still. This motion and the sound of my voice never failed to calm him.

I used some peppermint essential oil in the room that first day, and somehow Travis associated this aroma with a certain massage therapist he had visited several times. He was absolutely sure, even after coming home, that she had visited him in the hospital.

Travis fell on a Monday around noon, and by Wednesday afternoon he was awake and alert. As the tests came in, they showed that the bleeding in the brain had almost stopped and that nearly all other functions were returning to normal as well. So he was moved to a private room where he could have visitors.

The doctor said that it was looking as though we might be able to take Travis home the following morning, Thanksgiving Day. Since there was nothing to be done at this point but wait and watch, we could do that just as well at home. You would think I would have been happy to be taking him home, but it felt daunting and seemed early for someone with head trauma of this sort. The doctor returned to the room, gave us instructions for Travis's care, and released Travis—that very day.

We had been treated so well that I was upset at myself for thinking they might be rushing things by sending Travis home so soon. I suppose

I just wanted more tests run every five minutes or so, just to make sure the bleeding was not starting up again.

One week after the accident, I made the following entry in my journal, and again six days later:

December 2, 2002

It has been exactly one week since Trav's fall. He is at home now and is in a lot of pain. Not just his head, which is excruciating, but his whole body. Nothing seems to help! Because of the bleeding in his head, they can't give him any painkillers strong enough to help him much.

He has had very little sleep, although yesterday and last night were better. And he is finally holding down a bit of food and water. He has been promised in priesthood blessings that he will have a full recovery. I just wonder how much pain and confusion lie between now and then. It has been a horrendous experience!

Two friends from Trav's church just dropped in. One of them helped Val give Travis another blessing, and the blessing was beautiful. Once again, Travis was promised that the pain would "continue to subside" and that he would have a full recovery.

I have been guilty of being impatient about the demands on "my" time that family and friends so often make. As recently as two weeks ago, when Tara had the flu, I found myself annoyed because I thought she was being quite demanding, even for Tara.

I have since come to wonder if, when I am annoyed with someone else, it is not so much what they are doing that is the problem, but perhaps it is really some wrong thinking or selfishness on my part.

I am pleased to report progress in this area of my personality. I have felt virtually no impatience with the time that I am spending nursing Travis. This is particularly wonderful to me because he has required a lot from me. The head injury has resulted in his wanting his "Mommy" nearly every minute. Tara and Val have both been wonderful, so I have been getting a little more sleep—not nearly enough, but some.

I may not be feeling annoyed, but I am, however, beginning to have a bit of trouble with my emotions. I dread going to sit with him because I just want to break down and cry, watching him suffer like this and for so long. He is such a tough young man, but the constant pain is wearing him down. I pray every minute that I am by his side—and most of the rest of the time too—that this pain will soon pass. I pray that he will find the courage and peace to endure.

All in all, it seems like our world has gone from one crisis to another for many months, and I keep telling myself, "If I can only get to the end of the month. . . ." But then I say the same thing the next month and the month after that. Despite all the stress, I am happy. Or perhaps contented is a better word. My relationship with Val is strong, and our children all seem to be doing well in their faith and testimonies.

Nursing Travis these last days has been a wonderful experience! It is wonderful to catch glimpses of his temple covenants and his faith in his Savior. We have been richly blessed these past eighteen months: two temple weddings, three new grandchildren, and Travis. Marvelous, marvelous blessings, all of them!

December 8, 2002

There is something concerning Trav's accident that I wish to record here in my journal. With a head injury, we were told that the basic personality traits of the person can be expected to be more pronounced, at least for a while. I thought of Travis and his independence and stubbornness. His tendency to go, go, go until he drops. Considering his lack of patience and impulsiveness, we could be in trouble here.

What I have observed so far is another side of Travis, and more pronounced character traits like patience, appreciation, kindness, remorse at being a bother and needing so much care, and a desire to serve. When our children were growing up, if I went down with a migraine, they would come check on me. But Travis always came with something in his hands such as a bowl of soup or a sandwich, or an offer to rub the back of my neck.

As Travis seemed to turn the direction of his life over to the Lord just before this injury, he was noticeably becoming more tolerant, patient, and appreciative. It is this "new man"—the result of his personal efforts—whose characteristics have been more pronounced as a result of this injury and the pain he has suffered. It is as though the other, more impatient Travis no longer exists. It has been a great testimony to me of the power of repentance and the change that comes with forgiveness.

Within ten days, Travis was up and wandering around the job site, as he felt better when in motion and with his mind occupied by something other than the pain. But the pain often kept him awake at night. When the headaches would ebb, we would have long chats, and the injury seemed to have lowered his defenses. He told story after story, with little brakes applied to his recollections or his mouth. Some stories his mother perhaps would have preferred not to hear. I came to know his heart even better—the good and the not so good. It was a precious time. As much as I wanted to stay up late and listen, sometimes I just had to get some sleep in order to keep going.

Travis was gentle and grateful, witty, and appreciative—much more appreciative than I had ever known him to be. He was at times discouraged during the first few weeks and worried about what his future might now hold. Those first weeks were a very hard time for him.

Although there was no permanent damage to his neck or spine, a cranial nerve was damaged and he lost hearing in one ear. These residual effects are now part of who he is. He still takes responsibility for his choices in the same way he always has, and he doesn't cut himself any slack because of his injury. Travis was and still is a complicated man. As Val says, he has fought his own demons, yet has been on the side of angels just as often. If anyone needs a friend or a protector, Travis seems to be there, which is a pattern in his life. This trait has led him down some less-traveled roads as he has always looked out for the underdog and given to those he considers in greater need.

Travis sees the world and how cruel people can sometimes be very clearly. He recognized "man's inhumanity to man" as a young child and fought against it by intervening and taking on boys older than himself when they bullied other children. He has a habit of either pushing back against perceived cruelty or caring for people that cruelty has left behind.

Grandma Westover once gave Travis a small scarecrow figure that had "Scared of Nothing" printed on its shirt front. At the time, I thought that she had her grandson pegged all wrong. I have always understood that much of Trav's tough-guy act is a cover for the pain he feels for others and the fear that pain produces in his sensitive soul.

The Second Accident

The following summer, Tara was home from college for the weekend, so Travis came home also, arriving on his motorcycle. They decided to make a trip into town, and Travis suggested that they go together on his motorcycle, as they had often enjoyed rides in the past. Tara asked if he had a second helmet for her, but he didn't. Tara, being sensible, said that she wouldn't ride without a helmet and followed Travis in the small red car we had given her.

About ten minutes after they left we got a call from Tara: Travis had just been in an accident. Someone had left a gate open in a field along the highway and cattle were milling about on the road, and Travis had hit one of them with his motorcycle. Trav's helmet was on the back of the motorcycle when he crashed. He came off the cycle, sliding on the road with no protection for his head and little protection for his body. There is not much a mother can say about such a lack of good sense.

We told Tara that we would call an ambulance on our way there, but she said she had already loaded Travis into her car and they were just coming up Bear River Hill, putting them only about a mile away from the hospital emergency room. I believe that I yelled at Tara—not for taking Travis to the hospital, but for moving a man with a fairly recent head and neck injury without a backboard, and without the help of trained medical personnel. She was better taught than that.

Looking back on it again, however, I wonder how much say Tara really had in this decision. No matter what shape he was in, if Travis had set his mind to get in the car and go, there probably wasn't much she could have done but help him do what he was going to do anyway.

By the time we arrived at the hospital, they had cleaned up the blood from the scrapes on his head and the road rash on the side of his face. These scrapes required no stitches or even taping. His leg was scraped raw, but there were no broken bones and no cuts worth stitching there either. A scan of Trav's brain was ordered, and the hospital sent it electronically to the medical team that had handled his previous head injury. It showed no residual damage to the tissues of the frontal lobe and no new damage from this accident. It was a serendipitous outcome to what could have been a life-altering episode.

Whatever Travis and Tara had planned for the evening was, of course, canceled by this emergency room visit. We were grateful that Trav's injuries were so minor that no hospital stay was necessary. The worst part of this episode was the staph infection Travis developed on his badly scraped leg. The doctors and I fought this stubborn infection for several months. Even now, whenever he gets a cut on that leg, we sometimes see flare-ups of what looks like this old infection.

A while back I was feeling a little blue. Val had been quite ill for a few days and Valaree was out of town, and I quietly lamented that I didn't know where to go or who to talk to. The following day I mentioned this to Travis, and he said, "Mother, you can always come here to my house." *How could I have overlooked that?* He is raising a good family, his children adore him, and his wife is happy. All of them are in and out of our home regularly and are a blessing in our lives every day.

CHAPTER TWENTY-SIX

People, Politics, and Persecution

It takes a great deal of bravery to stand up to our enemies, but just as much to stand up to our friends.

—*J.K. Rowling*

A man must not only stand for the right principles, but he must also fight for them. Those who fight for principle can be proud of the friends they've gained and the enemies they've earned.

—*Ezra Taft Benson*

V*al and I decided* early in our marriage to walk our own paths, which led us to homeschool, herbalism, home birth, and eventually to our Butterfly companies. We have felt heaven's confirmation of these important decisions with every step we have taken.

Those around us, however, did not always see our choices in the same positive light. Judgment and gossip sometimes grew into ostracism and persecution. Our family had to bear the maltreatment meted out by those who were unwilling to make room for broader ways of thinking.

Thankfully, homeschooling children is much more common today than it was decades ago when Val and I sometimes felt like pioneers. The same can be said for using herbs and having babies at home; they do not seem to be as strange or suspect as they once were.

I love my neighbors and feel great appreciation for many of them. Our valley is home to so many good-hearted people, and I would not have wanted to raise our children anywhere else. This place and these people are home to us—and will always be so.

I want to relate this part of my history with as much candor and gentleness as possible. I certainly do not want to cause undue stress to anyone, even those who sometimes may have treated us less than kindly. Nor do I want to invite any sort of wrath on our children and grandchildren. With very few exceptions, my grandchildren have been very well treated. I will be forever grateful to those who have been kind and inclusive.

In writing this chapter, I will draw again from personal journal entries and will skip between how I wrote it at the time and how I see the situation now, with nearly fifteen years of hindsight.

Sunday, February 20, 2005

Today has been an emotional day for me, so much so that I finally had to leave Relief Society meeting [women's meeting at our church] *because I couldn't stop crying.*

I have felt for much of my life that I really don't fit in well in the area in which we have chosen to live out our lives. I am not sure, at least not today, that I made it a matter of prayer when we decided to move "home" all those years ago. I do know that, since then, our prayers about going somewhere else have been answered with the counsel to stay.

We have chosen to go in directions that are different from our neighbors. Home birth, my becoming a midwife, homeschooling our children, herbs, homeopathics, foot zoning, and the conservative political ideas we hold are just a few of the things that we seem to do very differently from our neighbors.

A special priesthood blessing that I received instructs me to "develop my talents and abilities" and "become an outstanding woman in Zion."

What I didn't realize when I was younger and walking the "middle of the middle of the road," however, was that by developing these talents, it would put me so far out of step with my neighbors.

Most of what I do every day is so foreign to the women around me that I can't even make it part of a simple conversation. Some days it is very lonely, and other days, it just plain hurts! I thought that I had gotten used to the loneliness and that, maybe, some of my neighbors were adjusting to and even enjoying my company a little bit. I have let myself pretend lately that the situation is different than it has been in the past. This pretense has made me happier.

But an incident this week—really a series of incidents leading up to one bigger one—has brought to my attention that nothing is really different at all. I am who I am, and I do what I do because I have followed the guidance of the Spirit to the best of my ability. I don't know all of the reasons why this walk has been required of me. I am both thankful for the things that I know and saddened that it places me somewhat at odds with my neighbors.

Long ago, Heaven made it clear to Val and I that we would need to live our lives with some "paranoia" if we were to be safe. If our homeschool was going to survive and we were to maintain the right to have our children born at home, we would have to limit what other people (even our own parents and siblings) knew about us.

We, therefore, kept our decisions and actions private as much as we could, and not because we were doing anything illegal, unbecoming, or dangerous. We had confidence that not going to doctors as often as our neighbors went would not endanger our children. Even though birth at home is historically safer than birth in a hospital, we were quite aware that some considered becoming a midwife to be too crazy. Our choices made some people very uncomfortable, so we tended not to share much information, and then, of course, we would be seen as deliberately isolating ourselves. When we were trying something new that was different than the cultural norm in our area, it would have been nice if the condemnation could have waited at least until the results were in.

We wanted to keep our family safe, in the multifaceted meanings of that word. Being *safe* can be as simple as avoiding being the hottest topic on the family or community grapevines. Subtle misinformation can have a devastating effect on a person's reputation and financial well-being. When these stories circulate throughout extended family, they can be particularly destructive.

Sunday, February 20, 2005 (cont.)

The need for paranoia has been a difficult lesson to learn. I have often forgotten to consider it in the past, but it has become almost second nature to me now; however, recently I have let my guard slip too much once again.

The events of the past few weeks and the past day or two, particularly, have brought to my attention that nothing has really changed after all. The fact is, there are some neighbors who seem to dislike me for who I am and would likely feel no remorse for any amount of trouble and inconvenience they could cause me and mine, so long as they could do it legally. Obeying the letter of the law seems to be very important to them; the spirit of the law, such as charity and kindness toward this family, not so much!

I have sometimes been remiss in following the counsel of the Lord in seeking His approval and not the approval and well wishes of my neighbors. I must shape up in this regard, right now. I must not forget the way things really are and the way they have been. It has not been so long ago that some homeschool families were seriously persecuted in this state, even though they were breaking no laws.

Likewise, many homeopathic physicians throughout history have had remarkable "cure" rates when compared to standard medicine. Nevertheless, this has often not kept them out of trouble with their governments or even kept some of them out of jail. I'm not sure I have the temperament, really, to be a pioneer! But it seems to be what I am meant to be.

> *We are different. We do things differently. The fact that I often relieve suffering, prevent undue drug consumption and side effects, and sometimes even save lives will not likely keep some of my neighbors from "persecuting" me and mine if they feel like it and can! Not all my neighbors. Most people, however, fear what they do not understand, and people often behave very strangely and unkindly when they are afraid!*

Val remembers our family going to church and sitting in an available pew and watching as people near us got up and moved away without speaking a word. At first, we thought it just a random action. Then we noted that for certain families such behavior was a regular occurrence.

Our children were often targeted with harassment because they were homeschooled. We would tell them, "Everybody gets picked on for something, so it might as well be for being homeschooled. Please, just do not ever be guilty of such behavior yourselves." I don't pretend they always took our words to heart, although they did repeat this advice back to us at times. I wonder if I really understood at the time the toll that such teasing and ostracism was taking on some of them.

Some of the worst offenders were adults, and one particular incident still makes me angry. Valaree once overhead our church congregation's youth leader tell her daughter not to associate with "that homeschooled girl" from the unconventional family. Up until then, Valaree had considered the daughter to be her friend and the leader to be someone she could count on and confide in. In the wake of that, Valaree understandably struggled with attending church activities for some time. Luckily, she endured.

As Val's health gradually improved, he could take on more money-earning work projects. Our improved finances allowed us to buy a newer vehicle, benefitting from Grandma Westover's bargaining skills. I made some velvety seat covers for this new station wagon. How I loved that little car.

Not long after the purchase, I took our children on a trip to Ogden,

Utah, but we only got partway there before the new car refused to run. I had no mobile phone in those days, so after a lengthy walk, I found a phone and called Val. When he arrived, the car started right up and ran fine. Baffled, he drove it around for a few minutes, then got back into his truck and returned home. We made it to Ogden, but the car stopped running again on the way back home. The children and I took another walk, called, and once again, the car ran just fine when Val got there.

This happened several more times before Val eventually gave the engine a complete once-over and discovered that someone had dumped sugar into the gas tank. It was impossible to clean it up sufficiently to eliminate the problem. We even tried converting it to propane, but that didn't work either as too much damage had already been done. I was heartbroken the day we hauled that beautiful little car to the salvage yard. It was quite some time before we could afford a replacement.

We couldn't help but ask ourselves, *Who would do such a thing to a family that had faced the struggles we had because of Val's health issues?* I couldn't think of anyone we had harmed or offended to deserve such retribution and began considering nearly everyone around me with a jaundiced eye. If we seem to be paranoid sometimes, we have come by such feelings honestly. I could share other similar stories.

The following entry in my journal caught my eye because it mentions witches. I have been called a witch more than once because of my herbal remedies—often in jest by Val and children, but more harshly by others.

One of my friends told me about a powerful lesson recently taught in her daughter's high school class. They were learning about the Salem witch trials, and their teacher told them they were going to play a game.

"I'm going to come around and whisper to each of you whether you are a witch or a normal person. Your goal is to build the largest group possible that does NOT have a witch in it. At the end of the allotted time, any group found to include a witch will get a failing grade."

The teens dove in to grilling each other. One larger group formed, but most broke into smaller, exclusive groups, turning away anyone they thought gave off even a hint of "witch" guilt.

"Okay," the teacher said. "You've got your groups formed. Time to find out who fails. All witches, raise your hands." No one raised a hand. The kids were confused and told the teacher he'd messed up the game.

"Did I?" the teacher asked. "Was anyone in Salem an actual witch? Or did everyone just believe what they'd been told?"

There never were any evil witches in our beautiful valley either, except for the periodic "evil witches" of gossip and mistreatment.

Please don't misunderstand and believe that our lives were a continual round of persecution. Some neighbors always offered kind and thoughtful service, especially after Val was seriously burned. We especially appreciated gifts of meals, garden produce, and treats. A dear friend, who is also our lawyer, showed up to finish a half-constructed greenhouse that was in danger of tumbling over. A neighbor sent over an entire case of blue hospital pads, and another who is a nurse brought a container of expensive burn salve. We only used a little bit of it, but that bit helped a lot and was much appreciated.

One particular gesture really touched my heart. A sweet widowed woman whom we knew lived on a very modest fixed income sent a $5.00 check, which reminded me of the Bible story of the widow's mite. I chose not to cash the check, but she called me to task for not doing so, and even sent another check in case I couldn't find the first one. She sent us a five-dollar check every month until she could see that Val was back up and getting around.

Many neighbors expressed their concern for Val, and most managed to avoid intimating that we were daft for dealing with a condition so serious at home. I felt more loved and supported than I had ever felt before.

Val's injuries made his construction work too difficult to return to. Many of our neighbors expressed delight to see that Butterfly Express was prospering and could provide us with a living. Such gracious comments lifted our spirits when they were most in need of lifting.

Success and Jealousy

Despite many of our neighbors wishing us well, not everyone seemed to cheer our success. We now had a little money to spare and were driving decent vehicles. We were employing local residents and paying them well. When our political conservatism involved us in a local election and in the debate over upgrading the Clifton city water system, we again found ourselves unpopular with some in the community.

Some influential citizens apparently couldn't keep people—and their differing opinions—separate, and made a list of those they considered "undesirable," and ought to be "encouraged" to leave the area. Westovers were on that list. Several people who had seen the list confirmed its existence. That, and subsequent political maneuvering, left us feeling confident that we were not imagining the harassment.

It was a rare month when the city council meetings failed to discuss what Val Westover was up to. One council member privately explained to us that others on the council worried that, with a little money behind us and land to expand on, we posed a danger to the community. Perhaps they feared we would bring in more strange homeschool, herbal families that might spoil the community. Or perhaps it could all be traced to the green-eyed monster of envy.

The Trailer House

Luke and his family had been living in a nice trailer house for about two years, one that could not be seen well from the road that runs by our farm. He had recently been blinded in one eye in a paintball accident, his wife was caring for their new baby, and they were striving to pay off medical bills from the early births of their twin boys.

One day, an eviction notice for the trailer arrived that was addressed to Val and me. This was odd since we didn't own the trailer or the land it sat on. And the timing could not have been worse for Luke and his family.

Eventually, we were informed that the matter was being dropped, but we soon heard from county officials instead. After unnecessary stress, hassle, and legal bills, it was finally settled in the end.

Fire Hydrants

Clifton city had installed a series of new fire hydrants, and within a short time three had been knocked over. The county sheriff came to investigate. A complaint was issued against Val. No hydrant sat on our property, nor were we the closest property owner to the damaged hydrants. Trucks do traverse the driveway daily leading to our business, but none come close to the hydrant. No evidence was found to indicate our, or any trucker's, involvement, so the sheriff dropped the matter.

Interestingly, families who lived close to the other damaged hydrants were not questioned by the sheriff or expected to pay for damages. This sort of behavior seemed to be reserved just for us.

Zoning Ordinances

Our little community is very rural and quite small, and a need for zoning ordinances had never been an issue. The Clifton city council, which included neighbors and members of our church congregation, attempted to pass a new zoning ordinance that would prohibit home-based businesses, applied retroactively. Ours was the only such business at the time. We had to get our lawyer involved to stop this effort to put us out of business.

One day, a certain highly respected council member walked out of a council meeting after saying she would never participate in another meeting in which Val Westover's name was mentioned. She said that she had seen more than enough persecution of this good man and his family. Persecution by the city council stopped, in large part due to the courage and common sense of this one member.

Even though just a few city officials led this particular bout of harassment, they nevertheless managed to create something of a mob mentality and stir up contention in our little community. The animosity they fostered toward us was distressing and made growing a business and financially surviving Val's injuries far more difficult than they should have been.

> Those who can make you believe absurdities,
> can make you commit atrocities.
> —*Voltaire*

Fight for Property Rights

I believe freedom is a cause worth fighting for. And strange as it may seem, sometimes we may still need to fight for it. In 2014, our county government was directly jeopardizing our property rights. This created more than four years of debilitating stress and had serious financial ramifications. More than that, though, it directly challenged our freedom. The father of our United States Constitution, James Madison, claimed that property rights and religious freedom are inseparable. If we cannot trust our local governments to respect those rights, where are we to turn?

In 2014 our business was booming. Val and I realized we needed a major expansion if we were to keep up with the ever-growing demand for Butterfly Express products. The planned expansion of our warehouse required improved power, so we contracted with Rocky Mountain Power to install expanded service. The power company required an easement over the property where the new power lines would run.

After the new electrical equipment had been installed at a cost of nearly $37,000, a close neighbor who was also a county employee sent a letter to Rocky Mountain Power falsely accusing us of not owning the property that our home, farm, and business occupy, or the land for which we had just granted the easement. She sent the letter from the county, with full authority from her boss, but without his adequate supervision and review.

Naturally, the power company needed this matter cleared up in order to keep the newly installed equipment in place and operational. It took nearly six months of expensive, time-consuming, and traumatic litigation to get the county to finally agree that they were wrong and that we had indeed owned the property in question when the letter to Rocky Mountain Power had been sent.

Even if there had there been a legitimate concern, a more reasonable course of action would have been for the county official—our neighbor—to contact us with any irregularity she thought she had found. If there had been an issue with the purchase of our property from Val's parents years before, this would have given us the opportunity to correct it. As a county employee, treating county residents fairly and courteously should have been a basic part of her job description. Government employees should strive daily to follow the letter—and spirit—of the law as outlined by the legislature.

The founders of our nation, drawing on the wisdom of such men as John Locke and others well versed in political theory, understood that certain pillars of freedom must be maintained if we are to remain a free and self-determining people. Among these are "life, liberty, and property." This unnecessary and unfounded slander of title—in addition to the misguided zoning effort aimed only at us—clearly interfered with our property rights.

Ezra Taft Benson, who served in Eisenhower's cabinet and later as president of our church, said, "While I do not believe in stepping out of the path of duty to pick up a cross I don't need, a man is a coward who refuses to pick up a cross that clearly lies within his path."

Local government officials sometimes allow personal grievances to become official ones, and in their official capacity they are often protected from personal liability for such petty governance. The adage "You can't beat city hall" has its roots in reality. The actions of our neighbor, backed as they were by our county government, can be seen as an incursion on freedom—a cross placed clearly in our path that both duty and courage required us to pick up and bear.

Val and I try very hard to live our lives according to the principles we believe in. We are not bullies prone to litigate, but at the same time we are not cowards. Nor are we afraid to stand up and be counted when we see something that is not right. Many citizens do not have the resources to stand and fight government overreach and poor conduct. We wondered who would take up this battle if we were not willing to do so.

Millions of immigrants have come to this country to have the right to own property and control their destiny. We believe it was worth the fight to try to ensure that governments respect individual property rights.

In our case, the Idaho state legislature had already recognized that some local governments were acting outside of the law. They passed legislation in an attempt to curb such a willful lack of concern for the rights and welfare of their citizens. The legislature also sought to balance the need for local leaders to be able to govern without fear of personal liability, with needed safeguards against government excesses. Newly passed laws required that legal damages for such government excesses be paid by the local county or city budget. The intent was for local governments to have financial "skin in the game" should they be brought into court as the result of their unlawful actions.

Citing this statute, our lawyer argued that the county could not hide behind their insurance company and were required to pay out of their own budget the legal fees we had incurred. Curiously, and confusingly, the court ruled that we—the citizens who had been injured by the unlawful conduct of a county official—could not challenge the county's use of its insurance policy. In other words, the courts upheld the county's hiding behind a large insurance company, meaning the county would not be required to pay themselves as specified by the legislature.

This was disappointing, as we had hoped for a more straightforward victory in maintaining freedom and following the statute. But we had done our best. We hope that our state legislature may see that further action is needed to curb local government excesses. They need to make clear their intent that injured citizens be able to act as private attorneys general (private citizens acting for the public good) in order to enforce the intent of the legislature and be able to seek redress for government wrongdoing.

> All the rights secured to the citizens under the Constitution are worth nothing, and a mere bubble, except guaranteed to them by an independent and virtuous Judiciary.
>
> —*Andrew Jackson*

From this expensive and traumatic experience, we learned that in Idaho there are no absolute property rights. With the stroke of a pen, a secretary in a government office can wipe out people's right to control their own property—without due process of law. We learned that some in our county would go to any length to avoid admitting fault and taking responsibility for the actions of their employees. We learned that a citizen has little or no effective recourse in obtaining justice from the misconduct of county officials.

This was a heavy and painful jolt of reality when it comes to justice and property rights in our county. I hope we have learned the lessons well.

I love my neighbors and cannot think of one whom I would not defend. Recent events, however, have made it easier to tell our many friends from our few enemies: our friends defend us. My grandmother taught me the following poem, the spirit of which I have tried to follow. Sometimes I succeeded; sometimes I failed. Our son Luke and his wife live this principle very well:

> He drew a circle that shut me out—
> Heretic, rebel, a thing to flout.
> But love and I had the wit to win:
> We drew a circle and took him In!
>
> —*Edwin Markham*

There were neighbors and their children who never participated in this kind of behavior. I will forever appreciate these families and what their children were taught and then lived. A couple of particular families come to mind because they have hearts of gold and live according to what they believe about kindness and judgment of others. The next generation in these families behave much the same.

If I am to be honest with myself, I have to admit that, when I was able to set aside my own anger and hurt and respond with love and caring, things seemed to get a little better, at least for short periods of time. I do know that when I do this, my heart heals and I am happier. Certainly, Val would tell you that I am easier to live with at those times.

CHAPTER TWENTY-SEVEN

Empty Nest

Let your dreams be your wings,
and your heart be your guide.
—*Unknown*

The most important thing a father can do
for his children is to love their mother.
—*Theodore Hesburgh*

T*he title of this chapter, Empty Nest,* is completely facetious! I have never experienced anything even vaguely resembling an "empty nest." The only way Val and I will ever experience an empty nest will be if we leave home and live in a small apartment far away. I would never want an empty nest to last any longer than it takes to serve a mission myself. The title, *Empty Nest,* refers to our children leaving home, especially the two youngest.

The new century brought many changes as our younger children left home and grandchildren were added to the family. The older boys had already left home for missions, college, jobs, or marriages. Valaree had left for college a couple of years earlier and then got married in 2001. Right after her wedding, Richard left on his mission. Luke, having shown very little interest in girls up to this point, met and married the girl of his dreams. Then Tara left for BYU.

Perhaps, instead of calling this chapter *Empty Nest*, I should have called it *The Demise of a Homeschool.* I knew that I would miss having our children at home, learning. I had seen my mother and other women pass through the stage of life where children leave home and thought I understood it. I was quite unprepared, however, for how badly the end of our homeschooling days would feel. Tara's going—the last child leaving—was more difficult for me than I had expected it to be. Building Butterfly Express didn't quite compensate for no longer teaching our children every day.

As the oldest, Tony was the first to leave home. I believe that his leaving was even harder on Val than it was on me. I had initially thought that after dropping Tony off at the Missionary Training Center in Provo, Utah, we would spend some time shopping or attending the temple on our way home. But as we pulled away Val said, "Let's just go home. I need to hug a child." I felt exactly the same way. It didn't get any easier as each subsequent child left.

When Travis left home and set up his own place, at times he would work on his own projects, and other times he was here working with his father on construction projects. He was home with us for a short while after his head injury. So, his leaving felt less abrupt and final than Tony's.

Sending Luke to far-away Australia to serve his church mission was even more difficult than when Tyler had left for Venezuela two years before. And since we have many grandchildren, I suspect we will have to endure many more such partings, and they may not get any easier.

The five older children were off on their own and doing well. I had confidence that our homeschool had given them a strong foundation. I felt that I could relax and enjoy these last two children more, giving them more freedom, including more support in pursuing their own dreams and goals.

Richard and Tara are particularly gifted, among our children, with musical ability and theatrical talent. Their singing voices are phenomenal. As the only two still at home, Richard and Tara had more opportunities for activities like music, dance, and theater. The three of us spent a great deal of time running to and from music lessons, play practices, plays, and performances all over the valley. We were having the time of our lives enjoying their talents and in hot pursuit of Tara's musical ambitions. I wish we had been able to provide similar opportunities for our older children as well.

Richard left on his mission just after Valaree's wedding, and when he returned two years later, he went right off to college. During Richard's first semester, being Richard, he obsessively studied certain textbooks that caught his interest from cover to cover. Then he suddenly woke up to the fact that midterms would be held in *all* his classes. So he did some cramming of the subjects and books he had not yet touched and did quite well on his tests.

Richard had always learned best by obsessively focusing on one subject at a time until he had grasped everything he wanted to know. While that method may work well in a homeschool setting, it is not as effective in public education or at the college level. He made more appropriate college study habits after that. Richard did very well academically and in other ways during the rest of his many years of higher education.

Tara is and always has been talented, beautiful, and intelligent. We seemed to enjoy even more memorable times together when the other six children had left home. This youngest daughter was a great joy to me, and I remember with fondness those good days and the relationship we shared. I find those memories a comforting place to visit.

It was particularly challenging to get Tara to focus on her education because she was so singularly interested in music. Her love of music was evident when she and Richard were very small, and they would sit in front of our old record player singing along with a record of *Peter and the Wolf*. Even at their young ages, they were trying to match their voices to the various parts they could hear.

Tara chose to take music and dance classes as a young girl. When she was eleven, she won the starring role in *Annie* with a local theater company. Val was hilarious as a proud "stage papa." He had so much fun watching her excel, and we all thoroughly enjoyed the production.

School seemed to be a bother and a chore for Tara, and she was interested in few things outside of music and performing. She loved reading J. K. Rowling's *Harry Potter* series, so I read the entire series myself, just to keep up with conversations between Tara and her friend on the way to voice lessons. Whenever Tara was in the car with Richard on the way to lessons and performances, he often bombarded her with whatever subject he was obsessively studying at the moment. One could argue that these unavoidable onslaughts may have indirectly helped in Tara's education.

TARA WESTOVER, daughter of Val and LaRee Westover, was awarded the Young Womanhood Recognition Award in July of 2003. She is a member of Clifton Second Ward.

Article on Tara in the local newspaper

As a teen, Tara placed a sticky note on her mirrored closet door that said: "I'm going." She was determined to go to college when the time came. Unlike her siblings, her only experience with public school was when she participated in music-related activities. Her sticky note came down the very day she received her acceptance letter and scholarship notification from Brigham Young University just a few weeks before her seventeenth birthday.

She left for BYU the day after New Year's; she was so excited to be starting on her dream that she couldn't wait even one more day. At just barely seventeen, she seemed so young to me.

Despite the inordinate amount of time she spent in plays and musical pursuits, Tara was as well prepared intellectually and educationally as any student I have ever known. My insisting that she puzzle things out and learn to think for herself, instead of wheedling me or a sibling into doing the thinking for her, is something I am proud of. I believe this insistence with each of our children, as stressful as it was to follow at the time, played a significant role in the many successful endeavors that she and our other children have undertaken since leaving home.

Tara leaving for BYU left a particularly large hole in our hearts. But the house was by no means quiet or empty, as our Butterfly Express business had started to grow. Valaree was often there, as well as her young children. Luke and his growing family moved closer to us. And employees were milling about as we were running the business from our home.

Worry—The Lot of a Mother When Her Children Leave Home

As our children left home, I worried as much—and possibly more—about them as I had when they were living under my roof. Upon realizing that my mother and Val's mother had gone through the same thing, I felt more compassion and understanding for them.

One of the things that concerned me most was whether these young people would eat regularly and nutritiously on their own. They had been well taught, but would they abandon—to the detriment of their health—the good habits they had learned? I need not have worried about my boys, as all are good cooks, and a couple of them pride themselves on their cooking skills. Valaree realized—after some backsliding—that good nutrition was key to feeling good and doing well in school. Valaree does an excellent job feeding her family and teaching them how to cook competently.

Valaree recently gave me a book about the nutrition and health benefits of freshly ground flour. Did you know that when freshly ground, whole grain flour has 40 of the 44 nutrients considered essential to good health? Only four essential nutrients are lacking in adequate amounts: vitamins A, C, and D and the amino acid lysine. Unfortunately, whole grain flour—even when refrigerated in air-tight containers—loses much of its nutritional value in less than an hour. The oil-rich portions of the nutrient-filled germ rapidly become rancid and bitter. Commercially milled flours, even when labeled whole grain, have had the bran and the germ removed to extend their shelf life and keep this bitter flavor to a minimum, but this also reduces the nutritional value.

When our children were still at home, we made pancakes with freshly ground flour most mornings. We placed wheat in the top of the grinder the night before, and the next morning while the wheat was grinding we would heat the griddle. It was sometimes a challenge to cook the pancakes fast enough to keep up with seven hungry children and their parents.

While Tony was on his mission, he met someone whom he invited to stay with us for a few days. Our visitor smiled with humor and appreciation when we served him pancakes made with freshly ground whole wheat flour on his first morning, as Tony had told him to expect them at least twice if he stayed three days.

Tara at BYU

Although only seventeen when she left for college, in typical Tara fashion she dove right in, excelled in her coursework, and was moving at almost breakneck speed toward her goals.

Just as I had more time to support our younger children's musical pursuits, I also had more time to visit them during their college years. With her encouragement, I visited Tara often during her years at BYU. It was great fun, and on most visits, we shopped until I dropped. I suspect I needed these visits more than she did, as I missed her and loved taking a day away to be together.

Originally, Tara had entered BYU intending to major in music and fine-tune her vocal talent. As I recall, she was advised to delay auditioning with the music department for a year or more, when she would be older and her voice more mature and less likely to be damaged by the rigors of the program. But before even the first year had passed, she had discovered a new passion in history.

Tara describes herself as completely lost in the world of BYU. I can appreciate at least some of those feelings as I felt somewhat lost at BYU in my own early days, even though I had been somewhat of a high-school success story with outstanding grades, extracurricular activities, earned college credits, and scholarship offers at graduation.

My first test-taking experience at BYU was in a botany class, and I thought I had studied more than sufficiently and expected to ace it; after all, I always aced tests. When I opened the test sheets, however, there were pictures of plants with blank labels, and I was expected to know the name of each part of the plant and how it reproduced itself. I had no clue about much of it. I had managed to learn the name of each plant, the basic family to which it belonged, and the habitat it preferred, and I thought that would be enough. It might have been in high school. My 30% score quickly woke me up to the fact that I "wasn't in Kansas" (or my small town in Idaho) anymore. I realized that getting good grades at college was going to take a lot more effort than it had in high school.

I suppose I could ace that same test almost in my sleep these days—in Latin. I could also explain what each plant is used for as an essential oil and as an herb, where it grows in the world, and what time of year is best for harvesting. At any rate, better study habits were born in that class that day. I arranged to retake the test three days later and aced it.

I had a generous scholarship during my first year at BYU. I assumed that as long as my grades were excellent the scholarship would continue. The scholarship renewal application for the following year was inadvertently delivered to the apartment upstairs, and no one bothered to bring it down to where I lived; it sat unopened until someone threw it away. Did my high school counselor fail to prepare me properly? Hard to say, but blame never fixes anything.

Though Tara may have seemed lost in those early days at BYU, I was confident that her innate competitive spirit would not allow her to fail. Whenever I visited or talked with her on the phone, she portrayed herself as happy. Except for food issues, we worried very little about how she was doing out on her own. And home was only a three-hour drive away if she ever needed something.

During the last part of Tara's undergraduate years at BYU, she informed me that she was seeing a therapist for depression. Tara said that the therapist firmly believed that her depression must be tied to some sort of abuse in her past, as it had been for other women he had worked with. The fact that she had no such memories or stories to tell him apparently made little difference.

I have worked with many abused women, sometimes at the request of their doctors or ecclesiastical leaders. I have seen depression up close and over extended periods of time, as well as schizophrenia, bipolar disorder, and very real cases of dissociative identity disorder. I am very familiar with some who grapple with opioid addictions, thyroid issues, and many other things that contribute to or mask themselves as mental health disorders.

Sadly, I have also seen cases of therapist-induced false memories. I know of one therapist who served time in prison for planting memories of nonexistent abuse in women during their treatment for postpartum depression. The results of her deceptive tactics had devastating consequences for these women and their families.

Many of the women who attend my classes are seeking help for health issues, which often includes depression and anxiety. They have previously tried many things to find relief and are desperate for help. In order to understand these complex issues better and offer sound counsel, I have had to study such topics in depth.

I have learned that health problems, poor nutrition, stress, working too hard, striving for a difficult or nearly unattainable goal—even living in violation of one's personal code of ethics—are just as often factors in depressive episodes as they are consequences of abuse.

When I visited Tara's college apartments, I was dismayed at her continuing disinterest in cooking healthy meals. Each girl had her own shelf of food, but it usually contained only meals that were easy to prepare and lacking in real nutrition. With my background, I knew that such a chronic lack of vital vitamins, minerals, and amino acids often leads to ill health, depression, and emotional disturbances.

I had growing concerns about Tara's eating habits and her hard-driving need to achieve perfection in almost every endeavor. And as Tara and I talked in more detail about her sessions with this therapist, I became even more disturbed. His diagnosis of depression was accurate, but I had deep skepticism about his understanding of its roots. The high likelihood the therapist was manipulating her memories worried me greatly. Nevertheless, I began to question the past—and the present, for good measure—just in case there may have been something I had overlooked.

Society has rightly taught us the value of watching for the warning signs of abuse. Val and I watched out for these signs as we raised our seven children, as all parents should. We never ignored even the potential for trouble. For instance, sleepovers were discouraged, and on the rare occasions when they were allowed, they were highly monitored.

I looked first at Tara's relationship with Travis. He had, after all, suffered a serious head injury while Tara was still living at home. Even when looking specifically for it, I saw nothing that caused me concern. Certainly, Tara had never previously indicated any such thing. I had never seen the slightest reluctance on Tara's part to spending time with Travis—just the opposite, actually.

Tara was so good to Travis after his head injury. When she came home from college, she sought him out soon after arriving. Often just the two of them would attend a play, go horseback riding, go shopping, or go swimming—despite my concerns because of Travis's head injury. They were very good friends, enjoyed each other's company, and looked to each other for support. She even went with him on long-haul trucking trips.

No one who knows Travis—not even Travis himself—will tell you that he doesn't have a temper. He had a temper as a child, and both before and after his head injury. He has fought as hard as anyone I have ever seen to master his feelings.

At times, Travis can be belligerent and obnoxious and intimidating. Valaree was working at a local fast-food restaurant in her teen years when a group of young men began harassing her. They would break into her car and give her a hard time at work, making her feel on edge. So Travis went to the restaurant one night, ordered something, and just sat there, making his presence felt. He didn't need to say, "This is my little sister—so back off."

In a debate, Travis can use careful reason and clear logic to win the day as well as anyone. He tends to be stubborn and doesn't easily give up or give in. And he is independent to a fault. He is also one of the kindest and gentlest men I know, deeply loyal, and looks out for the underdog. He is unselfish and does things for others regularly, giving what he has, even if it means there may not be enough left for him. Travis may not be a perfect man, but he is a very good man.

In addition to carefully scrutinizing Travis, I reviewed Tara's interactions with others in all aspects of her life over the years. While I thought I had always kept a wary eye, I analyzed everything anew very carefully. I considered her theater group, church groups, music lessons, friends, and every potential risk factor I could think of.

Then I took a good hard look at Tara's life, both as a child and as the grown woman she was becoming. Even as a child, Tara did not suffer any kind of intimidation from anyone. She did not tolerate any sort of criticism or advice, whether it was helpful or deserved. When asked to clean the fridge, she would throw out nearly everything—even if it was still good and would have been enough for another meal—with a go-ahead-and-comment-if you dare-Mom-and-Dad gleam in her eye.

I know several women who tolerated abuse for years, but when Tara lived at home, she was not of similar temperament. Tara would have fought back—loudly, if necessary—no matter who was involved.

There was a gentleman in our area that sometimes liked to give teenagers a hard time, especially about their driving. He once chewed Tara out for coming too close to his toes, which were hanging over the curbing around some gas pumps. Tara's reaction was to get back in her car, back up a few feet, and steer even closer to his toes when she pulled in the second time. And this was with me sitting in the passenger seat, telling her to be polite. Tara was never one to back down.

I talked to Tara again, extensively, and asked careful questions. I did the same with her sister, Valaree. Questions and more questions. Tara told me nothing of significance. I found nothing.

BYU Graduation

We were proud parents as Tara's graduation from BYU approached. She had done extremely well, and we wanted to celebrate with her. Tara told us that we were welcome to watch her walk across the stage to receive her diploma, but we were not invited to attend awards dinners or the meet-and-greet occasions with her professors and fellow students. Val and I were baffled—and heartbroken. On one visit home just before graduation, Tara rehearsed with her father what he could and could not say to her professors if we happened to meet them. She kept this up for so long we wondered if she was ashamed of us.

After further discussions with Tara, it occurred to me that she had likely been painting her parents to both professors and friends as backward, uneducated, and unintelligent. This may have been done to highlight all she had accomplished—made even more phenomenal because it was done in spite of her strange rural homeschool family. We realized that she had described her childhood as harsh, underprivileged, and even abusive.

This supposition was supported by comments made in a newspaper interview by a visiting professor from England. As closely as I can recall, he reported that Tara, although born to "eccentric" parents had "of *herself*, by *herself*, *made of herself* an historian of renown." The article included no acknowledgment from Tara of her family's contribution to her achievements. Even the many discussions of history, science, and other subjects that were part of our regular mealtimes and other times were given no credit.

At the time, we told ourselves that we should find this amusing rather than insulting, as there was not much to be done anyway. Her BYU days were over, and we did not expect to see these people again.

Despite her behavior, we made plans to attend those events that we were aware of. Tara was being awarded a bachelor's degree, graduating magna cum laude, and was receiving several honors. We were eager to be proud stage parents, just as we had during her childhood and teenage performances. We were so proud of our beautiful, intelligent, and talented daughter. But sadly, we did not get much of a chance to play this role.

We were not told about a certain awards dinner until it was too late for us to arrive in time. Looking back, I can see how our showing up, looking reasonably intelligent and presentable, probably went against her plan. What would her professors think of her and her stories if they conversed with us?

I had learned through hard experience that I should not run out and assist others until they have first asked for my help. This rule seems to apply in many of life's complex relationships. The feeling Val and I got was that she preferred not to have us in her life at this time and for these events.

When Tara left for BYU we had five grandchildren, including a set of twins. By the time she graduated we had fourteen, including another set of twins. My life was full with family and our growing business, but my heart, if not my "nest," felt so empty without her.

I tried to keep communication open between us without forcing my way past her obvious wishes. I wanted to maintain at least some sort of bond in case she ever needed us or changed her mind. Parents never stop being parents. To give space to a person you love so dearly is a very hard thing to do.

I expected to have time on my hands when our children finished their homeschool years—time to paint and journal, to read and work on craft projects. This didn't happen and it hasn't happened much yet. Spending a significant amount of time on these kinds of projects doesn't look likely in the near future, or any future, for that matter. But once in a while, when my heart hurts and I need a different sort of distraction, I turn to these pursuits and find a measure of solace and peace.

CHAPTER TWENTY-EIGHT

Heartbreak

I'm glad we had the times together just to laugh and sing a song, seems like we just got started and then before you know it, the times we had together were gone.

—*Dr. Seuss*

History would be a wonderful thing—if it were only true.

—*Leo Tolstoy*

I*t had been nearly a year and a half* since Val was burned, and we were beginning to recover from that setback, financially and in other ways. Our business was growing. Our youngest daughter was finishing college, and our other six children were doing well. We felt joy and optimism and had more than a little pride in our hearts.

In the summer of 2007, prior to her senior year, Tara had gone with other students to the BYU study abroad program at the University of Cambridge. The following February, she was awarded the prestigious Gates Scholarship, enabling her to return to Cambridge for postgraduate studies. Four of that year's recipients came from Harvard, two each came from Yale and Princeton, and one came from Stanford. Val and I were so proud of her, and Val's eyes glowed as he talked about his daughter with anyone who would listen.

From an article in the *BYU News*, February 27, 2008, Madison Sowell, director of BYU's Honors Program, said: "The Gates Scholarship is to Cambridge what the Rhodes is to Oxford: it immediately identifies Tara as a self-motivated learner, a disciplined and well-rounded person, and a stand-out student in her major." Way to go, daughter! Way to go, homeschooled child! I remember how excited Tara was. She didn't let on that she was also a little bit frightened about this new chapter of her life.

I had mixed feelings about Tara going to England. It was a huge step and she was still so young. England is also a very long way from Idaho! An ocean would lie between me and my baby girl. When I thought about it for too long, there were times that it would be hard to breathe.

It had been hard to send my boys on church missions, but Tara's going to Cambridge seemed to be harder. When young women and men serve a mission for eighteen to twenty-four months, they are focused on their work and are somewhat removed from worldly distractions. They are not, at that point in their lives, making any decisions about their futures. Tara, however, was leaving the conservative BYU ecosystem and going to be in a new environment with different values. She would be making decisions that would impact the direction of her future.

We raised our children to think for themselves, not just to fly but to soar. That did not make it any easier to watch my little girl soar so far away. Knowing what your children are capable of—and knowing that *they* know what they are capable of—is more than a little scary. Young people like that are likely to fly far, far away from home.

Sometime after arriving at Cambridge, Tara called and asked me to go to her personal small storage shed, find her journals, and mail them to her. She told me she had kept both her schoolwork and her journals in the same type of blue notebook and instructed me to open each blue notebook and read a page or two to determine that it was a journal and not a regular college notebook. I took a close friend with me on this assignment, and we dug through totes full of mementos of Tara's life trying to complete this assignment.

One page of one journal I read was an entry written before Tara left, expressing concern about going back to England, and noted that it had been easy to maintain her standards and live by her beliefs when she was with other BYU students, but she wondered how she would manage when she returned to England by herself. She even questioned if it might be a better choice to stay closer to home. I didn't read more of any of her journals than she gave me permission for, and we boxed them up and shipped them to England.

I wondered at the time and I wonder still if Tara wanted me to read that particular entry. I wondered if she wanted me to know who she had been and what she had feared. I wept at the thought then, and I am weeping now.

Tara had once told me during her first weeks as a freshman at BYU that she thought the most important thing a parent could teach a child before they went out into the world was to have confidence in themselves. "There are so many different voices, Mother," she said. "It would be so easy to lose sight of who you are and what is really important." At the time, I believed that she was paying us a compliment about the way we had raised her and her siblings. Tara appeared to be a very confident and self-assured young woman. And I trusted that her self-confidence would help protect her from being manipulated by others, as I had been as a teenager.

Comparing my own young life with hers, I wondered if Tara might also have been driven by a deep need to please and be well thought of. Was her desire to be the best, to shine in music and in plays a small indication of this? In my mind's eye, I could picture her arriving in the sophisticated and scholarly environment of Cambridge wearing the wrong clothes and the wrong shoes, with the wrong educational and family background—at least in her own eyes. And I can genuinely appreciate how playing the innocent child, so wronged by her eccentric parents, might have been used as a cover for any feelings of inadequacy. Traveling with a group of students she didn't know and trying to fit in with others from Ivy League schools must have been intimidating. It would have been so for me.

Perhaps finding herself in a foreign environment with different values contributed to feelings of insecurity. Being unsure of one's personal worth and the validity of one's opinions can make a person vulnerable to the manipulation of others. Did Tara *pose* as a lost soul, out of her element, grateful and eager to be molded, or was she genuinely vulnerable? This question torments me.

Tara tells of a certain professor at Cambridge who significantly helped to remake her into his ideal of the perfect *educated* woman. This professor pursued this course with little regard to the consequences such actions might have on Tara's sense of self or how it might affect relationships with people who were important to Tara.

As explained in a previous chapter, I once found myself trying to be what everyone else wanted me to be. I had appeared to be, in some ways—and truly had been, in other ways—confident and sure of myself during my teen years. Nevertheless, I had fallen victim to manipulation, and the molding of myself into something I really did not want to be. And it nearly destroyed me. The road back to my true self was not easy, and I would not wish that on anyone, and certainly not on our beautiful and talented daughter Tara.

Tara, this professor, and the Cambridge setting reminded me of the play *Pygmalion* that I disliked so in college, where the sculpted woman is left more than a little adrift, neither comfortable and happy in her old life nor content in her new environment. She finds herself estranged from former friends and family and uncomfortable with new acquaintances.

In the play *My Fair Lady*, in a similar way, Eliza Doolittle was not completely pleased with Professor Higgins and the changes he had made in her. Although she appeared presentable and was accepted by society, she was at odds with herself, uncomfortable and out-of-step with both her new world and the one she left behind. And she had questions about the direction her future should take and where she would someday fit.

I find my daughter's infatuation with Pygmalion and her gratitude to her own *sculptor* frightening and very sad. Learning and growing are so much different than being *remade.* As her mother who will always love her, I sincerely hope that she *is* happy. I hope she is finding herself and reaching her own stars and dreams and not the stars and dreams that were created for her during a vulnerable time in her life. Fame and fortune are not the only things that are required for happiness, and sometimes they stand in the way of happiness. The play *Pygmalion* can certainly give one food for a lot of thought.

An Ocean Apart

During my own college days at BYU, I came home nearly every weekend for the first year, but it was not because I was homesick. I came home to be near Val, as he was attending Utah State University, which was not far from my hometown. During the second year, after Val left on his church mission, I came home much less frequently and my parents, wanting me to be happy, were pleased to see me get more involved with college life.

I felt much the same way about Tara visiting home. She was excelling at BYU, which demands a great deal of time and study, and she had a part-time job. Like my parents had been, Val and I were happy she was involved in college life. During her first few years in Cambridge, Tara came home from England about as often as she had from BYU, which didn't seem odd to me at all. She enthusiastically claimed in frequent emails that she loved Cambridge and England. However, the young man she was very fond of was still attending BYU, and she missed him—and perhaps home too. She came home for Christmases, summer visits, and her boyfriend's graduation from BYU, and there was no hint of family strain during those beautiful visits.

When Tara was home with us on our own turf, our relationship and our time together went very well. Early in her Cambridge years, however, we were seeing some of the same signs of Tara not wanting us to visit her as we had seen at BYU. At first, whenever I mentioned our desire to visit her and see the country, her reluctance was low-key, and she would try to discourage us by noting how expensive it would be, or that she was planning to return to Idaho soon anyway, or that because of how busy she was she would have little time to take us sightseeing.

I watched, waited, fretted, and worried. I thought maybe my concerns were resulting from missing Tara. I began wondering what might be happening in her life or what there was about her new environment that she didn't want her parents to see.

We were continuing to recover from the effects of Val's burn; the business was growing into something that could soon support us, yet it was taking every spare moment and every penny we could scrape together to keep up with its growth. But we wanted to see her and her new life so badly. We wanted to meet the people and see the places that she described in her emails home.

Perhaps you are wondering about the title of this chapter, *Heartbreak.* "Heartbreak" is a fitting description for the worsening of my heart issues that occurred during this time as well. It is the best and only way that I can describe the pain of the estrangement that exists today between our beloved youngest daughter and ourselves.

Were the two—my pain at the tension that arose with our daughter and my physical heart problems—related? As a result of a great deal of experience with people over the years, I know that trauma and deep emotions have very definite connections to the physical distress that develops in our bodies.

More than One Kind of Heartbreak

From my journal:

> *About a week before Thanksgiving I came down with a cold, sore throat, and cough. I usually throw these kinds of things off quickly. This one just stayed and stayed, probably because I was out of sorts emotionally. Eventually, as this combination seems to do with me, it began to affect my heart function. There was intermittent pain in my*

chest and left arm, and I would often wake during the night with a pounding headache. If I lay there quietly, breathing deeply, the headache would back off enough and I would decide I was going to be okay.

I prayed to know whether damage was being done to organs. Did I need supplemental oxygen? The answer seemed to be a resounding "No!" At times, the cough and other symptoms appeared to be clearing. My heart, however, only seemed to do well if I moved slowly, was in a reclining position, or was holding still.

Christmas was coming and my heart pains seemed to worsen. With the help of employees and family, I managed to get ready for Christmas, visit some with Tara when she came home, and get a little work done as long as most of it was done sitting down. Walking stairs was getting increasingly difficult, and I was beginning to get worried.

Perhaps, at that last comment, you are saying to yourself, "Beginning to get worried? What is the matter with this woman?"

I had been here before, more than once, and thought I knew how to fix it, yet nothing I tried seemed to be working. The pain was often acute, but when I thought about what Val had gone through with his burn I didn't want to sound like a wimp. I felt like others might be thinking I was just "playing the heart card" to get attention, or get my way, or get left alone, or something, if I complained.

Having your children grow into adults and then assume they can tell you how to live your life can be stressful. I wasn't midwifing anymore, and Val was directing our business, so I was a little perplexed as to who I was supposed to be. Besides, when my heart acts up, my emotions tend to, also.

The family gathered for Christmas Eve, as was our custom. I enjoyed decorating cakes in the shape of trains with my grandchildren. Valaree did most of the work, and I was feeling better and had so much fun spoiling our children and grandchildren with presents that Valaree had helped me purchase.

Someone called and it felt like an emergency, so Val and I left the family party as the grandchildren were being gathered up to be taken home, and we drove to Logan. I was so very tired. When we got back home we saw that Valaree and the other girls had cleaned up the house, which I was grateful for. I did as little as possible and thought as little as possible and slept as much as possible.

On Sunday we went to church and I taught the Sunday School lesson. I was so very tired, and standing there for forty minutes felt so long! On the following Tuesday or Wednesday I finally had enough sense to ask for a priesthood blessing (or had finally reached the right frame of mind where one would help).

Blake Atkin came over to assist Val with that. I recall getting out of the chair by the heater and walking over to the middle of the big room to sit in a chair that Val had placed there. I tried to concentrate on breathing evenly even though my chest hurt so badly and I just wanted to gulp air. There were black spots in my vision and the veins in my neck felt like they might explode. I could feel my heart beating with big, slow thuds. I considered this to be an improvement over the fluttering feeling of a few minutes ago.

Blake poured a drop of consecrated olive oil on my head and, right then, I KNEW my heart was healing. The hard thumping settled into a regular beat and the spots in my vision cleared. After the anointing, my dear husband gave me a blessing. He said several things and then he very calmly and literally rebuked the "illness" and told my heart to heal. He told me that the healing I would experience was my reward—a gift—for a life of trying to be whatever God wanted me to be.

I felt it! It was incredible! I have had many priesthood blessings in my life. Some of them have even resulted in healing from that moment on, but the healing has always come slowly in little hard-won increments. This was not like that. I simply healed from one moment to the next!

Some other promises were made during that blessing.

One—that I would see into my children's hearts. I remember thinking that I didn't want to. I knew that me "seeing into their hearts" was bound to annoy the daylights out of most of them! Our children can be more than a little private about their thoughts and feelings! Travis once told me I should not check his math homework because it was his personal thoughts!

I was assured in almost audible words that refusing this gift of the Spirit, when given, was NOT the way to maintain the healing that I just experienced, and that I NEEDED to see into my children's hearts badly. Sorry, children.

Some of what I have seen is just as painful as I thought it would be. I have seen in each of your hearts (the ones that didn't already tell me verbally on their own) the sentiment that mom should mind her own business and stay out of things, and I am trying to do that. A conundrum. See into your hearts but mind my own business.

But some of what I have seen is inspiring. What I have learned is that the insides of our children's hearts are amazing places! Yes, there is dislike of some of my recent actions, but there is a lot of faith, a lot of love, a lot of pain, and many other things there as well. What amazing children I have been blessed with!

Anyway, promise two—I would be able to see important glimpses of the future. The reference to my seeing the future seems to be more to recognize that I do see what is coming quite often but that I, too often, don't trust what I know. I do not always act on such inspiration and guidance as I should.

The rest of the fulfillment of this part of the blessing has been a series of very personal experiences. I have recorded them in a very private place. Maybe I will share them with our children someday.

My dear husband said "Amen." I could see light glowing from his hands as he removed them from my head. I stood up to hug him and thank Brother Atkin. There was no dizziness. I turned and walked across the room. There was no pain, no black spaces in my vision, no need to gulp air. I felt great. To test this, I went downstairs and back up—about six times, the last several at a dead run.

I have had no pain or shortness of breath or anything since. I get strange sensations in my chest sometimes. It is like the entire heart muscle is changing, opening, turning somehow. When I tried the treadmill the next day, I got tired, but it was a nice kind of tired—the tired a person experiences when they exercise, especially if they have not done so for a while. I still feel really good. I am craving and eating chocolate and gaining back a little bit of weight and getting mad about it, but that is another story!

I have never in my life felt such a profound and immediate healing. The emotional and spiritual insights—and the glimpses into our children's hearts and into the future—have been a struggle. I hope I am finding peace and some direction here and that there can be healing, forgiveness, and peace in this family.

I feel very keenly the need for this family to stand together in the difficulties that life throws at every human soul. Trust me on this, if you can trust me on nothing else. This I know. But you children will have to do it in your own way and in your own time.

Living worthy of this blessing has been my goal and my quest for these last eight years. I ask myself every day if I am living worthy of this blessing. Am I receiving it to the degree and in the way that it was given? Sometimes I have been more successful at this than at other times.

Since I no longer had our children home with me, I thought that, perhaps, seeing into their hearts would prove to be a blessing. I am not sure it always has been. But I try to be grateful for it nonetheless.

Do I know my youngest daughter's heart? I have tried with all my heart and soul to keep communications between us open over the years. It has not always been easy. I have wondered, at times, if these communications have been good for either of us. But the God I love knows her and He loves her even more than I do. I pray that He has His eyes upon her and that He blesses and comforts her and that, someday, somehow, He brings her home to us again.

Christmas that year, 2011, was an amazing year of family parties. I treasure the pictures we have of everyone together, looking so happy. I look at these pictures and see our family playing games with each other and having fun. We made some amazing gingerbread houses. Thomas, our little grandson who was born so prematurely, looks healthy and happy. Val looks so good. Tara looks very happy to be home. There are grandchildren running about everywhere and so many of my homemade Christmas socks in our family lineup.

So many delightful memories and so many more good times to look forward to, I thought at the time. I didn't have the tiniest inkling that this would be the last of such happy family Christmases we would spend together. By the following Christmas, things were decidedly strained between us and our daughter and her boyfriend, who was now living in England. Visits home became less frequent and then ceased altogether.

CHAPTER TWENTY-NINE

Chasm

My heart is bigger than the distance between us.
—*Unknown*

The best thing to hold onto in life is each other.
—*Audrey Hepburn*

When you want to help people, you tell them the truth.
When you want to help yourself,
you tell them what they want to hear.
—*Thomas Sowell*

I*n the months following* this memorable Christmas with our entire family, there was a shift in our relationship with Tara. She hedged again when we said we were seriously considering flying to England. For a time, she avoided speaking with me and would only speak with Val. She sent him gifts from her visit to Israel, and her emails came to him.

Curiously, after some time, it switched. Tara began painting her father as the bad guy and I was cast as the one with the sympathetic ear. Tara subsequently asked if I would ever consider coming to her wedding without Val, if such an event should occur. She had to know that the very suggestion would hurt us both and make me angry. Was that her intent? It appeared Val and I were being played against each other, and I recalled times when Tara had worked family dynamics in similar ways to get her way on a certain thing.

I tended to downplay the worst of this to Val, thinking it better to insulate this man who had been through so much with his burns, the loss of some of the dexterity of his hands, and being unable to continue the construction business that had been his life. Besides, Tara had broken his heart once by not wanting us at her graduation, and I didn't want him to hurt like that again. This, however, was a mistake on my part. I should have demanded, for both of us, the respect we had earned many times over; I should have stood shoulder to shoulder as a team with my husband.

Whenever Tara was visiting from Cambridge, she would ask me to meet up with her—but without her father. I told Val that I really wanted to see her, despite the ultimatum. He did not agree; I went ahead anyway. I am not proud of the way I handled the situation. I would learn, to my sorrow, that doing the wrong thing even for what seemed like good reasons, would not turn out well.

Such visits with Tara were often tense. One moment we would be shopping and she would be happily trying on clothes, then, like a change of a scene on a stage, she would erupt, ranting and raving at me. We had not done enough for our children; we should not have homeschooled; our religious beliefs were all wrong; her father was too critical; we expected too much of our children; her father was overbearing; I was a mouse. The things she claimed did not match the reality of our family life, past or present. I was mystified and hurt, and these rants left me emotionally drained.

I remember one visit in particular. It was Christmastime and a winter storm had set in. Tara was in Salt Lake City visiting friends for the holiday season. As I prepared to drive to Salt Lake to see her, I saw the heartbreak in Val's eyes as I prepared to meet the beloved daughter that he missed so much without him once again. I also saw the concern he had for me, driving in that weather alone. Once again, against my own better judgment and in the face of my Val's unspoken pain, I went anyway.

Tara and I shopped and then went out to dinner. We talked and we laughed. After dinner we sat in my car to visit, which was parked next to her rental car in the restaurant parking lot just off the I-15 freeway. Tara started to rail at me once again; I tried to get a word in edgewise. She cried; I cried. She screamed at me for always trying to defend Val and myself. *Was she right? Was this denial on my part? No.* I had been present for so many of the events she was retelling with such bitterness, and the things she was claiming had no basis in reality.

She continued pouring out her feelings as if she couldn't stop. Suddenly, the power went out everywhere we could see; even nearby streetlights went dark. The outside world now felt as dark as our conversation, as dark as the future of our relationship appeared to be. Only the freeway offered any beacon. The freeway ramp was only a couple of city blocks away, and I ached—body and soul—to reach the light. I told Tara that I was going to try to get to the freeway and head home before the lights went out there too.

She calmed in a heartbeat and thanked me for listening to her, for "understanding." I was mystified, as I had heard little that I could understand or relate to the reality of our lives. And I could not see how such a diatribe had done either of us any good.

I carefully drove home through the winter storm, exhausted emotionally and physically and frightened for our daughter. Over the next few weeks we received a couple of dismaying emails that were very similar to her tirade that night.

Tara and I would repeat this scene a few more times before I decided that I would no longer meet with her if Val was not also welcome to come. To me, much of these visits and certainly her tirades seemed to be indications of something very awry in Tara's life. Was her boyfriend, who was now with her in England, attempting to isolate Tara from her family little by little—similar to what my former boyfriend attempted to do?

I asked myself if I was seeing signs of the early stages of a mental breakdown. I worried about her then; I worry about her now. I had no idea what to do to help my daughter, and I am discouraged to admit that in many ways I still don't.

During what would be her last visit home, Tara accused her brother Travis of being physically violent and intimidating toward her, yet she provided no details and claimed not to have any memories of these actions herself, only her former therapist's opinions. I remembered the therapist at BYU who had assumed and then tried to convince Tara that her depression must be the result of repressed abuse. We again asked her for details, but we received none, not a single detail. Not until her memoir was published.

We thought that a sit-down discussion with Val, myself, Tara, and Travis might be a good place to start, and so we discussed the idea with Tara privately. Her father's words were full of gentleness and concern. He wanted to do what was right. He wanted the best outcome for both his children.

Tara and Travis's relationship over the years had been especially meaningful and important to them both. They had spent so much time together, and Tara had never shown any fear of him. We felt Travis had the right to hear and respond to the accusations, so the four of us met together. It seemed the best thing to do.

This meeting went poorly. Tara would hardly speak. Travis was devastated. He could not imagine his "sittle lister" accusing him in this way ("sittle lister" was Trav's special name for his little sister). I think his head injury made him question his own memories, at least to some degree. He could not imagine ever having seriously hurt, to the point of abuse of any kind, his beloved little sister. We did not know what to do in the face of Tara's silence.

Soon after Travis left, Tara called her boyfriend from the kitchen. I could not help overhearing her describe the meeting. What she reported to him was not what had just happened at all. I was hearing lies. Her interpretation of this meeting was that of a powerless girl forced into a confrontation she did not want and was not prepared for. I rarely lose my temper or raise my voice, but after she hung up, I did both that night. I regret that I did not remain calm. I doubt it would have helped, but I am sorry regardless. Perhaps if I had remained calm we might have reasoned together, even though there was so little of reason in her claims. Perhaps much of what has occurred since could have been avoided.

Boston

Tara was required to spend a year at a "foreign" university to obtain her master's degree from Cambridge University. She chose Harvard University. By now, Tara had informed us that she had left the church we love. She thought this was momentous news, but we already knew it. She also told us that she was not happy about leaving England, her friends, and her boyfriend, not even for the impressive feat of attending Harvard. We knew that also. Val was concerned that she was putting off her acceptance to Harvard; *imagine anyone doing that*, we thought. He worried about her finding appropriate housing if she waited too long. She assured us that everything would be fine. "I will tell them I am coming," she said, "and all will be taken care of." We realized that our daughter was becoming someone of note in the academic world.

Val and I wanted to visit Tara in Boston and were surprised when she did not seem to strongly object. So we quickly made arrangements and left.

It was a beautiful trip, even though Tara seemed somewhat tense and out of her element in ways I had never seen before. We visited Niagara Falls. I will never forget the look on Tara's face as she reached the top step of the Bunker Hill monument and turned around to check on her mother. There I was on the next step down, almost nose to nose with her. We walked and walked and walked some more, seeing the sights. We shopped. We ate seafood.

Tara even insisted on going with us to some of the sites where events in the early history of our church took place. She was sweet and gracious, even when her father spoke at length of his great love of our religious heritage and the faith and testimony she had chosen to leave behind.

We learned to be quiet in the dorms as everyone is so serious and quiet there. We did not meet a single one of her instructors. On our last night Val offered to give Tara a father's blessing. She declined but said that he could give her some fatherly advice. He was ever so gentle, kind, and loving as he gave her advice based on the lessons life had taught us. I was very proud of him. This little speech lasted no more than five minutes, and then Tara hugged us good-bye. We were concerned about how the next few months would be for her, so far from her friends in England.

As we walked toward the bus station pulling our suitcases behind us, Val turned to me and said, "We have lost our daughter. You realize that, don't you, Hon?" I began to cry. I wondered what he had seen in her eyes and in her heart that I had been so carefully guarding myself against seeing. I wanted to go back inside and put my arms around Tara and never let her go.

Tara had posted some photos of our trip and shared them with me through Facebook. There were pictures of Tara and me laughing into the spray of Niagara Falls; Tara and her father racing up steps cut into the rocks, challenging each other and laughing together; Tara and her father standing with their arms around each other, looking upwards. Their faces shine with joy. The love they have for each other is unmistakable. Tara titled that album "Friends."

We heard nothing for several weeks, and when Tara's next email came it was full of invective, nasty and ranting. She informed us that we had visited her at a very low point in her life, when she had been pulled away from friends, from England, from her boyfriend, and from the life she loved at Cambridge. We were aware she was having a hard time, and that was one of the main reasons for our visit; we wanted to support her during this difficult season.

She said that we had come offering only criticism when she had needed solace. She called her father horrible names and informed us that she never intended to see us again; she would never come home again. I was flabbergasted and could not believe her threat was serious.

I felt the three of us had all had a good time, that we had built bridges, and so I could not understand how she could be feeling this way. Her description of us and of our time together bore no similarity to those precious days in Boston that I will treasure always.

> Do you know what hurts so very much? It's love. Love is the strongest force in the world, and when it is blocked that means pain. There are two things we can do when this happens. We can kill the love so that it stops hurting. But then of course part of us dies, too. Or, we can ask God to open up another route for that love to travel.
>
> —*Corrie ten Boom*

Trusting God in the middle of such heartache is difficult. Val and I try to help each other, and we also find peace through prayer. We receive tender mercies from heaven, family, friends, and especially grandchildren. What would our life be without our precious grandchildren? They love us dearly and often express it when we seem to need it the most. For us, they have been that other "route for that love to travel" of which Corrie ten Boom wrote so beautifully.

> Never be afraid to trust an unknown future to a known God.
>
> —*Corrie ten Boom*

I trust in the future God has in store for me. Some days this trust is the only thing that keeps my heart going. I want to know who Tara is these days. I want to hold her hand when she hurts and cry with her and laugh with her and spend time with her. I would apologize for any real or perceived wrongs I had committed. Our hearts are broken; we want our beloved daughter back.

CHAPTER THIRTY

Coming Home

May the bridges that have burned light
our way back to each other.
—*LaRee Westover*

If home is only a building, it will not long endure.
If home is a family, it can be forever.
—*Val D Westover*

I *first felt prompted to write my story* a few years ago but allowed the stresses of everyday life to get in the way. I can't help but wonder, *If I had shared my story then, would our family be living a different story now?*

Our story has been told *for us* by many people, and in these stories, I rarely find accurate representations of Val or me. The story I am telling now is *by us*. Our family deserves to be free from gossip, so my intent is to set the record straight; I believe that truth is the only thing that will set this family free from gossip and misrepresentation, both verbal and written. I have no expectation as to what proportion of those who read this memoir will believe what is written. It really doesn't matter.

It is important to note that many of the stories in Tara's memoir took place before she was born, so they are not her memories at all. Others refer to events that supposedly happened when she was still a little girl. And still others describe events at which she was not present. The most curious part of these stories is that so many of them contain the same destructive rhetoric that my sisters and other family members have long been guilty of telling to anyone who would listen. Our children—and particularly Tara, as the youngest child—have been subjected to colorful and twisted stories about their parents by extended family members for most of their lives. It is important to understand that when writing her memoir, it was to these family members Tara turned for information and encouragement.

With the words of Tara's memoir in my mind, and looking at many of the notes Tara has written to me over the years spread out on my desk, I simply cannot bring them into sync with one another. In her notes she thanks us as parents for all that we taught her and the life we provided for her and her siblings. She thanks us for our efforts to teach her. She praises us for trying so hard to prepare her for life.

I will share only two of those notes. The first was written a few years before Tara left to attend BYU. She apparently wrote this as an assignment from one of her teachers at church.

Mother,

I am supposed to write and tell you the things I appreciate about you. For a start, you work all day long and never stop to take a break. I doubt if I could ever do that for even one day, let alone 365 (sometimes 366) days of the year. You don't really complain, and you like to teach us things we never could figure out by ourselves.

I understand why God blessed everyone with a mother because life would be a mess without one. Plus, even the time when we were at the lake and I opened the door before the car stopped you didn't yell or scream.

Sometimes, when you go to deliver babies, if it took you longer than a week I question if the house would be standing when you got back home. I LOVE YOU!

I don't know what you will do with all of these little coupons [This note was accompanied by coupons for sweeping, dusting, doing the dishes, etc.] but bear in mind that they are only good once!

My life would be a shambles if something happened to you or you left for a month! I have been thinking, if you divided your life into fractions, ¼ of your life is spent sleeping, ¼ of your remaining time is spent teaching US. Another ¼ of your life is spent cleaning up after US, and the rest, you spend loving US! I LOVE YOU !!

Your daughter,

Tara Jane Westover

I received the following from Tara for Mother's Day in 2005, when she was eighteen (she wrote the date just below her signature). I have always assumed she wrote this insightful poem herself.

Once in a lifetime, a person may be,
a light in your struggles, as to ships in the sea.
Like an anchor, that person may teach you to care
for the parts of your life that time cannot wear.
If your focus you lose, through your shortness of sight,
that person will help you re-enter the light.
And you will find, oftentimes, by a wish or a prayer,
you will find she will come running and soon will be there.
Yes, once in a lifetime, we get to receive
the love of a mother that never will leave!

Happy Mother's Day

Thanks, Mom, for all you do for me—I try every day to live up to the person you taught me to be, and I thank you for what I know have been many sacrifices.

Thanks, Mom, for all you do. I love you!

In Tara's book, *Educated*, John Dewey is quoted as saying that "education must be conceived as a continuing reconstruction of experience." It appears that most of the events recorded in the memoir are a "reconstruction" of Tara's life in our home. Viewing these tales as reconstructions of fact and experience is the only way I can understand the digression from the love and gratitude evident in Tara's earlier notes to the stories in her book.

Maybe Tara has come to believe the things that she has written, for as Andrea Goodridge said, "What you focus on becomes your reality." We noted that occasionally a few beautiful crumbs were scattered our way apparently to reassure the reader that she was being fair and that she loves us. I find myself clinging to those crumbs as if they were true on the one hand, yet silently fearing that I am being played again on the other.

The Telling of Tales

> Three things come not back: the spoken word, the spent arrow, the missed opportunity.
>
> —*Proverb*

My mother, in her later years, would often repeat a story that her mother also used to share:

> *A woman who had spread false tales about a neighbor later felt regretful that nearly everyone in their community had heard the stories. So the woman asked a wise leader what she should do to make amends. The sage told her to buy a large bag of feathers and empty the contents into the wind. Then, the leader told her to go and gather all the feathers back into the bag. Of course, gathering all the feathers would be impossible. The lesson we children were expected to learn was that there is no way to un-say something once it has been said. And trying to undo the consequences of gossip, lies, and distortions is as impossible as trying to gather hundreds of wind-scattered feathers.*

Recently, Travis and I spoke early one morning. He was very discouraged, he said, as there was no place he could go, no job he could do, no place he could take his family, that the words of his sister's book would not follow him. Each member of our family knows what that feels like as we live it every day.

But then Travis said, should Tara ever "come upon hard times or difficulties," I could count on him to help with whatever she needed. He told me that there was a time he would have given his life, if necessary, for his "sittle lister." And then he added, "Mom, I have a family now, and my wife and children are entitled to my first loyalty and my best efforts. But you will always have from me whatever Tara may need that I can give."

I was grateful and, at the same time, amazed. I thought of the pain this book of lies has caused him. Nevertheless, I realized that I feel much the same way. In speaking with others of our children, I find them reaching within their souls for the same response.

Our family is moving forward with our lives with a brightness of hope, even though there may be remnants of fear and anger in our hearts. We pray that someday Tara may choose to come home and for the strength to welcome her with open arms. We pray to know what mistakes we have made so we might make amends. We pray for our daughter and for peace and family unity.

Tara sent an email to her sister, Valaree, not so long ago, as they were working on a project together. It was a picture of the "Princess" for their father's Christmas present. At certain times of the year, when the snow is just right on the mountain directly behind and above our house, the trees stand out in such a way as to form what has been referred to since Val's childhood—or maybe even before that—as "The Princess." This name refers to a legend about an Indian princess. Tara asked that these words be included with the picture of the Princess:

> And the end of all our exploring
> Will be to arrive where we started
> And know the place for the first time.
> —*T. S. Eliot*

We look forward to the day when our youngest daughter will return to the place where she started—her home and family. We hope—and count on—the coming of a day when she will "know the place" and us, perhaps "for the first time." We long to know her again as well.

If each member of this family can set aside anger and judgment, we can expect miracles. I believe in miracles, in truth, and in light. I believe in this family. I believe in Tara and in the love we have for each other.

I have written far more about Tara than any of my other children. Chances are, the other children will appreciate that they were not given equal space. Estrangement from my youngest and beloved daughter has been, by far, the biggest trial of my life. It has nearly broken me on so many days and in so many ways! It has changed me and shaped me and forced me to find my way and my faith. It could not be left unsaid in a memoir of my life, no matter how badly I might have preferred that.

The God I love has this family in the palm of His hand today, just as He always has. Just because I cannot imagine how He will work the miracles that this family needs does not mean that I have not felt the sweet assurance of the Spirit that He intends to do just that when—and if—we are all ready.

Val's Words

I believe in Tara. She will come home someday. She will mature and forgive. She will remember the good times. I may not live to see it. I will be here waiting just the same. My arms will be open—my heart as well. Whether you see or feel, I promise, I will.

You know, the Princess does not appear every year. Sometimes it is years in between. Her visits are short. Sometimes she is gone the next day. She is always facing south. I like to think that Tara will come home from that way—the Princess will be watching to welcome her home. Me too.

The Princess

This has been a strange year on Buck's Peak. As we look up to the mountain, the Princess has been visible all winter long this year. I don't remember a time when I have been able to see the Princess every day, day after day, all winter long like this. In fact, she was visible all through the month of April. She was even visible, if you knew where to look, for the first few days of May.

I must admit that it has given my heart more than a little bit of hope. Tara did not come this winter. Perhaps, she will not come in the upcoming winter or even the winter after that. Nevertheless, whenever she comes, her family and the Princess will be waiting.

A copy of this quote hangs on our refrigerator door, and means a lot to me and to Val:

> Be slow to judge for we know little of what has been done and nothing of what has been resisted.
>
> —*Rudyard Kipling*

The God I love is not a God of force. He will never force any of His children against their will. This I know to be true. Each of us, in our own way and time, will have to prepare our hearts for this miracle. We can do this. Someday, we will welcome our beloved Tara home!

CHAPTER THIRTY-ONE

Standing Up & Speaking Out

I would like to be known as an intelligent woman,
a courageous woman, a loving woman,
a woman who teaches by being.
—*Maya Angelou*

W*riting this memoir has been a journey* that has brought into focus the person I am now compared to the one I once was. Here I share two short stories that illustrate the "stand up and speak out" person I like to think I have become.

A Professional Organization

The state of Utah had just passed a new law governing the practice of foot zone therapy. Previously, Utah had a friendly legal situation for foot zone therapists, but under a new law, zone therapists would be required to be members of a "professional organization recognized by the State of Utah."

Apparently, the Utah Foot Zone Association (UFZA) was responsible for the introduction of the bill and its passage into law, and they expected to be approved as the *only* state-recognized professional organization in Utah. I was rather disgusted at the actions of this Utah association and the political maneuvering that had created this law. I considered the new law a mistake, and I was also concerned that one small group of people would be making the rules for all zone therapists in Utah. Through my lawyer, I arranged a meeting that included representatives of the Utah Massage Therapy Board, the UFZA, and a judge to discuss the law's ramifications.

At the meeting, my lawyer spoke for a moment, and then I stood, spread my pages of notes on the table, and paused. I stared down at those pages for a moment, then in a dramatic gesture gathered my notes together, turned them face down on the table, and began to speak extemporaneously.

Within a few moments, my lawyer was leaning back in his chair, completely relaxed, with his feet now up on the table. And a few minutes later the judge also leaned back in her chair, with a rather satisfied look on her face. I finished speaking and sat down, and the judge adjourned the meeting with a few concluding words. She expressed her opinion that even though the new bill should never have been proposed, let alone passed into law, she did not have the authority to overturn it. I was reminded once again that it is easier to get a bad bill to become law than it is to get a bad law off the books.

A few days later I was informed that my company, Butterfly Expressions, LLC, had been deemed a "professional organization recognized by the State of Utah." Also recognized were a national organization that had been formed years earlier in response to similar laws in other states and an organization in Montana associated with the beginnings of foot zone therapy in America.

The UFZA, even though they were also recognized by the state, lost the exclusive power to make the rules for foot zone therapists in Utah. Members of this association are still my friends, despite our disagreement and the results of this emotionally charged meeting. I learned anew that it is possible to disagree without being disagreeable. As for Butterfly Expressions, LLC, we make no demands other than those required by the state of Utah, charge no fees, or create any unnecessary difficulties in the recognition process.

At the first Utah Foot Zone Association Conference about a year later, I was voted "most influential member of the foot zone community" by my peers. This was a stretch in my opinion, but I appreciated their thoughtfulness. I will go to my grave believing that this new law had more to do with *control* than with the safety of either foot zone therapists or their clients.

The Courtroom

Several years ago, I had gotten a traffic ticket for something I had not done, and I had no intention of paying the fee if I could avoid it. As I sat in the back of the courtroom waiting for my turn in front of the judge, I was spoiling for a fight.

A young woman with her mother was standing before the judge. It was obvious that this young woman was outstanding. I listened as the judge ascertained that she was an "A" student, a student-council member, part of several service organizations, and in line for multiple scholarships.

A few nights previously, her parents had sent her to the store to buy a gallon of milk, but being seventeen, she had ignored her parents' instructions and driven by her boyfriend's house. The arresting officer claimed in his report that she had not come to a full stop at a stop sign; she claimed that she had. Either way, when she saw the lights of the police vehicle in her rear-view mirror, she continued driving for a block and a half before finally stopping. She did this so that the address on the ticket would not show her detouring off the main route to the store.

Disobedient? Yes. A matter for the court? Perhaps, but I didn't think so. And the court was throwing the book at this poor teen, talking about a ridiculous amount of community service hours and a large fine. The judge even mentioned—I suppose as a scare tactic—some overnight jail time. Such a blot on her record would almost certainly preclude her from receiving any scholarship.

I couldn't stand it any longer and moved to sit by the mother. I quietly asked if she wanted to discipline her daughter herself or if she wanted the court to do it for her. She answered that she just wanted the whole thing to go away since, in her opinion, a disagreement between the police officer and her husband was the real reason for the stop in the first place.

I asked if I could try to help, even though she didn't know me and had no reason to trust me. (Well, I wasn't even sure I trusted myself at this point.) But she replied that they had nothing to lose, and besides, I couldn't possibly make things worse. So I asked her to stand and introduce me to the court as her "next friend" and request that I be allowed to represent her daughter. *Next friend* is a common-law legal term, still in use today. It usually applies to a non-officer-of-the-court who wishes to represent a minor or a mentally incompetent person who cannot afford legal representation.

Permission was granted, and I proceeded to ask some questions of the judge. I requested the opportunity to question the arresting officer, but he was not present. I suggested rescheduling so that the officer could be questioned, as the law allowed, but the judge denied my request. This judicial mistake made me very happy.

I continued wrangling with the judge, and eventually he threatened to charge me with contempt of court. He shook his fist and raised his voice, saying that if I proceeded, he would give me a large fine and, quite likely, jail time.

The mother then found her voice, and stood and informed the judge that she and her husband would handle any expenses I might incur, would even tend and feed my children if he carried through with any such action, and that they would pursue legal action against the court on my behalf.

I then quoted a certain law that the judge was either unaware of or was hoping I was unaware of. The judge then loudly banged his gavel a few times, glared at me again, and said, "Young lady, I certainly hope, for your sake, that you are not on my docket today or any time soon!" Apparently, he was implying that when my turn came, I was to be found guilty—even if I was innocent, another serious judicial error.

I walked over to the court reporter and asked her to read the judge's last words back to the court, which she did. I then stated, innocently, that I thought that was what I had heard, but that perhaps she should read it one more time, so that we could all be sure of what we had heard. So she did.

The judge studied his docket, banged his gavel again, and then abruptly dismissed the remaining cases for that morning, which included the young woman's case, my own, and one other traffic violation. The mother and her daughter could not thank me enough. I was still somewhat jittery, but I was also very proud of myself for having found such gumption.

> Strong people stand up for themselves;
> stronger people stand up for others.
> —*Chris Gardner*

That same gumption has animated me to try to be a simple force for good in the world, and to live with integrity and intention. I readily admit that my story may be different than most, and that I have marched to different cadences from those around me. Nevertheless, both Val and I have marched in step with one another.

In writing this memoir, I have often asked myself: *If life were to offer me a do-over, what would I do differently?* It's an important question to consider. I would still strive to walk with faith and exercise courage, just as I have done in the past, but perhaps with a little less trepidation. And it would certainly be with the same good and dear man. Yet, I have come to realize, surprisingly, that even with my mistakes and personal weaknesses, I don't want a do-over. I only want to carry on, as I can now see the blossoming of astonishing possibilities for the future.

What will the eternities bring to the union between Val and me, and to this wonderful family that we—and God—have tried our best to educate and nurture? The prospects are breathtaking, and I am eager for us to continue learning and serving—together.

About the Author

LaRee Westover was born in southeastern Idaho and attended public schools and Brigham Young University. She was blessed with an inquisitive mind, and stories about her early childhood often end with her having said, "I can do it myself!"

She and her husband, Val, are the parents of two girls and five boys, all of whom were homeschooled. Six went on to receive more formal education, and three earned PhD degrees. Her family, which now includes 36 grandchildren, is the joy of her life.

LaRee prepared extensively and worked as a midwife for several years. She has published four books on homeopathic remedies, herbal remedies, and essential oils for the multimillion-dollar business, Butterfly Express. As an incorrigible optimist and consummate hard worker, LaRee continues to share her knowledge and experience by teaching classes about alternative health care modalities. She is an active member of The Church of Jesus Christ of Latter-day Saints and lives with her husband of 45 years in Clifton, Idaho.